PA Studies *for*

Advanced Secretarial Students

Carol Carysforth

Heinemann

...ucational Publishers
...t, Jordan Hill, Oxford OX2 8EJ
...n of Reed Educational & Professional Publishing Ltd
Heinemann is a registered trademark of Reed Educational & Professional Publishing Limited

OXFORD   FLORENCE   PRAGUE   MADRID   ATHENS
MELBOURNE   AUCKLAND   KUALA LUMPUR   SINGAPORE   TOKYO
IBADAN   NAIROBI   KAMPALA   JOHANNESBURG   GABORONE
PORTSMOUTH NH (USA)   CHICAGO   MEXICO CITY   SÃO PAULO

First published 1998
2002 2001 2000 99 11 10 9 8 7 6 5 4 3 2 1

A catalogue record for this book is available from the British Library on request.

ISBN 0 435 45512 5

Designed by Jackie Hill

Typeset by 🅰 Tek-Art, Croydon, Surrey

Printed and bound by Biddles Ltd, Guildford

Contents

Acknowledgements

The contents of this book owe much to all those who gave so freely of their time to advise me and make so many valuable contributions and suggestions over a period of several months. My express thanks are due to Cathryn Higham and her colleagues at Porter, Matthews and Marsden for their advice on tax and VAT, Bridget Swindlehurst of the Blackpool Gazette for her comments on press statements and press releases, David Williams for his practical guidance on rail travel and the very efficient and prompt assistance I received from Paul Richardson of Railtrack.

Particular mention must be made of the invaluable help and cooperation I received from Margaret Drew and Sue Tidbury of the Society of Teachers in Business Education in relation to the Society's own very successful conferences, where I have been made welcome on more than one occasion. Thanks are also due to Elizabeth Smaje, the current Chairman of the Institute of Qualified Private Secretaries, and for the cooperation of the Council over the inclusion of material relating to their AGMs.

Help and assistance was also provided by many other organisations and individuals including the British Travel Association, Lancashire Constabulary, the Environmental Health office, the VAT office and Thomas Cook – who gave me valuable assistance in understanding their computer systems and the intricacies of flight pricing. My thanks are also due to British Airways and Reed Travel Group, American Express, Tate Appointments and the Association of Colleges for permission to include copyright materials.

My appreciation is always due, in no small measure, to those at Heinemann who work so closely with me on the production of each book, but never more so than on this occasion when their assistance has been invaluable. Firstly, many thanks must go to Margaret Berriman for her kindness, patience and understanding when I was out of commission for several months, her awesome ability to readjust and juggle schedules and her foresight in solving some of the basic operational problems with which we were faced. Secondly, my gratitude is due to Jan Nikolic, who took a far more prominent role with this book than usual and did her job impressively well – combining her usual hawk-like eye for detail with flair, imagination and determination when it mattered. To them both I am very grateful, for their support and involvement has been a key factor in producing this book so promptly.

My love and thanks are, as ever, due to my husband Mike, who helped with much of the research and who unstintingly gave his time and energy to support and assist me.

Carol Carysforth-Neild
May 1998

The author and publishers would like to thank the illustrator, Ernest Curd of Tek-Art, and are grateful to the following for permission to reproduce photographs: Chris Honeywell (p. 5), Mary Evans Picture Library (p. 62), Empics (p. 126) and Eurostar (UK) Ltd (p. 248.)

Dedication

With love to Ann (Worcester) and Betty (Entwistle) – my friends, colleagues, compatriots and confidantes from way back, without whose help and support I could never have survived for so long!

SECTION 1 – Conference and meetings organisation

● Introduction

Every organisation in the world holds meetings, and many arrange conferences or other events on a regular basis. In every case these enable groups of people to come together to discuss specific issues of common interest.

A key role for many PAs and administrators is to arrange and organise these events – ranging from an informal meeting between departmental staff and their manager, to the company Annual General Meeting; from a sales presentation to a prospective customer to a three-day conference with many delegates. The success of any event is dependent on good planning and the abilities of the organiser. The PA concerned with these tasks benefits from a more varied job role, greater levels of responsibility and considerable job satisfaction when everything goes smoothly and efficiently.

Your understanding of such events, together with your organisational skills, are crucial to the success of any event with which you are involved. The degree to which your boss can depend on you to make all the required arrangements, offer useful suggestions and solve any problems are likely to be directly reflected in your manager's reputation and effectiveness, and your own career prospects and pay packet! Effective and experienced organisers are worth their weight in gold – not just because they can be relied upon to do a good job but also because of their ability to 'think through' potential requirements and problems in advance.

At this stage of your career, the thought of undertaking this type of responsibility might seem awesome. However, a useful first step is to understand what is required and why – which is the knowledge that this section aims to provide. The second step is to gain some practical experience. For this reason, suggested activities are also included to help you to develop your skills. You should note that an important learning experience is to review activities afterwards to evaluate the success of your arrangements and learn from your own mistakes. Even experienced PAs need to reflect on their current levels of performance, if they are to improve their expertise! Finally, revision and review questions are included at the end of each chapter to enable you to practise your examination technique.

Types of conferences and meetings

The types of events that you may organise in the course of your working life are many and varied, but they are mainly likely to comprise the following:

- meetings – both informal and formal
- presentations
- seminars
- conferences

In each case you need to know how to prepare for the event, what your role will be during the event, and your responsibilities afterwards. Obviously, there is a considerable difference between the organisational arrangements required for a three-day conference with 100 delegates from all over the world, and a half-hour meeting between three members of staff! However, certain broad principles are common to all events and it is often simply a case of developing existing skills to organise more complex activities.

The essential first step is to realise why an event is being held – in other words, what is the purpose of the activity? All your arrangements are then made with the objective of fulfilling this aim as effectively and efficiently as possible.

● Business meetings

One study of the way managers spend their time estimated that up to 65 per cent of the average working week can be spent attending meetings of one sort or another. In another study, psychologist Dr David Lewis estimated that people can spend up to two years of their working lives in meetings. Why do we hold meetings at all, and why so many?

Meetings are held for a variety of reasons – not least because they can be an excellent forum for face-to-face communication between a group of people who need to:

- disseminate or exchange information
- obtain views and opinions
- decide upon action to be taken
- solve problems
- dispel rumours or concerns and provide accurate, up-to-date information
- generate ideas and suggestions

- coordinate activities to be undertaken by different people

- report upon or evaluate an event or activity

- discuss current issues of mutual concern

- broaden participation and involvement in a project

- obtain assistance

- organise special events or occasions.

However, not all meetings are effective. Only well-planned, appropriately organised and properly controlled meetings achieve their objectives. A chaotic free-for-all simply wastes everyone's time and is extremely frustrating for those involved. The situation is even worse if the meeting has also involved external contacts, such as customers, shareholders or the press!

If a meeting is well planned and organised with clearly identified aims and objectives, then the following **benefits** are likely:

- an exchange of information takes place, so that each person present learns from his or her colleagues

- time is saved – as key issues can be debated amongst a group of people all concentrating on the same item at the same time

Communications for the millennium

An alternative method of communicating now used by most organisations is **electronic mail**. E-mail messages can be sent to any member of staff via a company's computer network, and to those in other organisations over the Internet. Many packages allow 'discussion groups' to be set up to exchange information on topics of common interest. Equally, e-mails can easily be sent to each member of a nominated group simultaneously. If a group of people work in scattered locations so that it is difficult to meet on a regular basis, this is a valuable way of 'discussing' an issue. If several members disagree on a solution, the person who is coordinating the discussion (in effect, the electronic chairperson) must control the debate and bring it to a conclusion. Today, e-mail is frequently used to save both time and money. Other alternatives include telephone conferencing, video conferencing and Internet conferencing – all discussed on page 100.

- an optimum conclusion is reached – given that a range of information, expertise and experience is on hand at the same time

- there is commitment by those involved to achieving the agreed objectives and undertaking the required action to ensure success

- the outcome is a deepening of mutual understanding and appreciation for each others' views. This is particularly true of effective meetings which involve both vertical and horizontal communications – vertical between a boss and subordinates, and horizontal between staff members.

✔ Check it yourself

Find out if your college has an e-mail system or a computer network, and whether you can set up a user group or a discussion group between yourselves and your tutor. If so, assume you are a group of PAs working for an organisation that proposes to close its existing smoking room and ban all smoking in the workplace. Each person should contribute towards the debate, with your tutor acting as chair, and you should decide on a **joint** recommendation to put forward to the main committee.

Chris Honeywell

Formal and informal meetings

Business meetings can be divided into those that are **formal** and those that are **informal**. The latter are the most common and the most frequently held. The degree of formality at a meeting is usually determined by:

- the type of meeting being held

- the reason for holding it

- the participants involved.

A meeting that is a legal requirement, concerns strategic issues relating to the organisation as a whole and involves the dissemination of information to governors, trustees or shareholders, will be formal. This means:

- its rules and procedures are clearly specified and pre-determined

- a formal record is kept of the proceedings.

The record is kept because organisations are *accountable* for their actions and have a legal responsibility to hold particular meetings and disclose certain information to their shareholders. The records – or **minutes** of the meeting – show the date and time when a meeting was held, list the participants, describe the items of business dealt with, and identify any agreed action. Such documents must be kept safely as they provide evidence of what occurred. In some cases, a press release or report on the proceedings is issued to the media.

Informal meetings, on the other hand, are held every day of the week in many business organisations. Some are **scheduled** or **structured** meetings which take place at regular intervals between a particular group of participants. Others are unscheduled or unstructured – held simply as and when the need arises. For example, a departmental manager may hold a scheduled weekly meeting with his or her staff to review work-in-progress and new developments. However, if a crisis occurs – such as the non-delivery of a component which will severely disrupt production schedules – a meeting may be called very quickly to discuss the issue.

You should note that the formal term for calling a meeting is **convening** a meeting. You could therefore say that a meeting was convened to discuss production problems.

Types of informal meetings

It is likely that the first type of meetings you will be asked to organise will be informal – if only because of their frequency. They are the easiest to arrange as there are no formal rules to be followed, except those that are customary in your organisation. The range of informal meetings you may be asked to organise include:

- departmental meetings between a manager and his or her staff

- staff meetings between groups of staff in a department or section

- cross-functional meetings concerning specialists or representatives from different areas in the organisation

- middle management meetings – between groups of middle managers

- senior management meetings – between the senior managers in the organisation.

In your own college, for instance, there are likely to be:

- weekly meetings of senior managers from across the college
- weekly meetings of faculty or departmental managers
- regular meetings of staff in different sections
- regular meetings of tutors involved in a particular course.

These will be interspersed with other meetings held for specific purposes. For instance, if your course team was asked to prepare a report suggesting changes to your course next year, the tutors would probably hold a special meeting to discuss and agree the action they wish to propose.

Structured or scheduled informal meetings usually have informal titles. Unscheduled meetings may have no title at all! In addition, they may be organised by a team leader or coordinator, rather than have a chairperson. The terms you may hear in relation to informal meetings include:

- working party
- task group
- project group
- quality circle
- team briefing.

In your college you may find there is a library working party, an IT task group and a quality standards group (if not several quality circles) in addition to management, departmental and section meetings!

All these terms relate to the type of **brief** given to a group. The brief is its role or remit. A summary of each of the main types of informal meeting is given in Figure 1.1, and a comprehensive explanation is given below.

Working party

A working party is a group that meets, often at the request of senior managers or of a particular committee (see page 21), to investigate and report upon a specific issue. If your college wanted to find out the pros and cons of introducing electronic and computerised equipment into the library to improve student access to information, then a library working party could be formed with the brief of investigating this issue and preparing a report outlining advantages, disadvantages and cost implications. Once the working party had produced this paper, its job would be done. The report would be submitted to the senior manager or the committee that had instructed the working party. The working party would comprise a variety of people representing different areas of expertise relevant to the issue, eg library resources, student requirements, IT equipment, and so on.

Project or task group

A project or task group is formed to oversee a particular job. This could be arranging a particular event (such as an Open Day) or putting into effect the recommendations made by a working party. For instance, if the college management agreed to proceed with the idea of introducing electronic equipment into the library, then it may propose the formation of an IT task group to implement the recommendations. The task group would be disbanded once the task was complete.

Usually 'projects' last longer than 'tasks'. Typical examples are the many millennium projects that have been proposed to introduce new initiatives before the year 2000. Many of these projects may take two to three years to complete. After the year 2000, when they are completed, the project teams will be disbanded.

Quality circle

A quality circle, in its truest sense, is a group of volunteers who meet, with the full support of management, to investigate and attempt to improve quality issues through a joint problem-solving approach. The issues can range from basic production-related problems, to safety and cost concerns, to the improvement of communications and employee morale. The aim is that each worker becomes a decision-maker in relation to his or her own work. Each 'circle' comprises between about five and fifteen employees from one area, and meets on a regular basis – say for about two hours each week. Electing a leader is usually optional. Each group may also meet with other quality circles in the organisation when the need arises. Each group selects its own problems for investigation, and members collect relevant information before participating in a brainstorming session, putting forward ideas. However, for the system to work, management must be prepared to accept the suggestions made. This factor has resulted in the failure of many quality circles. Other problems arise where the issues have been dictated by senior management, who have regarded quality circles as the easy answer to problems. This was certainly not what was envisioned by their founder, Professor Kaoru Ishikawa, who first launched quality circles in Japan in the 1960s.

Managers' meetings with subordinates

All managers hold regular meetings with their subordinates – either as small groups of individuals or as a large group, depending upon the size of a department or section and the number of subordinates under the control of a particular manager. A senior manager may hold a weekly meeting with his or her middle managers and then expect them to pass the information on to their own staff. Middle managers may hold meetings with larger groups of staff or with team leaders and, again, expect this information to be passed on. The aim is to **cascade** information from one level of the organisation down to another, and then to facilitate feedback upwards as staff respond.

In a flat management structure, a manager may hold a group meeting with all staff simultaneously. The cascading approach is more likely in a hierarchical organisation. The danger with this, of course, is that the message is changed or distorted (either accidentally or deliberately) each time the information is relayed, with employees receiving their own manager's interpretation of events rather than an objective report! Equally, staff responses may or may not reach the ears of senior managers – depending upon the stance taken by their own manager or team leader!

One way around this problem is to record the event in writing. Senior managers can then insist on receiving a copy and check that staff received the correct information. They can also note the action planned or the decisions made. This is why you will find that some record is taken at many informal meetings, even if these are not formal minutes.

Team briefing

A team briefing is a *short* session between a manager, supervisor or team leader and a group of staff to update everyone upon progress to date and current events. There should be an exchange of information so that everyone is involved. In some organisations team briefings are held once a week, or even more frequently, for about ten to fifteen minutes.

Working party	A group formed to investigate and make recommendations on a particular, usually short-term or current issue.
Project or task group	A group that undertakes a specific project or task and sees this through to completion.
Quality circle	A group of employees who voluntarily participate in problem-solving activities related to issues such as production, communications, safety, cost and quality.
Manager's meetings with subordinates	Meetings held on a departmental or section basis between a manager and a certain group of subordinates, or on a 'team-briefing' basis between a manager and a larger group of subordinates, with the main aim of disseminating information of mutual interest.

Figure 1.1 Types of informal meetings

Types of formal meetings

The different categories of formal meetings are summarised in Figure 1.2. You should note that often their rules and procedures have been determined by law. This is particularly the case where an organisation is using public money to run its operations, as is the case with county councils, charitable organisations, health trusts and public limited companies (which sell shares to the public in order to raise money). It is in the public interest to have a system that ensures the operations of such organisations are both controlled and publicised. As an individual shareholder in a company you have the right to know how your money is being used, to receive a report on the performance of the company and to participate in the taking of some decisions. As a voter and a council tax payer you have the right to know how your council is spending your money and to find out how decisions made by your council may affect you – although you don't have a legal right to attend council meetings. For these reasons, in many cases the minutes of formal meetings must be made public.

Type of meeting	Reason held	Rules and procedures
Annual General Meeting	A legal requirement for all public limited companies – private limited companies can opt not to hold these if all shareholders agree. All shareholders are invited to AGMs.	The Companies Act 1985, as amended by The Companies Act 1989, lays down the legal requirements. Each company's Articles of Association contain the specific rules and procedures relating to their own meetings.
Extraordinary General Meeting	A meeting held to transact any business with shareholders which cannot be held over until the next AGM.	As above.
Public inquiry	Inquiries held to investigate major accidents or other incidents of national importance, or to hear appeals against national or local government decisions, particularly in relation to planning applications.	The legal procedures are set down in the Tribunals and Inquiries Act 1992, and are also governed by other relevant legislation. For instance, planning decisions must be in line with the Town and Country Planning Act 1990 and the Planning (Listed Buildings and Conservation Areas) Act 1990.

Type of meeting	Reason held	Rules and procedures
Meeting of Board of Directors	Regular meetings held to discuss company policy and decide future action to link to the overall strategy of the company. Weekly meetings are likely, requiring the attendance of all executive directors and, less frequently, non-executive directors.	Meetings must be held in accordance with the Companies Acts (see above and this page) and as described in Table A or in the company's Articles of Association.
Committee meetings	Regular meetings of committees appointed to carry out specific tasks and duties on behalf of an organisation.	The procedures are usually governed by a **standing orders, constitution** or **terms of reference** determining those areas that are the remit of a particular committee.

Figure 1.2 Formal meetings

Meetings and the law

Many laws constrain the way in which organisations are allowed to operate, including health and safety regulations, employment legislation and tax law. If you work for a local authority or a health trust, the laws and regulations governing your meetings will be slightly different from those that apply to a commercial organisation. For the purpose of this book, however, we will concentrate on the laws affecting meetings held by companies.

The Companies Act 1985 distinguishes two different types of company – private limited companies (Ltd) and public limited companies (plc). In the first case, the company is privately owned and is often a family-run business. In the second case, the company offers its shares for sale on the Stock Exchange and these are purchased by institutional investors and members of the public. The Companies Act also recognises different types of meetings, primarily **General meetings** – to which shareholders are invited – and **Directors' meetings**, which involve only the directors and other officers of the company.

The Companies Act 1989 allows private companies to exempt themselves from certain requirements that are compulsory for public companies – such as holding an Annual General Meeting – because these can be an unnecessary formality for many small companies. However, such an

Refresh your memory!

If you have studied for a business qualification then you should already know that, when a company is formed, it becomes a distinct and separate legal entity – with the ability to enter into contracts, own property and employ people. The company will employ salaried directors who will be concerned with the day-to-day running of its affairs and will sell shares to shareholders in order to finance the organisation. In a private limited company the directors and the shareholders are often the same people, whereas in a public limited company they are not. The directors of Marks and Spencer, for instance, are employed to run the company, and may or may not own shares in it. Marks and Spencer shareholders will number many thousands and will include institutional investors such as pension funds and insurance funds which have large shareholdings, as well as private individuals who have invested their savings in the hope of receiving good dividends and seeing their shares increase in value if the company does well. Obviously all the shareholders cannot be consulted over every decision made, and the role of the directors is therefore to run the company on a day-to-day basis.

The law acknowledges that the Board of Directors has formal responsibilities towards the shareholders, the employees and the company as a whole. The law also recognises 'company officers' who have specific responsibilities, including the company secretary, senior management and, in certain circumstances, the accountant and auditor. The shareholders are expected to approve the appointment of directors and officers, oversee their activities and also have the power to dismiss them. Theoretically, shareholders have ultimate long-term control of the company. They meet together once a year at the **Annual General Meeting**, where the directors must provide them with an annual report and accounts. If urgent business must be put before shareholders at any other time, this is done by calling an **Extraordinary General Meeting**.

exemption has to have the agreement of all members. Any shareholder can insist that the company holds an AGM by giving notice of this request not less than three months before the end of a calendar year. If you work for a private limited company you are therefore likely to find that you will be involved only in meetings of the directors. If you work for a public limited company, the situation is rather different.

The statutory requirements contained in the Companies Act 1985 (as amended by the Companies Act 1989) give specific guidance on several issues relating to meetings. Certain points may be varied somewhat if the variation is specified in the company's Articles of Association (see below), which also stipulate the conduct and business of directors' meetings.

Check it yourself

Read through the main legal requirements outlined in Figure 1.3. Check that you understand the meanings of the terms used by reading the explanations below.

- The Secretary of State normally has no involvement with AGMs. This intervention would occur only if a company had failed to hold an AGM in the stipulated time period.

- The term **Articles** is used for the company Articles of Association, described below.

- The days counted in convening a meeting are described as **clear days** because neither the date of sending out the notice nor the date of the meeting can be included.

- The **quorum** is the minimum number of people who must be present before a meeting can be held. The Articles usually describe the procedure to be followed if a quorum is not present.

- The **chairperson** is normally the chairperson of the board, or another director or nominated officer in his or her absence

- A **poll** is a system of voting whereby members mark their preference on a ballot paper (see also page 153).

- **Special resolutions** relate to special items of business to be discussed, for which the shareholders may require more notice.

- The **registered office** is the official address noted at Companies House and specifically included on the company's headed paper.

The Memorandum of Association and Articles of Association

When a company is registered, two legal documents are drawn up: the Memorandum of Association and the Articles of Association. The Memorandum gives the name and status of the company and identifies its purpose for existence and its powers. The purpose for its existence (known as the **objects**) must be stated clearly and unambiguously, as this defines the type of business activities for which the company is allowed to raise

Annual General Meeting	Must be held by all public companies at least once every 15 months, or as otherwise directed by the Secretary of State.
Extraordinary General Meeting	May be called by members, subject to certain conditions. The directors must respond within 21 days of receiving such a request. This right of members cannot be waived through conditions in the Articles of Association.
Length of notice for calling meetings	Generally, 21 clear days for an AGM or a meeting required for passing a special resolution. Otherwise, usually 14 days unless there are special circumstances. The Articles may vary this requirement but only if there is general agreement of the members concerned.
Quorum	Unless varied by the Articles, two members present or represented by proxy constitutes a quorum. The number must normally be sustained until the end of the meeting, unless the Articles state otherwise.
Chairperson	Can be any member elected by those members present.
Proxies	Members who cannot attend can appoint a proxy, a person who attends and votes on his/her behalf.
Voting	Members have the right to demand a poll on any question other than the election of the chairperson or the adjournment of the meeting.
Notice of meeting	The company must provide all members with written notice of a meeting, giving details of any special resolutions to be discussed. In some cases, up to 28 days' notice may be required.
Records of proceedings	Minutes must be taken at all general meetings, all directors' meetings and any managers' meetings. They must be signed by the chairperson and kept available for inspection at the registered office. All members are entitled to receive a copy, within 7 days of making a request, although a charge may be levied.

Figure 1.3 Requirements of the Companies Acts

finance. If a company wishes to change its objects at a later date, this can be done only by passing a special resolution at a shareholders' meeting (see below).

The Articles of Association give details of the internal and administrative rules which apply to the way the company conducts its business. The Companies Act 1985 lays down standard Articles of Association, known as Table A. Companies can draw up their own Articles or diverge from Table A – provided that they comply with the minimum standards established in company law. The Articles can be amended or changed, subject to certain restrictions, provided a 75 per cent majority of shareholders is in agreement and a resolution is passed at a shareholders' meeting.

In practical terms the Articles of Association is the most important document, because it defines the scope of the directors' authority, identifying the amount of power they can exercise in the boardroom and those issues for which they require shareholder approval. The Articles specifically cover:

- the notice to be given for general meetings

- the procedures to be followed at general meeting (eg the quorum, the method of adjournment and the way in which a poll should be held)

- the rights of members when voting – including the right to appoint a proxy

- the nature and frequency of directors' meetings.

Studying a company's Articles enables prospective shareholders to identify the issues where they may be consulted for their views and those where they will not! Therefore, whilst all companies must operate within the same legal framework, the Articles determine the exact individual 'personality' of each company.

General meetings

Three types of general meetings may be held:

- Annual General Meetings (AGMs)

- Extraordinary General Meetings (EGMs)

- Class meetings

Occasionally you will see the term 'shareholders' meeting'. This description can be applied to any general meeting, given that shareholders are present at all of them. There is no such thing as a 'shareholders only' meeting! However, an extraordinary meeting may be convened by shareholders who control 10 per cent or more of the voting shares. On all other occasions, meetings are usually convened by the Board of Directors. One recent innovation is regional shareholder meetings, where shareholders in a particular area are invited to attend. However, these are mainly information and public relations events rather than meetings at which shareholders can exercise their legal powers.

Annual General Meeting (AGM)

As you saw above, an AGM is compulsory for all public limited companies (plc) but optional for private limited companies (Ltd). An AGM must be held each calendar year and no more than fifteen months must elapse between one AGM and the next. The business of the meeting is usually concerned with:

- receiving the report and accounts (as required by the Companies Acts)

- declaring a final dividend

- electing directors

- reappointing the auditors and agreeing their remuneration.

A controlling hand required for shareholders?

Directors of British Aerospace had to barricade themselves behind plastic shields at the company's AGM in 1997 when they were besieged by groups campaigning against the arms trade. Eventually security staff had to eject almost half the shareholders before order could be restored. BAe is not alone in having problems. RTZ, the mining company, struggled through interventions from Friends of the Earth and other groups of protesters. Shell, castigated for its human rights record in Nigeria, found protesters burning the company's flag at its AGM. HSBC discovered the World Development Movement had driven a tank to its AGM in protest over claims that Midland Bank helped to finance arms sales to Iraq.

In response to such problems, the Institute of Chartered Secretaries &

Administrators has issued a code of best practice on how the chairperson should keep order and complete the business on the agenda. This includes not only ejecting shareholders who create mayhem but also restricting repetitive questions and debates on irrelevant items. In Japan, some companies use a more devious ploy. There, the dates of potentially problematic AGMs are deliberately designed to clash so that protesters must divide their attentions! In 1996, UK utility companies were accused of using this strategy when six meetings of electricity companies took place on the same Friday at locations from Manchester to Dorset, and the following Wednesday three water companies held their AGMs on the same date.

All shareholders are invited – they are given advance information and notification of the meeting. This normally involves receiving the **notice** of the meeting, the Annual Report for the current year, the Report and Financial Statement (or Report and Accounts), and the **agenda** stating the business to be discussed. Shareholders who cannot attend have the option of voting by **proxy** instead. This means that they allow someone who will be present to vote on their behalf.

It is usual for the company to issue a press release containing the main points the chairperson will make in his or her speech (see page 98).

Generally, AGMs run smoothly – in fact they can be rather boring for many participants! However, there are occasions when more contentious issues arise, as the article on page 16 describes!

Extraordinary General Meeting (EGM)

EGMs are called to discuss urgent business that cannot wait until the next AGM. They may be called by the directors, or demanded by certain shareholders. Examples of EGMs held during 1997 include the following:

- an EGM demanded by the shareholders of Wigan Rugby League Football Club to decide the future of the chairman and vice-chairman, following alleged irregularities regarding a previous vote of confidence

- an EGM held by Shire Pharmaceuticals to approve the purchase of an American drugs company

- an EGM held by members of Interflora, who ousted eleven of the directors in addition to decreeing that the organisation should operate a postal balloting system in future

- an EGM called by Eurotunnel relating to the huge amount of debt owed to its bankers. At this meeting the directors' proposals were blocked by shareholders desperate to see a change in their fortunes.

Class meeting

Different 'classes' of shares are issued by most public limited companies, such as:

- preference shares, where the holders receive preferential treatment over dividends, but usually do not have any voting rights

- ordinary shares without voting rights (often called 'A' shares)

- ordinary shares with voting rights (the main category of shares)

- redeemable shares, which are shares the company can later buy back. They are often issued to employees as part of a share option scheme so that when an employee leaves the company they can be repurchased and given to a new employee.

You should note that only shareholders who hold voting shares can have a vote at an AGM or EGM, and that each shareholder has one vote for each share held.

The holders of a particular class of shares can meet in accordance with the Articles of Association or the conditions attached to the shares, whenever their rights are to be varied as a result of an action proposed by the company.

Check it yourself

1 Try to find at least one example in the press (or on the Internet) of a shareholders' meeting that has been held recently – either an Annual General Meeting and an Extraordinary General Meeting.

2 Discuss as a group and with your tutor why it is in a company's interests to make sure a press release is issued for an Extraordinary General Meeting.

3 The legal minimum rights of all shareholders are that they can:

- attend shareholders' meetings

- bring resolutions before the meetings

- vote on the appointment of directors

- vote on the appointment of auditors

- approve the directors' report and the accounts

- vote on any other resolutions brought before the meeting

- ask questions of the directors.

In practice, however, few shareholders usually bother to attend either AGMs or EGMs and therefore do not challenge the actions taken by the directors. Discuss with your group and your tutor why this is the case.

Directors' meeting

The Board of Directors is responsible for managing the company, and the conduct and business of their meetings is stipulated in the Articles of Association. Table A gives the directors the authority to meet as they think fit, and in private companies meetings will be held as and when considered necessary. In public companies the meetings will be held more frequently and usually on fixed dates. The frequency of the meetings depends upon the nature of the business and the composition of the board.

Many boards comprise both executive directors (who work for the company, such as the sales director) and non-executive directors (who are non-employees, paid a fee to attend board meetings, hired for their specialist knowledge and impartiality). Many organisations hold monthly meetings to which both executive and non-executive directors are invited, and hold intervening meetings of the executive directors only.

The length of notice for convening the meeting is usually stipulated in the Articles of Association – the norm is a minimum of seven day's notice, and a resolution of the directors may determine the quorum. Legally, a company does not need to appoint a chairperson for a directors' meeting, but in practice most Articles of Association make this appointment compulsory.

Check it yourself

1   Figure 1.4 shows a brief extract from Table A and a short extract from the Articles of Association of a private limited company. What differences can you identify and how will these affect any General Meetings held by the company?

Extract from Table A

Proceedings at general meetings

40   No business shall be transacted at any meeting unless a quorum is present. Two persons entitled to vote upon the business to be transacted, each being a member or a proxy for a member or a duly authorised representative of a corporation, shall be a quorum.

41   If such a quorum is not present within half an hour from the time appointed for the meeting, or if during a meeting such a quorum ceases to be present, the meeting shall stand adjourned to the same day in the next week at the same time and place or to such time and place as the directors may determine.

Extract from Articles of Association

General meetings and resolutions

6   (a) Clause 40 in Table A shall be read and construed as if the words 'at the time when the Meeting proceeds to business' were added at the end of the first sentence.

(b) If a quorum is not present within half an hour from the time appointed for a General Meeting the General Meeting shall stand adjourned to the same day in the next week at the same time and place or to such other day and at such other time and place as the Directors may determine; and if at the adjourned General Meeting a quorum is not present within half an hour from the time appointed therefor such adjourned General Meeting shall be dissolved.

(c) Clause 41 in Table A shall not apply to the Company.

Figure 1.4 Articles of Association

2 Your family owns a private limited company and your mother and father are the only shareholders with 50% of the shares each. Your twin brother and yourself have both been promised shares for your forthcoming 21st birthday although, as yet, the number of shares you will receive has not been decided.

a What would be the advantages and disadvantages in relation to voting rights and decisions made in running the company if

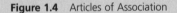

i your brother and yourself received an equal number of shares, but fewer than your parents?

ii the shares were divided equally between the four of you?

iii one of your parents held 55 per cent of the shares and the remainder were split between the three of you?

iv one of your parents held 40 per cent and the remainder were split three ways?

Discuss your ideas with your tutor.

b From the outcome of the above discussion, decide which division of shares you would recommend for the future good management of the company – and state why.

Committee meeting

A committee is a group of people meeting together to discuss a specific issue of common interest. Examples of committees include:

- those that run particular associations, clubs, societies and other groups, eg a local housing association, drama or golf club, charitable or social group (such as the Lions, Rotary Club and Round Table)

Executive	The most important type of committee as it has the power to make the decisions on behalf of the whole association or group.
Advisory	Given the responsibility of advising or making suggestions to the executive committee upon a particular issue. Cannot, therefore, make binding decisions.
Standing	A committee that has a temporary existence.
Ad hoc	A committee that has a temporary existence. It is convened for a particular (short-term) purpose.
Sub-committee	Reports to another committee and usually covers a particular set of criteria.
Joint	Formed for the specific purpose of coordinating the activities of two or more other committees, either on a permanent or temporary basis.

Figure 1.5 Types of committee

- those responsible for particular areas of your local council's work, eg the Planning Committee or Transport Committee

- those responsible for particular areas within an organisation, eg the Health and Safety Committee or the Equal Opportunities Committee.

There are several different types of committee, each of which has a different remit and/or different levels of responsibility. These are shown in Figure 1.5 on page 21.

Committee rules and regulations

Different terms are used to describe the rules and regulations that govern a committee, depending upon where it operates and the type of committee it is.

- Most **executive** or **standing** committees – whether for local councils, health trusts or other public bodies – are governed by means of their **standing orders**. These include details on

  - the usual place, date and time when the meetings will be held
  - any requirements relating to the convening of special meetings
  - the order of business
  - how decisions will be made
  - the rules of debate to be followed (see page 150)
  - the regulations governing adjournment (see page 152)
  - how votes may be cast (see page 152)
  - the power of the committee
  - how and when the standing orders may be altered
  - how and when the standing orders may be suspended.

- most **advisory, ad hoc** or **sub-committees** operate by means of specific **terms of reference**. These are simplified standing orders, designed by the main committee, which identify the precise remit and powers of any subsidiary committee.

- Committees of most clubs and societies are governed by a **constitution**. This states the rules that were established and agreed when the group was first formed.

Check it yourself

1 Look through your local Yellow Pages or Thomson Community Directory and identify at least **six** associations, clubs or groups operating in your own area. For one of these, make notes on the type of discussions they might have at a meeting. Check your answer with your tutor.

2　Ask your tutor for information on the formal meetings and committees operating in your own school or college. Find out their titles and the type of matters they discuss.

3　Assume your school or college has the following committees in operation. Refer to the types of committee described in Figure 1.5, and decide which type would be involved in each case.

　　a　The Marketing Committee is responsible for making decisions about marketing and publicity for the whole organisation.

　　b　The Curriculum Standards Committee is in permanent existence to check the quality of all courses offered by the institution.

　　c　The Festival Committee has been formed specifically to organise your organisation's participation in a local summer festival.

　　d　The Student Consultative Committee reports to the Curriculum Standards Committee. It is responsible for examining the standard of services offered to students.

　　e　The Equal Opportunities Committee also reports to the Curriculum Standards Committee and has the remit of making suggestions and recommendations of good practice to comply with equal opportunities policies.

　　f　The Safety and Security Committee meets once a term, and includes representatives from both the Health and Safety Committee and the Security Committee.

4　It is said that the first requirement of a good chairperson is to become thoroughly conversant with the rules that apply to the meetings he or she is chairing. Why do you think this is the case?

● Public inquiries

Public or statutory inquiries are held whenever there are major issues of national importance which the government feels are in need of thorough investigation. These include accident inquiries (such as the Southall railway accident), company inquiries (in cases such as fraud) and tribunals of inquiry dealing with matters of major public importance. These inquiries are always instigated by the government, and recent examples include those held to investigate the Hillsborough disaster and the tragedy at Dunblane.

Other public inquiries or tribunals are held to investigate decisions made by government departments or other bodies that initiate government action, such as your local council, the Data Protection Registrar or HM Customs and Excise (which oversees the collection of VAT). A person or organisation complaining of an unfair decision by a government department or agency can use the inquiry system to lodge an appeal. As an individual, you could appeal if you had asked for a state benefit and been refused or had applied for planning permission to build a conservatory and been turned down.

The majority of cases brought by commercial organisations and processed through the public inquiry system relate to decisions made by the local planning authority (LPA). Examples could include a local garage made the subject of a compulsory purchase order because of the building of new ring road, or a supermarket chain told it cannot build a new store on land outside the town centre, or your college if it were refused permission to alter one of its buildings because this was 'listed' as being of special historic interest.

All such appeals are controlled by the Planning Inspectorate, which is a part of the Department of the Environment and the Welsh Office. All appeals in England and Wales are dealt with through this inspectorate. Initially, appeals are in writing, through the submission of a form with appropriate evidence attached. This might include a statement showing why a proposal

For or against a fifth runway?

Recently, there have been calls for a review of the public inquiry system and a reduction in the time it takes to hear a complex case, following reports that the public inquiry over the proposed fifth terminal at Heathrow Airport is unlikely to finish until at least August 1998. The inquiry began in May 1995 and was originally expected to last for eighteen months. In the meantime, British Airports Authority (who have requested permission to build the terminal) and its opponents, represented by the Heathrow Association for the Control of Aircraft Noise, will have to wait to see who is the victor.

Even when the decision is announced, if permission is given to build the terminal there will be a considerable delay before it can open. Originally, the £1.8 million terminal had been scheduled to open in 2001, but now it will be at least 2005 before it could be completed. BAA has now lobbied the government to review the planning process for future major developments, such as additional terminals or runways at airports.

Nor has the inquiry been cheap. BAA estimates it will have spent about £200 million fighting its case, mainly on lawyers' and architects' fees. Its opponents have already spent £3 million and are now in danger of running out of funds.

should have been allowed and any evidence of similar proposals having been passed by the same local authority. In some cases the appeal is conducted solely through the production of written evidence. In other cases, the **appellant** (the person or organisation bringing the appeal) or the LPA may prefer a **hearing** to take place, particularly if the case is quite complicated. This is a relatively informal meeting at which both sides give evidence – although there is no cross-questioning as in a court of law. Finally, either the appellant, the LPA or the inspectorate can ask for an **inquiry** to be held. This is a more formal event at which evidence put forward can be challenged by the other party.

A long inquiry, with a company represented by a solicitor or barrister, obviously involves higher costs than a written appeal. The procedure to be followed will largely depend upon the importance and complexity of the issue.

At the end of the investigation, the inspector in charge of the case makes his or her decision, based on the evidence available, and submits this to the Secretary of State for the Environment. In the majority of cases, the Secretary of State agrees with the inspector's decision and confirms it to all parties in writing. On occasion, the Secretary of State may overrule the inspector. If the appellant still disagrees, then he or she may consult a solicitor to see if there are legal grounds for challenging the decision in the High Court.

✓ Check it yourself

1 Either by studying the newspapers or by browsing the Internet, try to find out the latest situation on Heathrow's fifth runway. Web sites to try include http//:www.baa.co.uk and http//:www.hacan.org.uk.

2 **As a group,** contact the Planning Inspectorate in Bristol on 0117 987 8935 and ask for a copy of their booklet *A Guide to Planning Appeals.* Study this carefully and then answer the following questions.

   a What is the time limit for submitting a valid appeal from the date of the original decision by an LPA?
   b How many copies of an appeal form must be made – and who receives each one?
   c Are photographs or plans acceptable as evidence?
   d Why is a certificate stating who owns the land required?
   e Is it allowable to fax an appeal if time is short?
   f What are the eight items listed in the checklist for sending off planning appeals?

g What is a 'site visit' – and who makes it and why?

h What is the difference between an unaccompanied site visit and an accompanied site visit?

i How many days' written notice are you entitled to, to inform you that an inquiry will be held?

j At the inquiry, who presents their case first – those bringing the application or the objectors?

k If your employer did not win his or her appeal and could not challenge the decision on legal grounds, but felt that the case had been dealt with unfairly, to whom could he or she appeal?

Now keep the booklet safely. You may need it again when you reach pages 135–137!

● Conferences and other events

In addition to meetings, you may be asked to arrange other types of events that involve **external** participants. Generally, meetings will mainly involve your colleagues and others in your organisation – apart from those to which shareholders are invited. Conferences and other events often involve external participants from different organisations and even from different parts of the world. The main three events we are going to consider are

- presentations
- seminars
- conferences.

Presentations

A presentation is an event normally scheduled by a host organisation for its customers – either actual or potential. It may take place on the host's premises or on the customers', or at a hotel or other location. Much depends upon the type of presentation, the number of people invited and the circumstances.

Generally it is the sales, marketing or PR departments in an organisation that are concerned with making presentations. The aim is to convince prospective customers that the company is honest, reliable and can offer a competitive service. Your college or school may give presentations to prospective students and their parents to convince them they should select your institution as a place of study.

If an organisation is making a presentation to *one* prospective customer, and is concerned with the specific product or service of interest to that particular firm, then the presentation is likely to take place at the location the customer would prefer. However, many sales people prefer to give a presentation on their own premises because they know the equipment and facilities that are available – and are certain they will be in working order!

If an organisation is making a more general presentation to a large group, this is likely to take place in a hotel or at another location, such as an exhibition. In this case, the presentation will either have to be geared to the facilities available, or equipment and visual aids will have to be transported.

Today a wide range of equipment can be bought or hired for both producing and giving presentations. This is discussed more fully on pages 93–95. The main things you should remember as a PA are that

- a poor or unprofessional presentation is worse than no presentation at all

- the treatment potential customers receive on arrival and departure is just as important as the type of service they will receive during the presentation itself.

To see why, you only have to put yourself in the customer's shoes! If you had arrived at your college to find the building in disrepair, a sloppily dressed receptionist had left you to wait in a draughty corridor for half an hour and you were then subjected to a presentation that told you very little and contained several spelling mistakes, what would have been the impression given to you and your parents? In today's world, such neglect can cost millions of pounds in lost business!

Seminars

A seminar is usually a one-day event comprising a 'learning experience' for those who attend. Invitations will be sent to those who are likely to be interested in the topics being covered. Some seminars are non-participative, in that the audience is invited to listen to an expert propound his or her views on a particular subject. More often, they comprise a more interactive programme – and in this case the number of participants is smaller. Seminar presentations usually require a similar aids and materials to sales presentations – and the same degree of care if the speaker and the organisation running the seminar are to retain a good reputation!

Seminars are usually organised to take place in external venues, such as in hotels, educational establishments or at the headquarters of professional institutions. A large, non-participative seminar may be held in a conference centre. Often organisers are concerned about the style of the event and will choose a venue in keeping with the image they wish to achieve. If, for instance, they wish to give the event an academic flavour, they may choose a luxury hotel, university or business school.

Seminars vary in that they can be quite formal affairs or relatively informal gatherings, depending upon the topics being discussed, the type of audience and, often, the size of the event. A seminar at which some advanced research papers are presented by leading specialists to a prestigious audience will be more formal than an evening seminar for a small group of business people about the Internet.

Another informal and abbreviated type of seminar is often a feature of exhibitions. These are sometimes termed 'fringe events'. For example, at an exhibition for top secretaries and PAs there may be short seminars on topics such as assertiveness, time management, travel arranging and so on. Those visiting the exhibition can reserve a place at the seminars of their choice, which usually operate on rotating time slots throughout the day in small seminar rooms off the main exhibition hall.

Finally, seminars are a feature of many conferences, as you will see below.

Conferences

The term 'conference' is usually used to describe a residential event where a number of delegates are invited to participate in a programme of activities organised in advance. A conference can vary in terms of size, scope, audience and length from a two-day conference for the company sales staff, to a week-long gathering of thousands of people from all over the world!

For very large and prestigious events, professional conference organisers are usually employed to make all the arrangements. Some professional associations employ their own specialist conference organisers. Smaller organisations, professional groups with fewer resources and companies that run conferences only for small groups or their own employees are more likely to expect their administrative or secretarial staff to make the arrangements.

Conferences are held in hotels, leisure complexes, public halls, universities, exhibition centres and large purpose-built conference centres, such as the Wembley Conference and Exhibition Centre, the Queen Elizabeth II Conference Centre and the Scottish Exhibition and Conference Centre. Some are even held on cruise liners! The venue is normally chosen for ease of access by delegates, and to match the space and facilities required and the budget for the event. In some cases security is also a major consideration, for instance at conferences held by the political parties (see page 85).

All conferences offer a series of activities and events to delegates – each of which is normally known as a **session**. These may include talks, seminars or presentations by visiting speakers, workshops, question and answer forums, visits to nearby places of interest, cocktail parties and formal dinners or dinner dances. The conference may be linked to an exhibition of products and services related to the theme of the event. Those conferences to which delegates are invited with their partners usually include a separate, alternative **partner programme**. These used to focus on traditionally female interests, such as shopping, but with the increase in women managers today's conference organisers have to take into account that partners will include men!

Check it yourself

1 The words 'meeting', 'conference' and 'seminar' may be used almost interchangeably in some organisations. For instance, what one organisation may call its 'three-day sales meeting' might be a 'sales conference' to another! To confuse matters even further, there are several other terms used to describe similar events. A list of these is given in Figure 1.6.

   Check that you understand when each might be used, and discuss any terms you are not clear about with your tutor.

Colloquium	An academic meeting at which specialists deliver lectures on a particular topic and then answer relevant questions.
Convention	The term often used in America to describe a large conference.
Road show	An exhibition event that takes place at different locations.
Symposium	A (usually informal) seminar at which several specialists deliver short talks on a topic or related topics, followed by a two-way question and answer session or an open discussion.
Trade Fair	An exhibition that often combines a conference, workshop activities, seminar sessions and entertainment for representatives from a particular trade or industry.
Summit	A conference of important and high-level officials, such as ministers representing various governments.

Figure 1.6 Event terminology

2 Assume you are giving a presentation about your course to next year's prospective students. Discuss as a group:

   a the information you would include
   b the visual aids and printed information you would need
   c the length of the event
   d an appropriate location

e an appropriate date and time

f how you would invite everybody.

Check your ideas with your tutor to ensure you have not neglected to consider anything of critical importance!

3 You have met several specialist terms throughout this section, mainly related to business meetings. There are some terms used specifically to describe certain activities that take place at conferences, seminars and other events. Below are given several such terms. Research each one to try to establish the correct meaning and compare your answers with other members of your group. Then check with the key on page 183.

- Registration

- Keynote address

- Workshop

- Simultaneous translation

- Open forum

- Fringe programme

- Plenary session.

4 Test your language ability! You work for a boss who is keen to retain traditional spelling and usage. He objects to your use of the words 'symposiums' and 'colloquiums'. What is the alternative plural form of each word?

● The role of the PA at meetings and conferences – an initial overview

The PA has a very responsible role in relation to the organisation of any type of event.

Before the event

The role of the PA before an event is that of planner, organiser, coordinator and 'doer'! You may attend meetings at which large seminars and conferences or formal meetings are planned – and you will no doubt leave the meeting with a considerable number of jobs to do! Smaller events, such as in-house meetings, presentations and company conferences you may be expected to plan and organise on your own.

It is often said that 'the devil lies in the detail'. Certainly, the potential success of *any* event is dependent upon excellent planning so that nothing is overlooked. Issues of concern – to name but a few – include:

- making bookings – for the venue, equipment, accommodation, speakers, refreshments, etc

- preparing and distributing pre-event documentation – from the notice of a meeting to conference programmes and correspondence confirming arrangements

- keeping lists of who is scheduled to attend, who has replied to correspondence and who has not – and following up the latter

- devising seating plans and arranging the production of place cards, if required

- checking continually that planned costs will not exceed the budget allocated for the event

- preparing event documentation – slides or presentation materials, copies of academic papers, documents to be tabled at a meeting

- preparing and checking that any equipment, special facilities or specific requirements are available

- making sure that everyone knows what is happening, when, what they are expected to do and how they are supposed to do it!

All these aspects are discussed in more detail in the following chapters.

During the event

During the event the role of PA may be that of note taker, press officer, customer liaison manager, problem-solver, trouble-shooter, coordinator, nerve soother and general factotum combined! If this seems daunting then rest assured that you are unlikely to be the only one in that role at a major event, and besides it makes for a very interesting life! The key attributes are unflappability, resourcefulness, patience, diplomacy, common sense and a good sense of humour!

After the event

After a large or complex event a review is usually made of its successes and failures. Even after a relatively informal meeting there may be something similar if the event was a disaster! These inquests are usually invaluable as they enable everyone to refine their skills for the next occasion.

Key tasks for the PA to perform routinely after any event include checking that all the bills match the quotations and are paid promptly, thanking people who helped, preparing and distributing relevant documents, and making sure all the documentation – including name and address lists and checklists – is stored safely in the correct files. It is also useful, if you do not have to provide a formal report on the event, to make your own notes on who was helpful, who was not, what went well, what did not – so that you can refresh your memory next time rather than repeat a mistake.

The role of the PA is considered in more depth in relation to each type of event later in this section. However, as the projected cost of an event is often the key criterion when making the initial plans, this is the area we will concentrate upon in the next chapter.

Review quiz

1 Identify FIVE reasons why meetings are held.

2 The proceedings at general meetings are constrained by the requirements of the Companies Act and the company's Articles of Association. Give THREE examples of items covered in these documents.

3 What is the difference between an ad hoc and a standing committee?

4 How would you describe the operations of a quality circle to a new member of staff?

5 A new employment agency has organised a presentation to be held in your College to which you have been invited.
   a What do you consider is the main purpose of this event?
   b What would you expect to be included, and why?
   c How would the standard of the presentation influence your opinion of the agency as a whole?

6 What is the difference between a working party and a task group?

7 Give three examples of informal meetings that may be held in your College.

8 What is a public inquiry? For what main reason are business organisations usually involved in public inquiries?

9 Match each of the following types of committees correctly with the rules that govern their activities.
   a sub-committee
   b executive committee
   c golf club committee
      i   constitution
      ii   terms of reference
      iii standing orders

10   Explain each of the following terms:

    a   to convene a meeting
    b   minutes of a meeting
    c   quorum
    d   clear days
    e   proxy

11   What is the difference between an Annual General Meeting and an Extraordinary General Meeting?

12   Identify FOUR potential benefits to be gained by holding an effective meeting.

2 Costing and budgets

Every event costs money – even a half-hour meeting of three members of staff in a manager's office. Interestingly, few organisations have any system for costing internal meetings, despite the obvious implications in terms of the salaries of those present plus the opportunity cost of their attendance – in other words, all the other jobs they could have been doing if they had not been attending the meeting.

However, organisations do usually operate a budgeting system to monitor all the other expenditure involved in running a meeting, and this is usually operated at departmental or section level. The stationery used will be set against one budget heading and the refreshments against another. If the meeting is run by the Human Resources department, refreshments ordered will be set against the total expenditure for that department; if special presentation materials were purchased by the Marketing department, these would be set against their budget and so on. For internal events and regular, routine expenditure you would therefore need to know the internal budgeting system in operation and how to book, cost and record the items you require.

If an external or large-scale event is being arranged, then you are likely to find that the event is allocated its own budget. This is sensible as the expenses (and income, if applicable) can be separately recorded and balanced. Not only is this more financially prudent than including the expenses of a large event in general organisational overheads, but this system simplifies matters for your accountant and your auditors who can check the figures more easily. In addition, separate accounts may be a specific requirement for VAT purposes (see page 53).

If you are responsible for organising such an event you therefore need to establish at the outset

- whether you have been allocated a fixed budget or are expected to submit forecast costings and bid for an amount
- whether any income will be accruing from the event and, if so, the amount of profit you are expected to make (if any)
- the system in your particular organisation for recording income and expenditure for an event
- whether your organisation is registered for VAT purposes
- the accounts you are expected to prepare after the event.

Normally, the sequence of events for PAs organising an event would be as follows:

1 Discuss outline plans with line manager and other relevant persons.

2 Prepare expenditure forecast in line with the above and calculate total.

3 Prepare income forecast (if appropriate) and calculate break-even point (see page 41).

4 Submit documents for budget approval.

5 Adjust forecasts and projections as required to comply with allocated budget.

6 Make bookings in accordance with plan.

7 Obtain and check invoices against expenditure forecast.

8 Check receipts against income forecast.

9 Pay invoices and bank receipts.

10 Prepare final accounts for event.

Note that at this stage we are not concerned with the VAT aspects of running an event. This is covered separately on pages 51–57.

Check your financial know-how!

If you have already taken (or are taking) a business qualification then you should already be familiar with the terms **fixed** and **variable costs**, **revenue** and **break-even point**. If not, then you should note the definitions below.

All costs can be divided into those that are fixed and those that are variable, and this division is essential to the concept of break-even analysis. Fixed costs are those that do not vary with output. In the case of running an event, the fixed costs are those **not** affected by the number of people attending. Variable costs, on the other hand, do vary with output. In the case of a conference or meeting, the more people there are in attendance, the higher the variable costs will be. Revenue, or income from an event, would also vary depending upon attendance if the delegates were paying a fee.

The break-even point is the point at which the **total costs** (ie fixed + variable) are the same as the revenue received. Costs are discussed in more detail on pages 37–39.

✓ Check it yourself

1 A meeting of the Health and Safety Committee takes place in your college on the last Thursday of each month at 12.30 pm. It is attended by the Safety Officer and up to ten representatives from across the college. From the expenditure items listed below, identify which would be fixed costs and which would be variable costs of the meeting:

   a heating the room
   b paper and stationery required
   c photocopying of leaflets for distribution to those present
   d sandwiches and coffee
   e lighting in the room.

   Check your answers with your tutor.

2 For a large event, the number of items required is obviously greater than for an internal meeting. A general list of items required for a conference is given in Figure 2.1. Study this list and, with the exception of the last item, decide which you think would represent a fixed cost and which would represent a variable cost – before reading the next paragraph.

Hire of venue	Printing of papers given out at the event
Accommodation, meals and refreshment for delegates	Cost of preparing videos and slides
Speakers' fees, travel expenses, meals and accommodation	Hire charges – flowers, stage settings, lectern, AVA and sound equipment, sign-posting
Staff costs (for interpreter, secretarial and security staff)	Insurance
Fees of professional conference organiser	Transportation expenses for equipment and displays from office
Advertising	
Pre-event publicity materials – preparation and printing	Transport costs for delegate visits
Postage and stationery costs	Entertainment which is a) individually priced, and b) generally provided
Delegates kits – preparation and printing of programme, name badges etc.	
	Contingency fund

Figure 2.1 Example expense list for a large-scale conference

Costing an event

You have seen an outline of costings for two different events in the exercise above. Note that for neither event were the salaries of permanent staff included, because these people would be paid anyway for undertaking other duties if they were not at the event and, as mentioned earlier, most organisations do not try to apportion internal staff costs when budgeting for an event. You should note that this usually includes ignoring the cost of the administrator's or PA's time! However, the situation is rather different if a professional conference organiser or any temporary staff are employed, when these costs must be offset against the event itself.

Generally speaking, the fixed costs of the event are likely to be the following.

- The venue itself. It could, of course, be argued that hiring a large hall for 2000 people will cost more than hiring a small room for 25. However, it is also the case that once the space has been hired, this cost is then fixed and will not vary if some people decline the invitation at the last minute or more delegates agree to attend than expected.

- Speakers' fees, travel expenses, meals and accommodation. Speakers usually charge a fixed fee that is not dependent upon the number of people attending. One way of saving money, however, is to book speakers who are promoting their own expertise or organisation – as they will often agree to appear for nothing. Conversely, celebrities or speakers who are renowned academically can charge tremendous fees, and their travel costs may include a ticket from New York on Concorde!

- Staff costs for interpreters, secretarial and/or security staff. Whilst the number of staff may depend upon the size of the event, it is usual to include all administrative costs under the 'fixed cost' heading.

- Advertising and pre-publicity costs, including the printing of tickets or registration documents, the stationery required and the postage involved in sending out invitations.

- Costs of preparing videos and slides.

- Hire charges – if you are going to need flowers, a lectern, special spot lights and stands, as well as audio visual aid (AVA) and sound equipment, these charges will be fixed.

- Insurance to cover injury to any person attending the event (public liability), damage to any valuable items being transported and kept at the event (property damage) and to cover cancellation of the event because of an unforeseen emergency (such as both your main speakers being stricken with 'flu or the conference centre catching fire the week before).

- Transportation expenses, for people and equipment.

- Any entertainment generally provided.

The variable costs will be the remaining items and can be calculated as the cost per delegate or per partner, to include the following.

- Accommodation, meals and refreshments for delegates.

- Delegate kits including programmes and name badges.

- The printing of any papers or other materials to be given out at the event.

- Any entertainment that is individually priced.

You should note that the fee charged by a professional conference organiser often has a fixed *and* a variable element, as the fee comprises an overall charge as well as an additional fee per delegate.

Once all the requirements are known, it is usual to prepare an expenditure forecast itemising all the fixed costs and giving the forecast total. The forecast can then be extended to include the variable costs for given numbers of delegates. Adding the fixed costs and variable costs together will give you the total cost of holding the event.

Income-generating events

Some events generate revenue or income. In this case you need to establish at the outset whether you are expected to make a profit (and by how much), can simply break even (make neither a profit nor a loss) or can make a small loss because your organisation is subsidising the event.

For a profit to be made, delegates must be charged a sufficient registration fee. However, people have expectations about how much is a reasonable price to pay – and this will depend upon the venue, the facilities, the speakers and the programme. It is no use arranging a conference in a draughty hall with terrible facilities and unknown speakers, and trying to charge a high fee! Most professional institutions charge for their conferences and the registration fee is paid by each delegate's employer. However, delegates are only likely to receive this financial support if their organisation believes it would benefit from their attendance because the programme is relevant to their area of work.

Other sources of income for this type of event may include:

- sponsorship of the event

- income from exhibitors

- advertising (eg in the conference programme).

It is usual to estimate how much income may be earned from additional sources *before* calculating delegate fees – particularly if you are trying only to break even for the event. In this case, you can calculate how much to charge as follows:

1 Calculate your **net fixed costs** by

- adding together all the fixed costs for the event

- deducting income from sponsorship, exhibitors and advertising.

2 Calculate the **net fixed costs per delegate** by

- estimating the number of delegates

- dividing this number into your net fixed costs figure.

3 Calculate the **delegate variable cost** by

- adding together all the variable costs for the event

- dividing this by the estimated number of delegates.

In some cases you will find that you have been quoted a variable cost per delegate. For instance, hotels normally quote a cost per person or per room and meal.

4 Calculate the **delegate fee** by

- adding together your **net fixed costs per delegate** and your **delegate variable cost**.

This is the registration fee you must charge to break even on the event.

Check it yourself

These calculations are easier than they might appear! Test yourself with the following example.

An organisation has estimated that 500 delegates will attend its event. The total fixed costs are estimated to be £60 000 and the variable cost per delegate has been calculated at £80. The income that can be raised through advertising and sponsorship is £15 000. How much would you charge each delegate if you wanted to

a break even
b make a profit of £15 000?

Check your answers with the key on page 183.

Coping with reality and complications

In real life nothing goes smoothly all the time – and this is particularly true if you are organising a large event. You would have to bear in mind the following possibilities:

- your estimated number of delegates may be either over-ambitious or over-cautious

- emergencies and problems may occur which affect your budget (a minor item forgotten at the costing stage, a sponsor withdrawing his support at the last minute, a taxi required to transport an item to the venue, etc)

- some delegates may expect a discount, eg members of a professional association or those who book early

- you may wish to offer variations of the programme, eg residential or non-residential, full attendance or just selected days.

All these complications will affect your calculations. Strategies for coping are given below.

How many delegates?

If your organisation has held similar events before, then you should be able to look back at the files to obtain a realistic estimate of the numbers likely to attend. If you are organising a new venture, you may be asked to start by calculating the minimum number of delegates who must attend to make the event viable. No organisation or association wants to invest thousands of pounds to host an event that attracts only a small number of people. Finding the break-even point will mean that a realistic decision can be made.

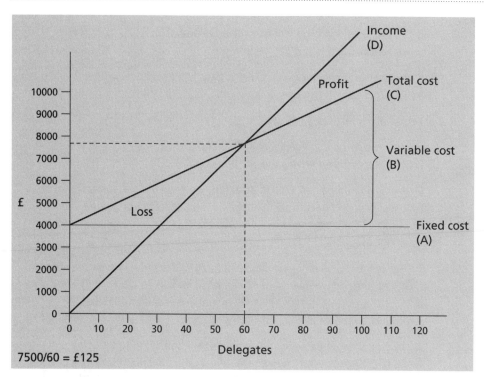

Figure 2.2 Break-even chart

The break-even chart illustrated in Figure 2.2 has been drawn up for a one-day event with estimated net fixed costs of £4 000, variable costs per delegate of £50 and with a projected charge of £125 per delegate. The fixed costs are shown by horizontal line A – this line never changes, regardless of the number of delegates. The total costs are shown by line C. This rises by £50 per delegate and is therefore sloping upwards above the fixed cost line. The difference between the two illustrates the variable cost. The projected revenue line at a charge of £125 per delegate is shown by revenue line D. At the point where this line crosses the total cost line the event will break even – it will cover all the costs but not make a profit. By extending the line downwards you can see that 60 delegates must attend, resulting in £7 500 revenue. More than 60 delegates would result in a profit and fewer than 60 delegates would result in a loss.

✓ Check it yourself

1 Study the chart in Figure 2.2 and make sure you understand it. Then answer the following questions:

a what would be the loss made by the organisation if only 30 delegates attended?

b what would be the profit made by the organisation if 100 delegates attended?

Note that you can work this out either by reference to the chart or by using a calculator.

2 Let us assume that £125 seems

   a too much of a bargain, or
   b too expensive for the event planned.

Draw two break-even charts yourself, one with an assumed charge of £100 per delegate and one with an assumed charge of £150 per delegate. Given the same costs, what will be the break-even point in each case?

3 To err on the safe side, professional organisers always assume that a maximum of two-thirds of those anticipated to do so will actually attend the event. In this case, how many people should be expected to make the event viable

   a in the case of the original break-even chart in Figure 2.2
   b in the case of your own break-even chart with £100 as the charge
   c in the case of your own break-even chart with £150 as the charge?

4 Break-even charts can be calculated very rapidly using a computer spreadsheet. The projected costs and revenue can be varied at the touch of a few keys to read out different break-even figures. If you are learning how to use spreadsheets as part of your course, then try using this method. You will find them much easier!

Emergencies and problems

Even the best-laid plans sometimes go wrong. This can be through a simple mistake, an oversight or an unexpected occurrence that must be handled promptly. Advertising costs might be slightly higher than expected, two members of staff could fall ill so that temporary staff need to be hired, or an important item of presentation equipment might need to be replaced at the last minute. Occasionally, major catastrophes mean that the conference has to be moved or rescheduled. It is prudent to take out insurance to cover such contingencies!

From the budgeting point of view it is sensible to set up a contingency fund for 'emergency and miscellaneous items'. This can range from 5 per cent to 10 per cent of the budget, depending upon the scale of the event. There is less to go wrong if you are organising a two-day conference for ten computer staff at a nearby hotel, than in the arrangement for a four-day conference at an overseas location for 2000 delegates! It is for that reason that a contingency item was included in the list of costs in Figure 2.1.

Discounts and related items

If you are arranging an event to which a large number of people will be invited it is sensible to see this as a marketing opportunity. In other words, you need to tempt them to attend. This is easier if you are offering a varied programme on relevant issues with reputable speakers at an appropriate location. However, in the majority of cases business people or members of a professional body will apply to their own company to cover the costs. In reality, few business delegates pay their own fees.

Offering a discount for early booking has two benefits. First, it reduces the cost for organisations sponsoring their staff. Secondly, it means you get a clear picture of how many people are likely to attend much sooner. Discounts are often offered to members of a professional association, and they are also invited to bring partners and friends – but at a higher charge.

You should note that most organisations sponsoring delegates will be VAT registered. This means that if VAT is charged on the fee (which is normal) then this must be shown separately in order that the organisation can reclaim the VAT paid. This reduces the overall cost to the company. This topic is dealt with in more detail on page 51.

Offering variations

Most conference organisers are aware that not everyone may want (or be available) to attend the full event. Equally, some people who live nearby may prefer to return home at night from a residential event. For that reason, most conference booking forms give a range of choices (often known as packages), together with the cost of each one. Different rates may also be given for members of an association or society, non-members and partners.

There are three main points to note.

1 Against each alternative you **must** clearly specify all the facilities offered, so people know exactly what they are paying for (see Chapter 5, page 171).

2 Once the booking forms have been sent out then these packages cannot be altered – so your costings must be right at this stage!

3 To help to calculate the projected revenue for a range of options you can either
   a estimate how many people will take up each package, or
   b calculate the 'average revenue' to be earned from each person. This is the easier option of the two!

Keeping records and preparing accounts

In some cases you may find your budget has been allocated on a line-by-line basis – with a maximum cost for different items. Alternatively, there may be a total amount for the event which you must not exceed.

Once the budget has been agreed, you can go ahead and make your bookings – although you should confirm, at this time, that the price has not changed from the quoted cost. This is particularly important if there has been any delay between receiving quotations and confirming your requirements. Make sure you confirm *everything* in writing (or through an official purchase order) and that the price is clearly shown. It is sensible to restrict the number of people who are allowed to place orders against a budget – so that responsibility is clearly defined. When the invoices are received, these must be checked before they are paid. For a large conference, planned over many months, the budget is checked regularly to ensure spending is on target.

For a large event, particularly one that has generated income, it is usual to prepare an **income and expenditure account**. This is an itemised list of income and expenditure which balances with the surplus remaining in your budget or any additional amounts you have had to request.

Normally, just the total amount spent on each item is recorded – even if there is a VAT element. However, some organisations prefer a separate VAT account to be completed, and only the net amounts recorded in the income and expenditure account. You would need to check the procedures in force in your own organisation at the outset.

Figure 2.3 on the next page is an example of a simple income and expenditure account of a one-day seminar for which delegates were charged a £45 attendance fee.

Check it yourself

1 You may like to consider how the offer of a discount would affect a break-even chart – in particular your revenue line – as in this case one group of delegates will pay a lower rate than the rest. Discuss your ideas with your tutor.

2 You have recently organised a one-day seminar at which participants paid £65 each to attend. Because it covered financial matters, it was sponsored by a local firm of accountants who contributed £100 towards the running costs. The room was free but your expenses included £35 per person for meals and refreshments, £150 for publicity costs, £50 for seminar materials and £55 for the hire of audio/visual equipment.

Draw up an income and expenditure account to calculate the surplus you made.

Health and Safety seminar held at Woodcrest Hotel, 14 April 199-		
	£	£
Income		
52 delegates @ £45 each		2340
Sponsorship by safety consultants		200
Programme advertising		200
		2740
Expenditure		
Seminar room	100	
Refreshments (morning and afternoon)	240	
Buffet lunch	720	
Advertising and publicity	1200	
Printing of booking forms/leaflets	100	
Printing of programme	160	
Postage	42	
Visual aid production	60	
Hire of audio/visual equipment	30	
Insurance	55	
		2707
Surplus		£33

Figure 2.3 Income and expenditure account

● The tax and VAT implications of organising an event

Tax and allowable expenses

Organising and arranging an event results in several expenses for a company, as you have already seen. Meetings for shareholders and events for staff, such as a training seminar and a sales conference, do not result in any income for the organisation – only additional costs. Such events therefore increase overall expenditure in the course of a year and reduce the potential profit.

The Inland Revenue allows for expenses incurred **wholly, exclusively and necessarily** in the performance of the duties of employment to be allowable against tax. Tax relief is given by the Inland Revenue to the person or the organisation sustaining the expense. Therefore, to give a simple example, if you had to wear a uniform paid for by your company, then your company would claim relief on this expense. If, on the other hand, you were expected to buy the uniform yourself, you could claim tax relief by including the expense on your tax return.

The key point for conference organisers is the phrase **wholly, exclusively and necessarily**. Only expenses incurred as an essential part of the business are allowable, and these include:

- car repairs and expenses

- hotel expenses

- protective clothing and uniforms

- training fees for courses to improve work-related skills

- essential reference books and business stationery

- travel on business trips

- work-related subscriptions to professional bodies.

Refresh your memory about profit!

When you are looking at how conferences and meetings are affected by tax and VAT, it is important that you understand the nature of profit. Virtually all commercial organisations are in business to make a profit. Professional associations and other non-profit-making organisations aim to make a surplus at the end of the year, rather than a profit as such – in other words, they aim not to make a loss.

In a commercial organisation profit is calculated by working out the value of sales and subtracting the cost of the goods that were sold. This gives the **gross profit**. From this figure is deducted the expenses incurred. This results in the **net profit** – on which the organisation pays tax.

However, for the purposes of taxation organisations are allowed to deduct certain expenses – reducing the amount of tax paid at the end of the year – and not others. Obviously, most companies wish to reduce their tax burden by taking advantage of those expenses that are allowable and minimising expenditure on those that are not.

Non-allowable expenses include:

- the cost of ordinary clothes
- travel between home and business
- gifts valued at more than £10, gifts without a conspicuous advertisement and any gifts comprising food, drink, tobacco or vouchers
- interest on credit cards
- ordinary meals (eg at the workplace)

However, the key point to note is that tax law is extremely complicated and also changes frequently! There are many grey areas (such as business entertaining). For this reason, you should check with your company accountant to ensure that you are operating within the current guidelines and in accordance with official company policy.

Check it yourself

You work for a firm of management consultants which organises several prestigious events each year. From the list above, decide as a group whether you think each of the following expenses would be allowable against tax or not. Check your answers with the key on page 183.

    a London hotel bill for accommodation of three sales consultants attending a national conference on corporate planning.

    b Air ticket for the MD to give the keynote address at a major conference in New York.

    c Lunch for staff hosting a seminar at a hotel for local business people.

    d Bottles of wine given as gifts to all those who attend a seminar.

    e A new outfit for the MD's PA who is accompanying staff to New York.

    f Air ticket for the MD's wife who is accompanying him to New York.

    g Hotel bill for rooms booked during a firm's AGM.

    h Postage costs for sending out the AGM notice and agenda and the company report and accounts.

    i Stationery costs for all documents required for an AGM.

    j Drinks and nibbles for journalists at a press conference.

    k Cost of producing slides and a video for a major sales presentation.

    l Insurance premium paid against the non-appearance of a famous American management guru at a forthcoming conference.

    m The American guru's speaker fee.

n Drinks party given by MD at his own home for overseas visitors.

o Cost of Institute of Directors' membership fees for the Board of Directors.

p Printing of conference kits for 500 delegates at a forthcoming conference.

q Your own travel to the conference venue 150 miles away.

r Your own travel to a conference venue that is nearer to your home than your employer's premises!

Perks and benefits

The Inland Revenue does allow all employees to receive some benefits tax free. These include:

- luncheon vouchers up to 15p per day

- canteen facilities at the place of work

- crèche places and nursery facilities run and operated by your employer

- retraining if you are about to leave your employer or have recently lost your job

- a car parking space near your place of work

Suspicious minds?

The Inland Revenue is forever concerned that some conferences may be more of a 'jolly' for staff than hard work! In some cases, the conference may be viewed as a fringe benefit or a perk – rather than an arduous business activity. This perception is important, because it affects the way in which the Inland Revenue treats the expenses incurred.

Preparatory arrangements, official programmes and detailed costings are very important – as the Inland Revenue may request copies of such documents to decide a doubtful case. Interestingly, the location is irrelevant – whether your conference is held in Manchester or the Maldives influences the decision much less than the activities that take place! Moreover, if the Inland Revenue considers that part of the trip comprises private enjoyment, then you may be personally responsible for declaring these as benefits on your self-assessment form and paying tax on them. Each year, your employer must give the Inland Revenue details of all your expenses and benefits by completing a P11D form. You receive a copy so that you can check that benefits listed match the entries on your own tax form. This is important – a mistake made by your employer can mean a fine of up to £3 000 – and you, too, can be charged interest and penalties for incorrect completion. Further difficulties can arise if you receive benefits from a third party – such as a client. If you are in the position of receiving a P11D then you must remember to check it carefully and to include on your own tax return any taxable benefits you have received from any source.

- Christmas parties and similar events provided that the cost is not more than £50 per employee

- up to £5 per night for miscellaneous expenses when staying away from home on business

- employer contributions to your pension

- workplace sports facilities.

If you earn less than £8 500 per year then you may be able to receive other tax-free benefits. If you earn more than this amount then you are likely to be taxed on additional items such as:

- a company car and the fuel it uses

- mobile telephones

- equipment (such as a laptop computer) regularly loaned to you by the company

- private medical insurance
- gifts (from your employer or from a third party) or discounted products and services
- vouchers and credit cards for personal use
- season tickets for travel
- most employer-provided accommodation.

Check it yourself

This next exercise is not meant to be taken too seriously, but may help you to remember some of the points above. Read the following and identify all the areas where naive Noreen may find herself in serious trouble!

Noreen Organising this year's conference isn't half as bad as everyone made out. It's quite fun putting the programme together. Taking home that spare computer out of Sales has helped as well, as I've been able to do a lot of work at home.

Paul I hope we're going somewhere decent this year. Last year the food was awful and the waiters looked like they should have been pensioned off years ago. It took them about an hour to serve the soup.

Noreen You wait until you see this place. (*Hands over brochure.*) There's a heated swimming pool, squash court, golf course, fitness centre and beauty clinic! I bet most of the managers spend the week on the golf course. I've booked in all the staff as honorary members of the fitness centre for the three days we're there and booked a beauty session and manicure for Pamela, Jenny and me. I'm hoping to lose a bit of weight while I'm there.

Paul If the food's as bad as last year, that shouldn't be difficult.

Noreen No – you should see what they have on offer. I've told them we don't want the set menus – we'd rather order à la carte each evening. That way, if I want fillet steak or lobster there isn't a problem.

Paul If you're losing weight, you'll have to stop drinking.

Noreen That's a point. I've already booked a champagne reception for staff on arrival and told them to offer us the full wine list each evening, and the bar does some fantastic cocktails. The last night I thought we could do with a bit of entertainment. I contacted an after-dinner speakers' club to see who would liven things up a bit. You wouldn't believe the fees some of the famous people charge.

Paul Someone suggested a dinner dance for the last night. I hope they forget that idea – I'd rather have a disco.

Noreen I quite fancy a dinner dance – I've never been to one. It could be quite romantic. Mind you, I'd need something special to wear. (*Thinks.*) I know, I could ring a few of our clothes suppliers. I bet for a free advertisement in the programme at least one of them would offer me an outfit to wear.

Paul You're getting carried away. It'll be too cold for nights under the stars. Perhaps you should arrange it somewhere with sun, sea and Sangria next year.

Noreen Now that's a good idea . . .

VAT regulations – an overview

Most people are well aware of the existence of value added tax (VAT) and the fact that it is levied on most of the goods and services we buy. However, you may be less familiar with how the VAT system works and why it is important that you keep an accurate record of any VAT payments you make.

VAT rules and regulations are complicated and may vary according to the type of business with which you are involved. Detailed study of different aspects of VAT is outside the scope of this book. However, you should be aware of the basics, which are given below.

- VAT registration is compulsory for businesses that exceed a specific value of taxable supplies over a certain period (generally twelve months). At 1 December 1997 this value – known as the registration limit – was £49 000.

- The VAT definition of 'business' is quite broad and includes sole traders and partnerships, as well as limited companies, clubs, associations and charities.

- Not all supplies are 'taxable' supplies. Some are exempt from VAT and an organisation that only provides exempt supplies cannot normally be registered for VAT. Examples include insurance, betting and gambling, supplying credit and loans, certain education and training and the services of doctors and dentists.

- Taxable supplies are all goods and services that are 'rated' for VAT. In most cases this is at the standard rate, currently 17.5 per cent. A reduced rate (currently 5 per cent) is charged on supplies of fuel and power used domestically and by charities. Some supplies are zero-rated and no VAT is charged on these, eg most food (except restaurant meals and take-aways), books and newspapers, children's clothes and shoes, exported goods and medical prescriptions.

- Once an organisation has registered for VAT it must charge VAT at the correct rate on the items it supplies.

- The VAT charged by a company is added together at periodic intervals (usually quarterly). This is the total **output tax** that has been collected by the company, and this tax is payable to HM Customs and Excise.

- VAT-registered organisations can reclaim the VAT they have paid on most of their own business purchases and expenses, such as raw materials, equipment purchased for business use and general business expenses. This is also totalled over a period and is classified as **input tax**.

- Each period the company must complete a VAT return and show the output tax and input tax, as well as the value of their taxable supplies. The **difference** between the output and input tax is the amount owed to HM Customs and Excise.

Reclaiming VAT

If you are buying goods and services on behalf of your organisation, then you must keep a full record of all VAT payments so that the input tax can be reclaimed. This applies whether you are paying for stationery supplies, settling a bill for conference accommodation or monitoring expense claims submitted by staff. Obviously, you cannot claim for any exempt goods or services (because you won't have paid any VAT), nor for any expenses not allowed for VAT purposes. Allowable and non-allowable expenses for VAT in relation to conferences and meetings are discussed below.

For those expenses that are allowable, you must follow the rules and regulations for reclaiming VAT.

- First, a VAT invoice must be received and retained by the purchaser. This must comply to VAT regulations (see below). It must be made out to the registered organisation, except in the case of hotel bills and similar expenses where the invoice may be in the name of an employee.

- VAT invoices can only be issued by VAT-registered organisations. If you do not know if an organisation is registered for VAT, *always ask* at the time you are making your initial enquiry. The VAT invoice must show the name, address and VAT registration number of the supplier, the date of issue, a description of each item or service supplied, and – again for each item – the charges made exclusive of VAT, the VAT rate, the VAT amount owed and the total charge. Any cash discount must also be clearly shown and VAT must be calculated on the discounted price. Each invoice must have a separate identifying number and show when the goods or service were supplied. The invoice should be issued within 30 days of this date.

- Supplies of under £100, inclusive of VAT, can be shown on a less detailed tax invoice giving the name, address and VAT number of the supplier, the time of supply, a description of the goods or services, the overall charge made *including VAT* and the rate of VAT. Invoices for petrol and diesel fuel should show the registration number of the vehicle involved.

- Credit card vouchers can be adapted to serve as VAT invoices provided that the voucher clearly shows the supplier's name and address, the charge made including VAT and the date of sale. The supplier must then also add the VAT registration number, the rate of VAT and a description of the goods or services supplied.

Ideally you should summarise all the payments you have made, in date order matching your copy invoices. Your summary should show the VAT rate charged, the VAT-exclusive value of the purchase, the amount of VAT paid and the total amount paid. You should note that if you later receive a credit note for any items, this amount should be deducted from the totals above.

Calculating VAT

In most cases you will find that VAT is calculated for you on a VAT invoice. In other cases, you may need to work it out yourself. One important point to note is that, whenever you are in any doubt, you should always check whether quotations you receive are **exclusive** or **inclusive** of VAT. If they are exclusive of VAT then you will need to add 17.5 per cent to the quotation. If they are inclusive of VAT then you may have to calculate how much of the amount is VAT. The same applies if you receive a VAT-inclusive invoice.

Example one

Hotel A quotes you the rate of £80 per person per night for each of your 25 guests, exclusive of VAT. In this case you need to calculate how much the total bill will be including VAT. You calculate the price × the number of guests + the VAT, ie

$80 × 25 = 2000 + 17.5\% = 2000 + 350 = £2,350.$

Example two

Restaurant B quotes you a price of £282 for a buffet inclusive of VAT. In this case you need to calculate how much you are paying for the buffet and how much you are paying in VAT.

This calculation is done by applying a simple formula. For the current rate of VAT this formula is 7/47. If you are mathematically minded and wonder how this formula has been derived, then see below. For the moment, we will concentrate on applying it to the task in hand. You must divide the price quoted by 47 and multiply by 7, ie

$282/47 = 6 \times 7 = £42$.

You can check your answer by applying the formula 40/47 to find the VAT exclusive amount.

$282/47 = 6 \times 40 = £240$.

The two figures added together should equal your total. Therefore

$£42 + £240 = £282$ – which means we are correct.

Of course, not all amounts divide by 47 as precisely as 282! Do not be alarmed if you find your answer is a rather long decimal. You are allowed to round VAT amounts down to the nearest whole penny.

Check it yourself

1   Work out the VAT that will be charged on each of the following quotations, which have been issued **exclusive** of VAT:

  a   an advertisement costing £62
  b   a computer costing £1450
  c   accommodation and meals for staff for a two-day seminar costing £750.

2   Calculate the VAT on each of the following bills you have received **inclusive** of VAT:

  a   train fare to Manchester for three managers, costing £141
  b   restaurant meal following a sales presentation costing £320
  c   taxi fares to the train station for visitors costing £35.

3   The formula for calculating any rate of inclusive VAT is as follows:

  $$\frac{\text{rate of VAT}}{100 + \text{rate of VAT}}$$

  For the current rate of VAT the fraction is therefore

  $$\frac{17.5}{117.5}$$

  This is cancelled down to give the formula 7/47.

  From this explanation, calculate the formula you would use if:

  a   the VAT rate was lowered to 15%
  b   the VAT rate was increased to 25%.

VAT-allowable expenses

You may also be asked to check expense claims for staff who have attended events – and to enter the VAT amount where appropriate. In addition to checking the amounts and entering those that are missing, you must also be able to check whether the claims are for allowable or non-allowable items. We have already covered tax-allowable items on pages 45–47. In this case we are concerned with those items, relating to meetings and conferences, on which the VAT office is prepared to allow your organisation to reclaim the input tax. You should note that the list is *not* identical to the expenses allowable by the Inland Revenue, and that regulations relating to allowable expenses do change. Therefore, you must not assume that just because an expense is allowable against tax you can automatically claim the VAT back! Unless you are absolutely certain you know what you are doing, check with your company accountant or with your local VAT office – the number is in your local directory.

Broadly, however, some similar rules apply.

• The VAT criterion is basically whether each expense is **wholly for business use**. Private purchases cannot be counted for input tax. If goods or services are used both for business and private purposes (eg a car or a telephone) then some part of the input tax may be reclaimable but the proportion must be agreed with the VAT office beforehand.

• Input tax *cannot* be recovered for expenditure on business entertainment. This category includes:

  – the provision of meals and drinks to anyone who is not an employee
  – the provision of accommodation or facilities for sport or recreation
  – visits to theatres, nightclubs, etc
  – goods purchased purely or partly for the purposes of entertaining (eg a private yacht).

  Expenses incurred by employees acting as hosts on such occasions are also not allowable.

• Input tax is recoverable on staff expenses incurred for meals, etc when business trips are made away from the normal workplace, *provided* that any entertainment is secondary to the main purpose of the trip. The same applies to expenses incurred by temporary staff or casual helpers but *not* to VIP guests, journalists or other invited guests.

• Input tax may be claimed on certain events classed by the VAT office as 'staff entertainment' if the event is held wholly for the purpose of business, eg a working lunch or breakfast meeting. In other cases, the basic rule applied is to assume that only 50 per cent of the input tax can be claimed, to reflect the 'personal benefit' received – unless the organisation has negotiated a different proportion with the VAT office.

- Input tax cannot be reclaimed on any food and drink purchased purely for business entertainment. That consumed by staff at a function may be reclaimable according to the negotiated proportion, that consumed by their guests is not.

- Input tax may be recovered on room hire or equipment hire for the running of seminars or other training courses. Input tax on accommodation and meals for such an event is recoverable only if the guests are charged to attend and the 'inclusive nature' of the event (ie accommodation and meals) is stated in the promotional literature.

- Professional bodies, learned societies and other clubs and associations may be able to recover any VAT on the events they hold or may be able to claim exemption. The regulations are quite complex but, broadly, entertainment offered must be free to members as part of their subscription benefits. Normally VAT incurred on expenses for non-members cannot be recovered, neither can exemption be claimed.

Going over the limit

You may work for a small organisation that is not registered for VAT because its income from taxable supplies is usually below the limit for VAT registration. However, if it decides to hold a conference or other income-generating event that would create an increase in its taxable supplies over a short period, it may be that the organisation must register for VAT.

Generally speaking, the VAT office looks at **trends** when recommending whether registration is necessary or not – mainly because it does not want businesses registering for one period and deregistering the next! If an event would create a minor blip in income then it is likely that registration will not be necessary. If more events are planned so the overall trend is upwards, registration may be necessary. It is important to contact the VAT office if you are uncertain about what to do. Otherwise the organisation may be subject to stiff penalties for non-compliance with the regulations!

1 Your predecessor has left you some notes about VAT charges relating to conferences and meetings (see Figure 2.4). Use this, together with the information given on the previous pages, to

---

VAT on conferences and meetings

Notes you may find useful

1 VAT is charged by hotels on sleeping accommodation, meals and refreshments at the standard rate. It doesn't matter whether they quote for providing meals as an inclusive charge or for an additional payment.

2 Hotels charge VAT on any deposits but NOT on cancellation charges.

3 Some places charge VAT for supplying a room and some do not! It depends whether they have waived their exemption or not – you'll have to check when you enquire about a booking. However, if they serve refreshments the catering must be subject to VAT.

4 Additional services provided by a hotel, such as equipment or car parking, are also subject to VAT.

5 Any tips collected at the time of the event and given freely by those present are not subject to VAT.

6 If you use a booking agency and then cancel the booking, you will still have to pay a basic charge plus VAT.

7 Most printing is zero-rated. This means you will have no VAT to pay on the printing of items such as location maps and conference programmes.

8 Don't forget there is no VAT on postage charges!

9 Most speakers and interpreters are not registered for VAT, so there shouldn't be a VAT element in their fees.

10 You won't pay VAT on insuring the event, unless you pay a 'surcharge' to the hotel to avoid any cancellation fees. Contact our insurance broker instead.

11 Virtually every other item you purchase will have VAT levied at the standard rate. This is reclaimable in most cases.

Hope this helps!

Figure 2.4 A PA's notes on VAT

decide which of the following are acceptable, or correct, and which should be challenged.

a A hotel charges you a deposit of £50 + VAT.

b You receive a bill after the event for VAT on the tips that you and your colleagues collected to give to the waiters and waitresses at the event

c The hotel sends you a separate bill for hire charges for audio/visual equipment, the lectern and flowers placed in the conference hall.

d One organisation quotes you a charge of £120 for the hire of a seminar room + VAT, another tells you there is no charge for VAT for the room, only for any refreshments provided.

e You cancel a room booking at the last minute. You are charged £20 for the cancellation but told that no VAT is payable.

2   From the information given in this section, decide which of the items on Melinda's claim form (Figure 2.5 on page 60) can be allowed *for VAT purposes* and which cannot. Then calculate the VAT for each of the allowable items.

Finally, calculate the total value of the claim and the total amount of the VAT reclaimable.

Check your answers with your tutor.

Review quiz

1   Briefly describe the value of calculating the break-even point in relation to organising an event.

2   List SIX fixed costs likely to be incurred by a conference organiser and TWO variable costs.

3   Identify THREE reasons why the price charged to different people attending a conference may vary

4   What is a P11D? Under what circumstances would you receive one?

5   Your boss is interested in the idea of giving all conference delegates a small gift at the end of the event. What advice would you give him to ensure the gifts could be classified as a tax-allowable expense?

6 As a conference organiser, what precautions would you take to ensure that your event could not be challenged as a pleasure trip by the Inland Revenue?

7 List FIVE items which must be included on a VAT invoice for items costing more than £100.

8 Your boss settles a hotel bill using a credit card and supplies you with the voucher. What items must be included for the voucher to be acceptable for VAT purposes?

9 You have received two quotations for a one-day seminar. Hotel A has quoted you a price of £25 per person + VAT. Hotel B has quoted an inclusive price of £380 for the event.

   a What is the VAT amount you could reclaim if you visited Hotel B?

   b How many participants would you need for Hotel B to be the more cost-effective option?

10 After a business presentation, your boss takes six important clients out to a nightclub. The bill comes to £550. He asks you to calculate the VAT so that it can be reclaimed. What would you tell him and why?

11 You have been given the task of organising a conference at a nearby hotel. List FOUR types of expenses you might incur on which you would expect to be charged VAT, and TWO types of expenses on which you would not.

12 Briefly describe how you would explain to a new employee the calculation of VAT from a VAT-inclusive petrol bill.

Expenses Claim Form

Name: Melinda Joyce

Department: Sales

Month ending: 30 June 199-

Date	Description	Amount (ex VAT)	VAT	Amount (inc VAT)
6 June	Train fare to Coventry to view conference centre	£35.00		
10 June	6 bottles white wine for hospitality	£23.00		
16 June	Postage on invitations for seminar	£16.25		
20 June	Bill for staff working breakfast (preparing for seminar)	£24.20		
21 June	Printing of seminar programme	£16.00		
22 June	Taxi fare to client	£4.70		
23-24 June	2-day stay in Bristol to see clients – accommodation and meals	£185.00		
	TOTAL			

Claimed by . . . .

Authorised by . . . .

Figure 2.5 Melinda's expense claim

Planning and organisational skills

3

This chapter is concerned with the organisational and administrative skills needed to plan different events. It also contains information on general issues – such as selecting the venue, deciding on the main requirements and facilities, and aspects such as security and health and safety that can apply to any type of event. In the early stages of your career it is unlikely that you will be expected to organise a highly sensitive and important meeting without advice and guidance, or to arrange a major conference single-handedly – at least, we would hope not! Most people progress from arranging small, informal meetings, to larger or more formal meetings and finally to large-scale events. This enables new PAs or administrators to apply their knowledge and skills to progressively more complex and important occasions. Very large, prestigious conferences or those organised on an international basis are usually arranged by a team of people. In this situation, good communication and coordination skills between team members are vital. Alternatively, the role of the PA or administrator is to work with a professional conference organiser to provide all the information that is required.

Rudyard Kipling – and his relevance to organising events

If you studied English literature at school and know that Kipling was a nineteenth-century author and poet, you may well wonder what relevance he has to this book! The reason for his inclusion is that one of his famous rhymes should be learnt by heart by all aspiring organisers.

I had six honest serving men,
They taught me all I knew

Their names were **What** and **Why** and **When**
And **How** and **Where** and **Who**.

These six key words are very important – consideration of each one should result in a 'key facts' sheet for any event and prevent you from forgetting anything essential.

Rudyard Kipling
Mary Evans Picture Library

At this stage it is important to develop a technique you can use to enable you to transfer your skills from one event to another. Trying to remember a hotch-potch list rarely works and usually means something will be forgotten. For that reason you need to develop good planning and organisational skills from the start.

● Planning and organisation – the basics

Before the planning starts

As a first step, use the 'Kipling list' to focus yourself on what is being planned and, broadly, what you will have to do.

Why is it being held? In other words, what are its aims and objectives – what is it trying to achieve? This can affect the choice of venue, the facilities required and the overall style of the event. For a conference, it may influence the theme reflected in both the programme and the social activities. It also helps you to focus on the reason for all your work and to help the manager or chairperson to run it successfully.

Where is it to be held? In-house or at an external venue? Is there a recommended list of venues you must use? If not, how can you assess which venue would be appropriate? If it is in-house, will it be in someone's office or in a particular meetings room?

When will it take place? This is essential information as it tells you how long you have to make all the arrangements! You also need to check how long it will last as this helps you to identify the accommodation, food and refreshments required. In addition, if you are booking an external venue, the time of year may influence your choice.

Who should be invited? This gives you information on the number of people who will be likely to attend (which affects the choice of room or location). The status of those being invited will be crucial to many of your plans. The name of the person chairing the meeting or running the event is also important, as he or she is your key liaison person.

What will be needed? All events require different facilities and services. In addition, there will be a variety of documents concerned with both the event itself and the organisational arrangements. There may be some limitations on your choices depending upon the budget. It is essential to make certain that you know exactly what your own responsibilities are, ie the aspects of the event you are to organise on your own and those where you would need your manager's approval.

How does it operate? Experienced PAs are confident organising a variety of events because they know the format followed for different types of meetings and conferences. They also understand the roles of the different people involved. Knowing what to expect helps to dispel anxiety, means you can plan more knowledgeably and increases your effectiveness on the day itself.

Aids to good planning – checklists and planning schedules

Some people are inveterate list makers, others try to work without them. Invariably, good organisers and administrators have a list (or even several of them!) somewhere in the background for virtually every event. Even if the event is a small, informal meeting they regularly organise, having a list means that they will never forget anything even during a particularly hectic time.

The two types of lists you are likely to find most useful are checklists and planning schedules. Each of these is discussed separately below.

Checklists

Checklists are vital to good planning – although they can be overdone. The aim is to have a 'master list' which reminds you of everything you must do. However, the last thing you need is a file full of old checklists that simply confuse you. The ideal is to have *your own* tried and tested checklist for each type of event you organise. Each should be as simple as possible and set out clearly under specific headings. As you gain in knowledge and experience, you may adapt the headings and entries. A short checklist for an informal meeting is likely to look similar to Figure 3.1. You will see it has been divided into the tasks to be done before, during and after the meeting. A checklist for a formal meeting would have additional items and one for a residential conference, of course, is likely to be much longer. If a team of people is involved, against each item on the master checklist it is usual to insert the initials of the person responsible for the task.

In some cases, meetings secretaries and organisers prefer to photocopy a copy of a standard checklist for each new meeting or event and then tick each item as it is done. Others prefer to enter the date alongside each task to identify when it has to be carried out. Whilst this is useful, it is easy to

BEFORE THE MEETING

Venue
Book meetings room
Check furniture
Ascertain/check layout
Check OHP and flipchart

Food
Order refreshments

Documentation
Send e-mail or memo calling meeting
Prepare Agenda (if required)
Prepare/photocopy papers for circulation
Prepare/photocopy papers to be tabled
Prepare visual aids

Other
If external visitors involved

Book car parking spaces
Prepare visitors' badges
Send location maps/letter confirming details

AT THE MEETING

Obtain room key (if required)
Check room before event
Take spare copies of all documentation
Arrange for phones to be switched through (as required) and messages taken
Take notes, as required

AFTER THE MEETING

Type up notes
Distribute notes
Distribute relevant paperwork to absentees
File papers in relevant files

Figure 3.1 Checklist for an informal meeting

miss an item if you are busy – unless you have had the foresight (and time) to transfer each job into your diary to remind yourself to do it on a particular day. For that reason, alongside a basic checklist, most organisers also prepare a planning schedule.

Planning schedules

A planning schedule is similar to a rearranged checklist, written in date order with the first activity to be undertaken listed at the top. Alternatively the list can be written in week or month order, with tasks grouped under each heading, but this gives a less precise schedule. A mixture of the two may be used, with tasks undertaken early in the process grouped under monthly or weekly headings, and key activities for nearer the time allocated to specific dates.

Usually schedules for major or complex events are created by taking the following steps.

- Identify those activities where a specific length of time is required, add some time allowance for safety, and enter these activities under the dates for action and completion. For example, if it takes your printing section (or external printer) at least three weeks to print a conference programme, you should make four weeks (to be on the safe side) prior to your posting dates the deadline for finalising the contents and giving the text to the printer.

- Identify those activities where you are under a legal obligation to observe certain time constraints, for example if you have to give fourteen clear days' notice for a formal meeting.

- Decide which activities are interlinked and dependent upon one another. For instance, you cannot advertise a conference until you know

- where and when it is being held
- who is speaking
- what the outline programme will be.

  All these issues need to be clarified first, earlier in your schedule than preparing any advertisements, programmes or internal memos.

- Schedule the remaining activities to be undertaken in a logical order, in all cases allowing a good safety margin.

An example of a monthly planning schedule for a one-day seminar is given in Figure 3.2.

Check it yourself

You have been given the job of organising a one-day seminar at a nearby hotel for the sales representatives in your organisation. The event will take place six weeks from today. The speakers will be the MD, the Sales Director, the Technical Director and the Computer Services Manager.

Event: One-day seminar on Time Management for PAs

Date of event: 28 May 199-

January

Prepare initial costings and agree with JW
Finalise programme for event with RT
Book speakers, agree topics and obtain biographies
Visit and book venue and confirm
Prepare flyers and advertisement copy

February

Place advertisements for February and March
Prepare and post mailshot to members
Confirm speakers' slots in writing, check audio/visual aid requirements
Prepare information pack/location map for delegates

March

Receive and process firm bookings – send out information pack/location map
Commence log of firm bookings
Select and confirm buffet lunch menu plus special requirements
Check transport arrangements and meal requirements for speakers
Book photographer

April

Finalise list of attendees
Confirm numbers to venue for seating/catering/refreshments
Visit and confirm final arrangements/requirements for venue – refreshments,
    parking, visual aids, reception facilities, etc
Arrange transport for additional equipment
Receive, prepare and photocopy speakers' papers and OHTs
Prepare seminar packs, name badges and attendance list

May

Obtain summary of talks for press release and in-house publication
Check list of attendees
Send location pack to all speakers with prepared material

June

Pay invoices
Prepare and balance accounts
Send letters of thanks to speakers
Prepare follow-up marketing material as required

Figure 3.2 Planning schedule

1 Using Figure 3.2 as a guide, as a group decide on the tasks you would need to undertake.

2 On your own, make out a planning schedule, entering specific dates against each task. Remember to sort the tasks into an appropriate order before you start to enter your dates!

3 Compare your schedule with someone else's and discuss the reasons for any differences you find. Finally, assume the two of you are jointly organising the event. Allocate the jobs fairly between you and insert an 'Action' column at the right-hand side of your schedule showing who is responsible for each task.

Developing your organisational skills

You can hardly work to high standards if you are constantly in a muddle and only do each job at the last minute! Being well organised is a key requirement of all PAs involved in making arrangements, and usually involves the following.

- Operating an efficient and effective filing system, with a place for everything and everything in its place. PAs arranging various events simultaneously often have a colour-coded system to enable them to identify the relevant files quickly and easily. At the very least, you need

  - separate files for separate events
  - a new file opened and labelled on the first occasion a new event is discussed
  - storage files for regular items, eg agendas, minutes and supplementary papers for different meetings
  - reference files for your key sources and feedback sheets, eg venue details, hire companies and other suppliers, completed questionnaires and checklists
  - work-in-progress files for events currently being arranging. Many PAs clip a copy of the planning schedule to the front of each folder.

- Using a good reminder system so that you do everything in good time. This could be your diary, a purpose-designed 'tickler' system or a wall planner.

- Carrying a notebook with you at all times. This means that you will never forget to make a note of something someone tells you – even if it's a hasty request by a colleague in a corridor!

- Having a good memory! This enables you to answer queries quickly without always having to look things up or check your files.

The consequences of inadequate preparation

One consequence of failing to plan or of adopting a very relaxed approach to making arrangements is that a variety of things will go wrong and you will take the blame. You are also likely to be regarded as anything from a scatterbrain to an utter fool – depending upon the tolerance of those with whom you work, and the regularity with which you repeat mistakes! Such a reputation may take you many months to live down and will obviously do very little for your promotion prospects.

The more formal the event, the greater the danger of serious consequences – particularly if external people have been in attendance. For a formal meeting, for instance:

- the notice could be sent out too late to comply with the required 'clear days', so that the meeting has to be postponed.

- if some of the members were mistakenly left off the list, the meeting may not be quorate or legitimate

- if an important procedure is not followed, the meeting may be invalid

- if a meeting is chaotic, people may refuse to attend another

- adverse press reports about the meeting may damage your organisation's reputation

- your boss or the chairperson may be made to look foolish because he or she does not have the necessary papers to hand

- delays and confusion could mean much of the business has to be deferred to the next meeting, and some important and urgent decisions cannot be made

- if shareholders decide that the directors could be running the company as poorly as they run a meeting, they may press for a vote of no confidence in the senior management team!

The last point is extreme, but there is obviously a PR side to any event that involves other people – your mistakes are made public for the world to see! Not only that, but since you are representing your organisation, it will be judged on your performance.

Quite apart from the embarrassment of trying to cope at the time, having to admit to making a serious mistake is not a task anyone relishes. Imagine, for a moment, having to tell the Principal of your college two days before a governors' meeting that you forgot to send out the notice! Such a salutary thought should be enough to make you realise the importance of developing your planning and organisational skills to a high level!

Check it yourself

1 From what you have read so far, identify the type of events which you think could be managed effectively using a diary system, and those that would be easier to schedule using a wall planner.

2 You are organising an informal meeting for your tutor, for a week on Tuesday. He or she has informed you that

- the Refectory Manageress requires three (working) days' notice for refreshments

- the room must be booked immediately

- some papers will be needed – the draft will be with you on Wednesday but your tutor will not be able to check for accuracy before Monday week

- a memo calling the meeting must be sent today, because one person will be away next week

- you will need to book an OHP and a flipchart from the administration office and they like at least two (working) days' notice

- you are required to attend the meeting to take notes.

   a Draw up a planning schedule to make sure that everything is done on the right date.
   b Assuming your tutor requires coffee and biscuits for six people, write a short memo to the Refectory Manageress asking for these items. The room for the meeting is T26 and the refreshments are required at 2 pm.
   c The furniture in the room is normally arranged as a boardroom, whilst your tutor would prefer the horseshoe arrangement (see page 75). Write a short memo to your caretaker or building custodian making this request.

3 Naive Noreen has been given the job of organising a seminar. From the script that follows, identify all the things that could go wrong with the event – and the possible consequences!

Noreen Papers, papers everywhere! Sometimes I think I'll never see the top of my desk again. Have you seen the name and address list that was on here yesterday? The one with 'speakers' on the top of it?

Paul No. I've given up going anywhere near your desk. I never know what I might find. There was a half-eaten apple mouldering away under three files last week.

Noreen   Damn. That guy who was running the Internet session cancelled yesterday so Fatima suggested a replacement. I scribbled the name and address of her suggested speaker on the bottom. Oh, well, I'll have to ring or fax him when I find it.

Paul   Internet session? Presumably you'll be taking a lot of equipment to the hotel. Are they wiring it up to show on a large screen? They did that at a seminar I went to recently, and it looked very impressive.

Noreen   Don't even *talk* to me about the equipment. It's unbelievable. I got so fed up trying to understand what Computer Services were talking about I told them to sort it out themselves and liaise with the hotel direct. Between them they should be able to arrange for someone to take it there and set it up as well.

Paul   How many people are you expecting? Is anyone important going?

Noreen   I'm not sure – my VIP list went missing last week. I can't remember how many invitations went out – it seemed like thousands, especially when my computer went funny in the middle of printing the address labels. We've had a good response though *(triumphantly brandishes box file and rifles through contents)* – there must be at least 200 booking forms in here.

Paul   Aren't you supposed to know the *exact* number? *(Picks out a form.)* This guy will need attention, he's put here that he can only attend if there is wheelchair access. Oh, it also says he's a vegan.

Noreen   *(Irritably)* Look, just put it back will you, I've lost enough stuff already. I haven't time to cope with things like that at the moment, it'll have to do later.

Paul   *(Equally irritably)* OK, OK, I was just trying to help. If you ask me you're not managing to cope with very many things at the moment.

Check all your answers with your tutor.

● Key issues in planning – factors to consider

No matter what type of event you are organising, there are certain similarities in the planning process. All events are held for a reason, in a particular location, at a certain time and with a particular group of people. All require facilities, services and documentation and all are held according to certain conventions or formats. Therefore, if you consider the planning under the 'Kipling' headings, you will cover all the angles.

The reasons for holding meetings and different types of events were described in Chapter 1. It is important that you keep these in mind at all times. Events held for legal reasons often have strict procedures to be followed and you would need to pay attention to these at all times. Often the best contributions from PAs are made because they are concentrating on the overall event and its purposes, rather than focusing purely on the details.

More fundamentally, the purpose of the event is a vital consideration for the type of venue to be chosen and the facilities required. In this section we will consider:

1 **When and where** an event should be held – and related issues such as health and safety and security.

2 **Who** must be invited (members, guests, participants, delegates, guest speakers, VIPs).

3 **What** else will be needed (catering requirements, equipment, transport, publicity, miscellaneous items).

You should note that the role of different participants and the documentation required is linked to **how** the event will operate, and will be discussed in Chapters 4 and 5.

Selecting the venue

Choosing where to hold an internal meeting may take five minutes. Selecting an external venue for a large conference may take several weeks. However, the basic considerations are the same:

● how convenient is the venue?

● how suitable are the rooms?

● what facilities are available?

● how much will it cost?

Generally, events such as meetings are held internally because this is the most cost-effective option. Only high-profile or large events would take place at an external venue – or a meeting that had to be held in secret.

Choosing an internal venue – basic considerations

Any event can be adversely affected if the venue is unsuitable. Even a small, informal meeting can be ruined if the room is too small, people have nowhere to sit or are unable to take notes comfortably, hardly anyone can see the projection screen, or no-one can hear what the speaker is saying because of traffic noise outside. Basic considerations such as heating, lighting, ventilation and sound proofing are all important if those present are to concentrate on the matters in hand rather than their physical comfort (or lack of it). It goes without saying that any room should be clean and tidy – and not cluttered with dirty coffee cups from the last meeting!

Most informal meetings are held in-house which means that the organisation's own rooms or offices are used. Even the smallest firm usually has one room set aside for this purpose, but it must be large enough to accommodate the expected numbers, preferably to the preferred seating plan (see below), and must be equipped with the required facilities. If groups of people will be working on different issues and reporting back later, it is sensible to have separate rooms available near to the main meeting room or to divide the room into different working areas with grouped tables and chairs.

Most organisations have a Board Room, and some also have Committee Rooms. In other cases you will find that committees are convened in small meetings rooms on the premises. Some senior managers have large offices containing a meetings table and chairs. This enables them to host meetings in their own offices, which saves their PAs from having to find accommodation. It is likely that their rooms will be booked by other groups on occasions when they are away on business or on holiday!

You are likely to find that the company Board Room is furnished more luxuriously than the other meetings rooms – in order to enhance the company's image. Usually, in addition to the meetings table and chairs, there are side tables used primarily for refreshments, which also serve as useful repositories for papers. In some cases you will also find a drinks cabinet and glasses. This is not because it is normal to serve alcoholic drinks at a formal meeting but because, after it is over, directors may relax for a while and chat informally. For that reason, it is wise not to expect all the members of the Board to leave the room when you do, as there might be one or two discussions they wish to have in private. A word of warning, however! If you attend a meeting where alcohol *is* served (especially to take the minutes), you should strictly limit your intake. Notes scrawled when you were rather the worse for wear are almost impossible to understand the next day!

Some organisations have appropriate facilities for giving presentations to clients, particularly if this has to be done frequently. Because audio/visual equipment is normally used, it is important to use a room with blinds or curtains at the windows to black out the light. Alternatively, on some occasions, presentations may be held at the client's premises or at an external location.

Choosing an external venue – basic considerations

Large meetings (such as the AGM or an EGM), seminars and conferences are usually held at an external venue. This may be a hotel, an educational establishment or a purpose-built conference centre. Much depends upon the type of event, the numbers expected and the facilities required.

At external venues the range of issues involved in selection can be more complex – particularly if customers or other guests are invited. It is an unfortunate fact that many events are remembered for their shambolic surroundings long after the reason for attending has been forgotten. Typical problems can involve not being able to find the venue in the first place, having nowhere to park, not finding anyone to assist on arrival, having various meetings rooms in completely different parts of a freezing cold hotel, and being served cold coffee or inedible food! Basic considerations when selecting an external venue must therefore include the following:

- easy access for those attending (to reduce travelling time and costs)
- conference, meeting and function rooms and sleeping accommodation of the right type and size for your needs (see below)
- the appropriate facilities
- a good safety and security record
- friendly and professional staff
- places of interest in the surrounding area (if there are to be excursions or other trips for delegates)
- your budget!

Bear in mind the time of year when selecting an external venue. In the middle of summer, it might have seemed a wonderful idea to hold the January sales conference at a country house hotel, situated in beautiful grounds, miles from anywhere. On the day itself, the choice may be rather more questionable if no-one can navigate the icy roads and at the sight of a first snowflake everyone panics about being able to get home. In this case, somewhere local, with roaring log fires and a cosy atmosphere, would be far more appropriate!

Rooms, seating plans and facilities

The first thing to establish is the number and type of rooms you require. Options include

- conference rooms – which may hold up to 3 000 in some venues!
- lecture theatres

- meeting, seminar or syndicate rooms – which are smaller

- a separate reception area for greeting and registering guests

- a press room and/or office for the organisers

- VIP suite

- 'break-out' rooms or areas where people can relax, such as a lounge or coffee area

- exhibition space

- sleeping accommodation (single rooms, double or twin rooms, suites, private facilities, rooms for disabled guests)

- dining rooms, function rooms and banqueting suite.

Most venues can mix and match the space and rooms you require – sometimes through the judicious use of partitioning. However, if this is the case, do make sure that your event won't be disrupted by another one separated by only a thin partition!

Seating arrangements

The number of people who can be accommodated in any given room will depend upon the seating arrangement. Generally organisers have six options to choose from, as illustrated in Figure 3.3.

- **Cinema or theatre style** – delegates are seated in rows, preferably tiered for good visibility. This is the most economical arrangement for seating large numbers.

- **Boardroom style** – all participants sit around a table

- **Classroom** – each participant has his or her own desk and chair

- **U-shaped** – participants sit around a large table consisting of a top section and two legs. If the table is wide, seating can be placed at each side of each leg.

- **Hollow square** – the tables are positioned as a large hollow square, with participants facing the centre.

- **Discussion groups** – groups sit around separate tables.

A venue is usually able to tell you the maximum capacity of each of its rooms, based upon any of the above layouts.

Facilities

Your requirements for an event can be as basic as a flipchart and coffee for a short meeting, or be an extensive list for a large conference. In this case you would expect that most of your needs could be met by the venue provider.

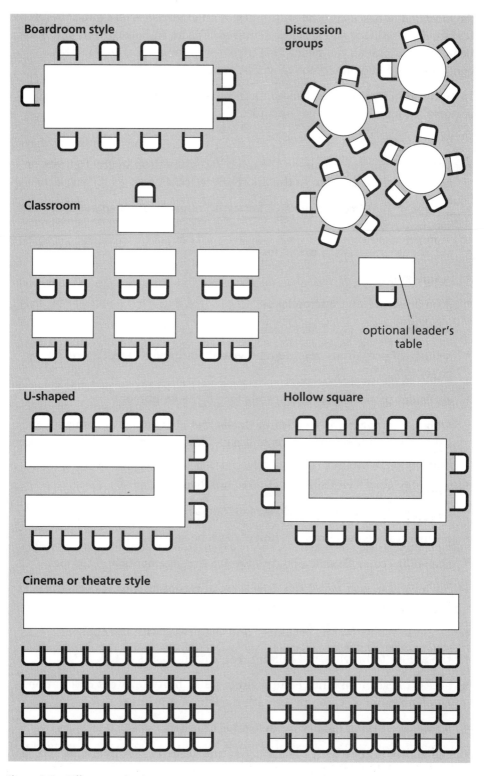

Figure 3.3 Different seating layouts

Any method of assessing the suitability of an external venue must therefore include the facilities and services required. For an in-house event you must book any equipment you need. This involves finding out who must be contacted, and how much notice will be required.

In addition to meals or refreshments (discussed below), the facilities and services for a major event can include:

- plenty of car parking spaces
- a friendly, helpful person on the main reception desk to greet guests on arrival and direct them to the appropriate location
- a stage or platform for the speakers with appropriate displays and stage settings
- sufficient chairs (with arms) for the audience
- suitable lighting
- good acoustics and microphones
- a lectern and/or gavel and block
- a range of presentation and audio visual equipment (see Figure 3.4, pages 93–95)
- sufficient power points and stands for all the equipment
- a host of minor items – eg water flasks and glasses, floral displays, ashtrays in public areas, pens and pads, lettered name cards for speakers and chairperson
- a display area for exhibition stands and displays
- an appropriate number of cloakroom and toilet areas
- a separate area where refreshments can be served
- the ability to be flexible about tea/coffee arrangements and timings
- the ability to post signs and directions in reception and at necessary locations in the venue
- separate rooms for the organiser and the press (with telephones)
- the ability to provide and link up translation booths
- access to essential office equipment (or the ability to site it on location), eg photocopier, fax, computer with modem and printer
- a message taking facility for delegates or others
- the ability to cope with special needs and security requirements
- honesty and discretion amongst the staff.

Given this list, you can see why some of your local hotels may be quite good places at which to hold a small meeting but may struggle to cope with a large and important event. Venues familiar with the needs of event organisers normally employ a specialist member of staff to guide you through your requirements and will arrange for you to hire most of the equipment you need, which simplifies matters considerably.

Making a selection

If you are arranging a staff-only event at an external venue you may find there is a recommended list of local places for you to use. For a large-scale event, such as a conference, you may need to find out more information about suitable venues in appropriate locations.

The English Tourist Board publishes a useful guide called *Conference Venues in England*, which includes separate listings for town and city locations and country venues. Similar guides are produced by other national tourist boards. Assistance can also be obtained from the British Association of Conference Towns, in Birmingham. However, you may find that some of the recommendations are unsuitable for smaller gatherings (or too expensive) and, in this case, you should contact the local tourist board for the areas in which you are interested, who will be able to give you information (and often advertising material) on appropriate hotels in their area. If you live in a city, you will usually find that the local council has a Conference Officer who will help you to find a suitable location.

One word of warning – many people are tempted to ask their friends and colleagues to recommend suitable places nearby. Do be wary of making a booking at a hotel because someone's friend remembers enjoying a wedding reception or dinner dance there! As you have already seen, your requirements for a business event are likely to be considerably different!

There are two ways in which you can check if a potential venue would be suitable. The first is to visit it yourself, preferably with a checklist that enables you to 'rank' it for suitability. Ideally your checklist should include both the physical environment *and* your impressions of the service you receive. Bear in mind that if you are enquiring about holding a large event, and visit a hotel or conference centre on a quiet day, you might find that you are given wonderful treatment – and even wined and dined during your visit. Try not to be overly impressed by this, because the establishment will obviously be keen to obtain your booking. One method of checking your impression is to ask for the names of other organisations that have held events there recently (or note them yourself, if there is a list of those currently being held in reception). Then ring one or two to obtain their personal feedback.

The second method is more tried and tested but can only be established over time. Many organisations provide delegates with a questionnaire at the end of an event. This should check satisfaction with the content of the event *and* the venue – together with the services and facilities provided. This will give you better feedback on the suitability of different locations than any amount of visiting or asking around and, in time, you can create your own list or database of appropriate venues for the different events you hold.

Making a booking

If you require a room within your organisation then you need to find out whether a formal booking system operates – and who is responsible for recording your requirements. Unless the person concerned is extremely reliable and efficient, you are well advised to confirm your requirements in writing – usually a simple memo or e-mail will suffice. Always include both the day and the date as a double check. Allow sufficient time for people to assemble – and for the gathering to possibly over-run by 10–20 per cent of its scheduled time. Experience will usually tell you those members of staff who are likely to finish promptly and those who will not, and you can fine tune your arrangements accordingly. What you should avoid, however, is having one group of people waiting outside a room until another group have finished – apart from anything else, this leaves you no time to check that the room is tidy, to set up or check any equipment or to assemble any papers that are needed.

You would not, of course, make a booking for an external venue until you were assured that all the additional facilities you need would be available and that your catering requirements could be met (see page 89). However, once you have made a decision you are wise to book promptly, rather than delay and then find your first choice is no longer available. It is quite customary to make a reservation first and confirm exact numbers and specific requirements later. This is one occasion when you *must* put everything in writing. This is because you are entering into a contract with the venue to fulfil your requirements, and if there is any dispute later you would need proof of your request. Equally, you should insist that you receive confirmation in writing.

Bear in mind that if you later cancel, you are breaking the contract and the venue will still be likely to charge you. Some hotels will quote you separately for accommodation and food. You cannot be charged for any food (as you will not have consumed any) but you can be charged for accommodation or other rooms that the hotel was unable to re-let. In the case of a quotation that includes food, you would be charged about two-thirds of the original bill. Therefore it is sensible to ascertain the exact amount of accommodation needed as quickly as possible and not book rooms you do not need. A final point to consider is whether you will be requiring the hotel to let double rooms as singles, or whether you will expect people to 'double up'. If this is the case, some conference organisers will allow a discount. Do note, however, that this practice is *not* customary for staff events!

Check it yourself

1 With the agreement of your tutor, survey the meetings rooms available in your college. Draw up your own checklist by which you can evaluate them in terms of size, comfort, facilities, location, etc. Visit each room at an appropriate time (you may have to agree this with the person responsible for the room) and make your assessment. Then type up a list ranking the meetings accommodation in order of suitability if you were responsible for arranging meetings for a group of between ten and twelve people throughout the year.

2 Find out the system used in your college for booking a meetings room. This includes establishing who to contact, the amount of notice that has to be given, whether you must obtain a key or whether the room is normally open, the hours it is available, etc. Add this information to the list you prepared for (1) above.

3 What type of seating arrangements would you recommend for each of the following events, and why?

   a an informal meeting of a group of staff of equal status
   b a meeting of departmental heads, chaired by the General Manager
   c a large conference with 150 delegates
   d a seminar at which people will be learning and taking notes
   e a relatively large group, meeting to brainstorm ideas
   f a large meeting, chaired by the MD, and comprising all senior and middle managers in the organisation.

4 a Draft a letter to the Manager of the Peartree Hotel, Riverside Place, Hightown, HG2 3PS, confirming your telephone reservation for their Riverside Meeting Room for a date four weeks on Thursday, from 9 am to 4 pm, to be set out in a U-shaped formation. Also confirm your request for fourteen single rooms with private facilities for the previous evening. The rate for the meeting room is £40 + VAT and the accommodation is £70 + VAT per room including breakfast.

   Ask for some sample buffet lunch menus to be sent to you and explain that you will confirm your catering requirements and the exact number attending the meeting within the next two weeks.

   b Assume that you receive a call the day before the meeting that two members of staff who required accommodation were ill, and would not be attending. If the hotel could not re-let the rooms, how much would you have to pay for them?

Check your answers with your tutor.

Health and safety and trade descriptions

One consideration for all event organisers must be health and safety. No-one wants to stay at a venue which is a fire risk or where there was an outbreak of food poisoning last week! It is also useful to know your rights if the venue does not provide the facilities you were promised, or if the rooms are much smaller than described.

All organisations in the UK are bound by the legal requirements of the Health and Safety at Work Act 1974. This is an over-arching Act which encompasses a variety of Regulations, and full details of these are given in the companion book in this series, *Administration Procedures for Advanced Secretarial Students*. This section therefore only considers issues that would be of particular interest to event organisers.

Under the Management of Health and Safety at Work Regulations 1992, all organisations – whether shops, factories, offices, hotels or conference venues – must undertake a risk assessment of their activities. This means identifying potential hazards and the likelihood of each occurring. The organisation must then take steps to control the identified risks to prevent harm to any individuals. Where there is a risk that cannot be controlled by any other means, a Safety Sign must be erected that complies with the Health and Safety (Safety Signs and Signals) Regulations 1996. The individuals who may be affected by risks include employees (in any category of work), outside contractors, members of the public and visitors.

The Workplace (Health, Safety and Welfare) Regulations 1992 covers many general issues of concern to all organisations. These include:

- ventilation, temperatures and lighting – which must be appropriate in all areas

- general cleanliness and housekeeping matters – all areas should be cleaned regularly and waste removed promptly

- washing facilities – which must provide running hot and cold or warm water, soap and clean towels or a hot air dryer with (usually) separate facilities for men and women.

The following requirements are applicable to all organisations, but are likely to be specifically relevant to establishments such as hotels and conference venues.

- Visitors should not be put at undue risk through any cleaning or maintenance operations that are undertaken. This means careful consideration of when and how cleaning and maintenance work is done.

- Any electrical hazards must be identified and a system of maintaining portable electrical equipment should be implemented. Organisations usually do not allow untested or unchecked electrical equipment to be brought on to their premises.

- There must be safe access and egress for individuals – which usually means a separate area for loading and unloading, in addition to speed limits on drives or car parks and the provision of crossing points or barriers where pedestrians must cross a vehicle route.

- Internal traffic routes must be kept clear and floors must be appropriately covered and not be uneven or slippery. There must be handrails on stairs, landings and galleries.

- Doors that open both ways and ordinary doors on main traffic routes should have a transparent viewing panel. Where a glass door may be hazardous the glass must be marked so it is clearly visible (eg with criss-crossed black wires) and the quality of the glass must conform to the relevant Regulations.

Organisations that deal with large numbers of people or provide catering facilities or sleeping accommodation also have other factors to consider.

- Any establishment that undertakes **catering** must abide by the requirements of the Food Safety Act 1990 and other relevant Acts and Regulations, such as the Food Safety (General Food Hygiene) Regulations 1995 and the Food Safety (Temperature Control) Regulations 1995.

- The requirements for a **fire certificate** are more stringent for establishments that provide sleeping accommodation. There are also special requirements for those establishments that hold a public entertainments licence – such as the width of exits to cope with large numbers of people.

All organisations must comply with the requirements of the Fire Precautions Act of 1971, the Fire Precautions (Places of Work) Regulations 1995 and the Fire Precautions (Workplace) Regulations 1997. Obvious requirements include the provision of fire doors, exit signs, emergency lighting and exits, fire alarms and fire equipment. In a large hotel there should be smoke alarms, heat detectors and a sprinkler system as well as fire-fighting equipment such as extinguishers and hoses. In addition, a clear fire notice must be placed in every bedroom, showing the quickest escape route. The fire certificate lists the equipment installed, shows a plan of the building, and gives details of the fire precautions taken, the method by which the alarm is raised and other relevant information. Again the Regulations require all organisations to undertake a risk assessment and to check there is an adequate warning system, means of escape and appropriately maintained and tested equipment, and that all staff are trained to know what to do in an emergency. In a responsible establishment, the management frequently undertake fire safety checks and make certain that all employees receive ongoing training.

- To prepare for **accidents and emergencies**, health and safety guidelines relating to the Health and Safety (First Aid) Regulations 1981 require that organisations train an appropriate number of staff as first aiders and provide facilities relevant to the degree of risk involved. A large hotel or conference centre will have more trained staff and a wider range of facilities than a smaller establishment. However, all staff should be trained to cope with emergencies. The Home Office recommends that

An inspector calls

Trading Standards officers are not the only inspectors to monitor compliance with legislation. All organisations possessing a fire certificate are routinely visited by a local Fire Officer who will inspect the premises and check that fire equipment is regularly serviced and that safety standards are being maintained. Organisations failing to conform to the required standards can be issued with an improvement or enforcement notice detailing the action required, or even prosecuted in the case of a severe breach of regulations.

Hotels also receive regular visits from a local Environmental Health Officer who has the task of checking compliance with all health and safety and food legislation. These officers have both an advisory and an inspection role, and will assist by giving information and advice as required. In many areas Environmental Health departments also run courses on health and safety and food hygiene. Again, if organisations fail to comply with the required standards, they can be issued with an improvement or enforcement notice forcing them to take action.

You should note, however, that in England, Scotland and Wales there is no compulsory registration or inspection system for the grading of hotels. Grading is carried out by a variety of organisations (eg tourist boards, the RAC and the AA) but generally focuses on the range of facilities and services available – not issues such as hygiene or health and safety. The situation is different in Northern Ireland, where specific Tourism Regulations introduced in 1992 have resulted in the inspection and compulsory registration of all establishments offering accommodation. An NI Tourist Board Certificate is granted only if all statutory requirements, including those relating to fire, health and safety and environmental health, are met and the relevant documentation is available for inspection. Without a certificate, the establishment cannot continue to trade.

Finally, do note that standards in other countries (even within the EU!) may be very different from those in the UK. If you are organising a large event to be held overseas, you should obtain expert assistance in selecting an appropriate venue.

all organisations have a disaster plan stating the procedures to be followed in the case of an emergency from fire, power failure, flood or bomb warning, particularly if there is a need to evacuate or contain a large number of people quickly. All staff should be aware of their role and their duties to other people in the building, particularly visitors or members of the general public. Under the Reporting of Injuries, Diseases and Dangerous Occurrences Regulations (RIDDOR) 1995, serious accidents and incidents involving either staff or visitors must be reported to the Health and Safety Executive (HSE).

- The Disability Discrimination Act 1995 states that all employers have a duty to provide any reasonable adjustments for **disabled** employees *and* visitors. You should therefore find, for instance, that wheelchair access is available and clearly signed, and that any evacuation plan includes provision for the disabled and those with any physical impairment.

- All organisations which sell goods and services to the general public must abide by **consumer law** – such as the Trade Descriptions Act – which means you must never be misled by false descriptions relating to an external venue and its facilities, including the size of rooms or the number of people who can be accommodated. There are obvious safety implications here. If too many people were crowded into a public area then it would be harder to evacuate them in the case of an emergency. In addition, the Development of Tourism Act 1969 requires that all hotels display their accommodation prices in the reception area. Compliance with these requirements is monitored by local Trading Standards officers.

✓ Check it yourself

1 In March 1997 the Health and Safety Commission published a revised Approved Code of Practice on the Health and Safety First Aid Regulations, and produced two useful free leaflets – *First aid at work: your questions answered* (ref IND(G)214L and *Basic advice on first aid at work* (ref IND(G)215L). Obtain a copy by ringing the HSE on 01787 881165.

2 As a group, decide on the checks that you would make, both visually and verbally, if you were
   a visiting an external venue and assessing it for health and safety, and talking to the manager about your requirements
   b staying in a hotel yourself, to check that you would be safe if a fire broke out.

Check your answers with the key on pages 184–185.

Security

The final consideration in relation to your choice of venue is security. It is unlikely that you would ever knowingly select a venue in the middle of a troublespot or war zone! However, there are other more subtle aspects of security to be considered when you are organising an event.

Security usually falls into two categories – security of belongings and the security of people. There are also different levels of security, depending upon the degree of risk involved.

Routine security devices are installed at all reputable venues and hotels, such as locks on bedroom doors, suitable lighting in corridors, night porterage and mini safes in bedrooms. Larger establishments will have their own security staff responsible for reporting suspicious persons, for monitoring the lobby, corridor areas and car parks through CCTV cameras and walking surveillance, and for undertaking routine security checks both inside the building and in the grounds. They will be trained to take charge in the case of an emergency (such as a fire, bomb threat or medical emergency). Frequently, security staff are trained first aiders. There will also be a formal security policy, which may include – for instance – the requirement that all baggage or personal items are removed promptly from public areas and not left unattended. Venues specialising in 'high risk events' will also have a system for vetting job applicants, particularly for responsible positions. They will also be familiar with procedures for liaising with the police when VIPs are expected.

The police are usually only involved in providing security protection in one of three circumstances:

a   where there is a high degree of risk associated with a person (or persons) attending an event
b   where there is the risk of public disorder, for instance through protesters demonstrating on an issue such as animal rights
c   where there is a threat to national security.

The police are usually only concerned with external threats, and private security staff are responsible for controlling any problems inside the building. The degree of risk will be assessed by police in relation to the type of event, current political issues, the people involved and the location. Any public meeting (open to everyone) held in a public place is automatically their concern. A private meeting or event is not, unless there is specific risk under a) or b) above.

If a conference or meetings organiser has any security concerns, the local police constabulary would need to be informed and will give advice. Government departments can also give advice, and they liaise with the police over security for government ministers and other VIPs. Foreign embassies will provide information relating to their own visiting diplomats.

The political conference timetable

Political parties' conferences are held at the same time each autumn at large venues usually in Brighton, Blackpool and Bournemouth. Each of the county police forces involved has a special Conference Planning Unit responsible for the security at these events. The hotels used are familiar with the need to cooperate with the police on security procedures, and over issues such as which staff can be allocated security passes. As an additional precaution, each political party takes over the entire hotel for the duration of the conference, so that no other guests are present, and the area is usually 'swept' beforehand to check for explosives. This should prevent, for instance, a terrorist from planting a bomb some days before the event. Needless to say, given the security requirements, the dates and locations of party conferences are fixed years – rather than months – in advance!

Who will be involved – thinking about the people

The type of event being held will determine the people involved and the way in which they will be invited to attend.

- An informal meeting will involve various members of staff, and notification will usually be by telephone (if time is short), e-mail or memo (see Chapter 4).

- A formal meeting will involve the members of a committee or association, the Board of Directors and/or other officials, and may involve external guests such as shareholders. Members are notified through a notice of meeting or a notice and agenda (see Chapter 4).

- A presentation or seminar will involve, chiefly, the presenters and the invited guests, although other staff may be on hand to welcome guests on arrival, assist with serving refreshments and undertake other general duties. The type of invitation issued will depend upon the scale of the event, and may be a letter, invitation card, leaflet or a general advertisement in the press (see Chapter 5).

- A conference will involve the organisers, internal staff and/or external delegates, guest speakers and, possibly, VIPs or local dignitaries. An in-house conference is likely to be announced to staff in a memo, whereas an external conference may be advertised through letters and leaflets to members of a society or association, or advertisements in the press.

Some basic considerations always apply when thinking about the people involved.

- The longer the notice you give for an event, the greater the chance that everyone whose presence is vital will be able to attend. This is just as true for a small meeting as a large conference when you may be desperate to obtain the services of a particular speaker. If you leave it until the last minute, it is likely that some of the key people will have made alternative arrangements or have other commitments on the day(s) in question.

- Everyone prefers arrangements to be confirmed in writing as this enables them to check the time, day and date and to put the event in their diary.

- Knowing who is attending has several implications for the organiser. First, you know in advance who needs special facilities so that you can make the appropriate arrangements. Secondly, for a large event, important visitors may mean there are security implications (see above) and a newsworthy item or the opportunity for good publicity may mean the press should be invited. Finally, you can check that the venue is large enough, sufficient accommodation has been booked and conversely that you are not likely to have problems of a shortfall in numbers – and the consequent bill for overbooking! Note that it is usual for members of a meetings group to send their apologies beforehand if they cannot attend (see Chapter 4).

Guests with special needs

Dietary needs are discussed on page 91. Other group members or guests may have physical disabilities or an impairment which means you will have to pay special attention to their needs. Some guests may suffer from a hearing impairment, although if this is minor you may not even know! If someone is profoundly deaf then you must establish whether he or she should receive additional written information, whether a signer should be present (either next to the deaf person or on the platform) and how to make contact in an emergency (usually through the Typetalk service). If you have any guests who use wheelchairs then you need a venue to which there is appropriate access and to reserve adequate space for them in the room (rather than struggle to remove chairs at the last minute). If wheelchair guests will be staying overnight, their requirements must be discussed with the venue at the outset. They will need more space to manoeuvre (along corridors, through doors, in the bedroom and bathroom) in addition to special fittings in the bathroom. They would also need assistance in the case of an emergency. Some hotels are better than others in this regard and if you are planning an event where you are concerned about the requirements of people with disabilities then you would be well advised to contact a specialist advisory service such as DIAL UK, the Disablement Information

Minicoms, Typetalk and textphones

If you are involved with making arrangements for guests who are hard of hearing, profoundly deaf or have a speech impairment, you may find that you are expected to communicate with them using the Typetalk service. This is a National Telephone Relay Service which links textphone users to ordinary phone users. A relay operator types the hearing person's reply and this appears on the textphone of the other person, who can either speak a reply or type it out, depending upon the nature of the impairment. Another term often used for textphones is minicoms – and you will often find organisations listing their minicom number separately for users with special needs. Today, text payphones are available in airports, railway stations and motorway service areas. Try to spot one next time you are travelling.

and Advice Line (see your local Yellow Pages) or RADAR – the Royal Association for Disability and Rehabilitation on 0171 250 3222 – who provide specialist information and practical guidance. Alternatively, obtain a copy of the free booklet *A Practical Guide for Disabled People: Where to find information, services and equipment* by writing to the Department of Health, PO Box 410, Wetherby, LS23 7LN.

Dealing with VIPs

There are two aspects to consider under this heading. First, what special arrangements must be made for VIPs and secondly, how you should deal with the people themselves?

The arrangements will depend upon the particular VIPs involved. Those who are renowned in the business world are unlikely to besieged by fans outside the hotel or to be a specific terrorist target. Your arrangements will focus mainly on providing a first-class service – such as a chauffeur-driven car, a suite of rooms (rather than a single room) at a top hotel, and the constant attention of your own chairperson and important staff during the event itself. Anyone who is *very* famous is more problematic. If your event involves the attendance of either royalty or a top politician, there will be special security aspects to consider (see page 84).

Your attitude towards VIPs should be one of courtesy and slight deference, rather than fawning sycophancy! Some will be a pleasure to meet, others

will not! Ironically, it is usually the case that the more eminent the person, the greater his or her charm and courtesy. Comfort yourself with this thought if you are ever the victim of a particularly obnoxious VIP throwing a tantrum – while you struggle to remain polite and attentive!

Check it yourself

The Principal of your college has informed you that David Blunkett, the Secretary of State for Education and Employment, will be visiting the college and is interested in attending a meeting of the Equal Opportunities Group, for which you are currently meetings secretary.

1 She is aware, as are most people, that David Blunkett is blind. What special facilities do you think you should consider for his attendance at your meeting? If necessary, research the topic and (as a group) contact some of the specialist organisations that may be able to advise you.

2 She is also concerned that some students, concerned about the issue of tuition fees, might try to sabotage the meeting. Discuss, as a group and with your tutor, the security measures which might be taken to limit any problems.

What will be needed?

General facilities likely to be needed were covered earlier in the discussion on venues (see page 76). However, there are still other key considerations to be considered – not least the food you will provide!

Catering requirements

Requirements will depend upon the length and type of event, and the time of day when it is held. They may range from tea/coffee and biscuits mid-morning or mid-afternoon, to sandwiches for an internal lunchtime meeting, to a buffet lunch for a one-day seminar or a five-course dinner or banquet at the end of a conference.

Catering and internal events

For internal events there is a system for ordering light refreshments or sandwiches in most organisations, which often means completing an internal order form or requisition. This enables the Catering department to enter the cost under an appropriate budget heading (ie yours!). There may be specific internal regulations to take into account regarding expenditure on refreshments for meetings.

The food, like the venue, can be critical to the overall success of any occasion. People rarely remember a good meal, but always remember a poor one! In addition, offering some refreshments is often a social courtesy that helps any occasion to run smoothly – which is why visitors are normally offered a coffee on arrival. Equally, whilst the American practice of breakfast meetings hasn't yet taken off in this country, if staff are asked to come in early to attend an 8 am meeting, then coffee, tea and hot toast are likely to soften the blow somewhat! Do ensure that the type of food served at a breakfast or lunchtime meeting is such that it is possible to eat and talk at the same time – otherwise the whole proceedings come to a halt, which is not the idea. Sandwiches served on several plates in the centre of the table is better than one huge stack which is continually having to be passed around. Sticky or messy food (including cream cakes!) should be avoided. Serviettes help, and reduce the number of crumbs that get spread around the room.

In a small firm there may be no Catering department and only the ability to provide tea, coffee and biscuits in-house. In this case you are likely to find that one of your duties in relation to lunchtime meetings is to visit the local sandwich bar! A useful tip, if you regularly do this, is to keep your own list of people's preferences so that you can always guess correctly if you haven't time to contact them personally on that particular day.

For larger events held in-house, either the Catering department or outside caterers will be involved – depending upon the facilities available in-house. In the case of the former you would need to contact your Catering Manager to find out what was available and within your budget. You may then need to type out the menu yourself to give to those involved – particularly if there are options they must choose before the event. If you are using outside caterers it is normal to contact several firms and compare sample menus and prices unless, of course, your organisation regularly uses the same company.

Catering and external events

If you are using an external venue, you will arrange your catering requirements directly with them, probably by liaising with the Catering Manager. It is likely that your choices will be largely determined by your budget – and this will be strongly influenced by the importance of those attending and who is paying.

You have three decisions to make:

- where people will eat
- what they will eat
- what they will drink.

Where to eat   For some events, such as a seminar, it is usual to have lunch on the premises. For others, such as a presentation to important clients, it may be more appropriate to book a table at a local restaurant. At a residential conference in a hotel most meals may be taken on the premises but, especially during a long conference, people enjoy a meal elsewhere at least once. Often the decision will be based on the quality of catering and the dining facilities available at the venue – for instance, whether a private dining room is available or if a small group would have to use the main dining room, along with other guests. It may also depend upon the number of people who can be seated and served simultaneously – known in the trade as the number of 'covers'. It is worth noting that some large conferences end with a special meal, such as a banquet or dinner dance or dinner and entertainment. If this is organised properly it can often be the highlight of the event.

What to eat   External caterers and external venues will provide a selection of menus, covering a range of prices, from which you can make your choice. Buffet menus are priced per head and range from basic finger foods to a carvery selection of cold meats, fish, vegetarian dishes and salads. Restaurant menus are either table d'hôte or à la carte. The former is more usual for group bookings, where guests have a limited selection of starters, main courses and desserts from which they can make their choice. A la carte means guests can choose anything from the full menu, which is a far more expensive option! If you are trying to plan an event on a limited budget, do take advice from the Catering Manager, who will be able to recommend a reasonable choice, based on varied and seasonal foods that can be obtained without difficulty. For lunches, lighter foods are often preferred and opting for a buffet means that people can circulate and talk to one another. A dinner is more likely to be a sit-down occasion, when you would also need to check the number of courses to be served.

Before you make your choice, note that you need to take account of any special requirements of those who will attend. Most caterers today offer vegetarian options as standard. You would have to be more specific, however, if any guest is a vegan or is restricted by dietary requirements or religious beliefs. You can establish these by including an appropriate question on the booking form (see Chapter 5, page 172). On occasions where it is impossible to check special requirements beforehand (such as the company AGM), you are wise to opt for light refreshments or a buffet with a wide variety of salads.

What to drink At lunchtime people tend to shy away from alcohol, if only for fear of falling asleep in the middle of the afternoon session! Even if alcohol is available make certain that you also arrange for a plentiful supply of non-alcoholic drinks as well. For a dinner, you may wish to be guided on both the type and amount of drinks to be served with the meal. A choice of red or white wine is normally offered to guests, but it is not usual to order the most expensive bottles available – 'house red' or 'house white' is more normal, particularly for staff events! Bear in mind that people are likely to consume rather more if they are staying overnight and therefore not driving home.

For a residential event, you also need to establish some rules regarding the payment for drinks consumed in the bar area. A private, or paid bar, is one where all the drinks are free to guests and paid for by the organisers. This has obvious disadvantages, particularly if some guests over-indulge (most hotels will keep the bar open until the last guest goes to bed!) A cash bar is one where people pay for their own drinks. A compromise option for many functions is that the first drink is free and any subsequent drinks are paid for by guests. This needs to be made clear beforehand.

Finalising the arrangements

Finalising the catering and payment arrangements must be done in liaison with your line manager, who may also ask you to submit some draft menus for approval. Often these will have been sent to you in advance and can simply be copied. Only if the presentation or format is poor, or you wish to customise the items on offer, should you reproduce them yourself. Make sure that you confirm *all* your catering requirements in writing with the supplier.

Check it yourself

1 Find out the system used in your college for ordering refreshments for a meeting. In particular, find out any budget limitations, who must authorise the expenditure and the amount of notice that must be given.

2   As a group, select *either* a buffet *or* a three-course table d'hôte meal that could be offered to participants in a seminar. Prepare a menu listing your selection, in a suitable format, for displaying on the noticeboard at the entrance to the dining room.

Equipment and related requirements

Today there are very few meetings or events at which no equipment is required. Most people wish to record decisions or ideas on a whiteboard or flipchart, and anyone giving a formal talk or presentation may ask for a range of audio/visual equipment to be available, not least because a talk without them is usually very boring for the audience.

Your precise requirements will mainly depend upon the type of visual aids to be used, which can range from simple text and graphics, to complex text, photographs and elaborate graphics, to a full multimedia show combining a computer-based presentation with video and sound!

Basic equipment is available in most organisations and all reputable external venues. Otherwise, equipment can often be hired for a special event – either by you or by the venue. It is, however, important to check whether your own electrical equipment would be acceptable for use in an external venue – bearing in mind health and safety regulations. If it would, then you need to arrange for insurance and transportation. If it would not, then you need to find out whether the venue will provide or hire what you need.

Make sure that all equipment is well maintained and in working order. A major crisis can ensue if a key item of equipment will not function on the morning of a presentation. A 'dry run' with all equipment is an essential part of preparing for any important event.

Check it yourself

Read through the list of equipment and terms in Figure 3.4.

1   Discuss with your tutor the type of equipment available in your college and try to arrange for a demonstration of any types you have not seen previously.

2   Find out whether your college has any computer presentation software available that you could learn to use. This is often a very valuable skill to have listed on your CV.

Audio visual aids (AVA)	A general term used for all types of audio/visual equipment.
Back room projector	A projector sited at the back of a room, often in a projection booth.
Back lighting	Illuminated buttons on a remote control which enable it to be used by a presenter working in a darkened room.
Blackboard	The most basic device for writing and drawing simple diagrams. Because chalk dust is messy and chalk cannot be used near a computer, blackboards are losing popularity and have largely been replaced by the **whiteboard.**
Blackout curtains	Special black curtains that block out lighting from windows or from corridors and darken the room.
Brightness	A major factor in the success of any presentation. The brightness of presentation equipment is measured in **lumens**. Note that surrounding brightness (e.g. from a window) can ruin a presentation.
Copyboard	Combines a **whiteboard** with a projection screen which enables information written on the board to be downloaded on computer, printed out and even transmitted to a distant location.
CRT projector	A projector that operates using a cathode ray tube (as in your television). These are large pieces of equipment, sited in permanent locations, used where high-quality images are essential.
Dimmer switch	A special lighting switch that enables the intensity of lighting to be reduced.
DLP projector	Projectors that operate through a system of digital light processing – often considered to be the technology of the future.
Fader	An audio device that enables the sound to be faded out during parts of a presentation.
Flip chart	A large (A1) pad that stands on an easel and is affixed by means of screws at the top. As each page is used, the speaker can flip over to a new page.
Front room projector	A projector sited near the screen.

Keystoning	A common problem on **OHPs** and front room projectors, where the top of the image is much wider than the bottom because the distance to the top of the screen is greater than to the bottom – which is often parallel to the placement of the OHP or projector. Some devices have a keystone correction facility. On those that don't, the problem may be lessened if the device is placed at mid-screen height – but this often obscures the audience's view.
Laser pointer	A pointer that projects a small, high-intensity laser beam visible on the screen.
LCD panel	A panel placed on to an **OHP** and linked to a computer. The computer images are transmitted to the panel and projected onto the screen via a high-intensity OHP.
LCD projector	A portable projector that uses Liquid Crystal Display technology and can be linked to audio speakers to give stereo sound.
Microphones	The most basic are stand-mounted and are usually adjustable up and down. Roving, halter or radio microphones enable the wearer to walk around without losing sound capability.
Multilingual interpreting	A sound system through which interpreters, sitting in special booths, listen to a speaker's presentation through earphones and transmit the translation simultaneously to delegates who also wear earphones.
Multimedia	Presentations that combine various types of media, such as text, clip art, graphics, photographs, sound and video.
Overhead projector (OHP)	A device that illuminates and transmits the images on OHTs (overhead transparencies) via a glass screen and a lens to a projection screen. To work properly the glass and the lens must be scrupulously clean.
PA system	A public address system that transmits sound over a wide area.
PC presentation	A presentation devised on computer through the use of a **presentation package** and transmitted through a linked computer and projector, or computer, LCD panel and OHP.

Pixel	The smallest component on a computer image or graphic. A pixel is a tiny dot, the whole of which makes up the **resolution** of a computerised image.
Power focus	A device that allows the presenter to adjust the focus through the remote control.
Presentation package	A computer software package that produces presentation images and enables them to be projected and/or printed out on an inkjet or laser printer, such as PowerPoint, Freelance Graphics, Harvard Graphics and Corel Presentations.
Rear screen projection	A projection system that uses a special opaque screen. The projector is sited behind the screen and cannot obscure the view of the audience.
Remote mousing	The ability to operate a computer mouse by means of a joystick or trackball on the remote control.
Resolution	The clarity of the image on a computer screen, defined by the number of pixels. The most common today is SVGA (Super Video Graphics Array) which is 800 × 600 pixels. However, there must be compatibility between the computer and the projector for the resolution of a computerised presentation to be maximised.
Slide projector	A projector that projects 35 mm slides. Now going out of favour as **PC presentation** systems become more popular.
True colour	A term used in relation to **PC presentations** which means it uses 24-bit colour (ie 16.7 million colours!)
Universal power supply	A device that can operate internationally under a wide range of power supplies and voltages. Essential for presentation equipment being used overseas.
Video projector	A projector that shows video recordings on a large screen.
Whiteboard	A large white screen on which the presenter can write using *non-permanent* colour pens. Note that the use of permanent markers produces an image which can only be removed by special solvents!

Figure 3.4   Audio visual equipment and related items

3 Arrange for one of the technicians responsible for maintaining standard AVA equipment (such as OHPs) in your college to give you a short talk on his or her duties and the checks made to ensure the equipment is functioning and sited correctly before an important event.

Transport requirements

Transport may be required for equipment and for people. The type of transport may range from a chauffeur-driven car for a VIP, to a taxi for a visiting speaker arriving at the local station, to a mini-bus or coach for a group of delegates visiting a nearby place of interest. You need to ensure you make any bookings with external transport providers in good time – particularly if large numbers of people are involved or if you have any special requirements.

In some organisations, transportation of important customers and VIPs is arranged internally or through a particular firm. You will need to check that you comply with any existing requirements. If you are arranging coach transport it is usual to obtain two or three quotations from reputable companies before making your choice. Bear in mind that coaches vary in size, so firms may need a fairly accurate idea of the number of people involved before they can specify the exact cost.

Publicity

It is interesting to note that press interest in an event is often in inverse proportion to the amount of publicity desired by the organisation! This paradox means that when you want massive publicity for a seminar or conference you may find that you have been given four column inches on the back page of the local paper, whereas when a contentious meeting takes place which the Managing Director wants to keep secret, you find you can't move for journalists!

Generally, therefore, you have two major considerations:

* how to encourage the press to give you free publicity when you want it (thereby reducing your advertising costs)

* how to cope with unwelcome attention when you do not.

Obtaining coverage of an event

Coverage is obtained through the issue of **press releases** to interested media organisations. This tells them that the event is going to take place – and gives a summary of what is going to happen. Local newspapers are usually keen to report on the proceedings of local council meetings, the AGMs of local firms and any public meetings or events. However, unless the business being discussed is of particular interest, or the paper is having a very quiet day, they will rarely guarantee that a reporter or photographer will attend. This means that you are wise to book your own photographer so that you can provide photographs and a **press statement** after the event has taken place.

Note the difference between a press release and a press statement. Usually a press release is issued before an event occurs and gives prior notice, together with a few brief details. This is termed advance publicity. A press statement is issued either at or after the event. Organisations do this to ensure that:

- all sections of the media receive the relevant information

- press coverage will take place even if no journalists are present

- the 'company line' on a particular topic is communicated (this may be different from earlier reports in the paper).

Different organisations use different terms and phrases (eg news release) and there is no hard and fast ruling, but you should note the following facts about press releases and statements.

- Local papers, in particular, dislike having the same information as anyone else. Therefore you are sensible if you tailor your releases for specific recipients.

- It is possible to put an embargo on the document to prevent the information being issued or reported until after a stated date and time.

- A press release or statement should be worded so that it can be 'cut' from the bottom upwards. This way, the sub-editor can use as much text as he or she has space for, without destroying the main message you are trying to communicate! A useful way of providing additional information is by including 'notes for editor', which can be used to include more details if there is space in the paper.

- Quotations are useful as these enable the newspaper to report and attribute remarks directly.

- Don't worry about thinking of a catchy heading – more often than not, the newspaper will write its own.

- Press releases can be sent by post, by hand, faxed or e-mailed to a news agency or a particular paper. If you have any queries, ask for the business editor rather than the news desk, unless you happen to be in the news at the time!

- There is a specific layout for press releases and press statements. This is shown in the example press release in Figure 3.5.

Coping with unwelcome attention

On some occasions, far from trying to persuade the press to cover an event you may have problems dissuading them! If a meeting is likely to be very contentious (such as potential protests at your AGM), if you have a famous guest arriving or if you work for a newsworthy organisation such as a football club or political party, you may find that not only are the local press interested but also the national press and even television companies. A good rule of thumb is that it is better to assist the press rather than try to block them – which usually makes them more interested rather than less. For this reason,

---

PRESS RELEASE

17 January 199-

UK COMPANY CHIEF SAYS GROWTH THE KEY TO FUTURE PROSPERITY

Brian Halloran, Chairman of Polax Systems, will announce an investment programme of £4 million over the next few years at today's Annual General Meeting in London. The money will be used to develop IT systems for businesses and education.

Mr Halloran will tell shareholders:

'Our strategy has continually been one of meeting new challenges and being a leader in our field. This has resulted in record profits for the year of £13 million and an increased dividend to shareholders. We will continue to increase our market share and prove that a UK company is capable of being at the leading edge of technology as we enter the new millennium.'

He considers that the additional investment will lead to a substantial increase in jobs, and the company is looking for new sites at different locations in the UK.

Notes for Editors

1   Profits show an increase of £2.4 million from the previous year and an increase of 15% above forecast levels.

2   Number of jobs is forecast to increase by between 200 and 400 between now and 2002.

3   Meetings currently taking place with Economic Development Units in Sunderland, Greater Manchester, Norwich and Cardiff.

4   Main product success this year has been Quantipro system, now installed in 90% of educational establishments in the UK. A key feature of this system is its ability to be cheaply upgraded, which has reduced the replacement and updating cost of IT equipment by up to 75%.

– ENDS –

Figure 3.5   An example of a press release

it is not usual to attempt to ban the press from attending unless absolutely everyone involved is in favour (otherwise, reports will be leaked by disgruntled members who simply put forward their own point of view). Special arrangements are often made to accommodate the press on these occasions.

One strategy for defusing the situation is to hold a press briefing before the main event – with appropriate refreshments. In addition, an official press statement is usually provided (and sent out to news agencies) either immediately before or after the event, and questions are answered as diplomatically as possible. Normally this will minimise any potentially hostile coverage as journalists will have tangible facts to report, rather than resorting to filling their column inches with speculation.

Most large companies have PR specialists to deal with the press and it will be their job to prepare and distribute press statements and look after any journalists. If you are involved then try to restrict your conversation to small talk so that you are not unwittingly indiscreet. If you find yourself cornered it is useful to remember the phrase 'off the record'. This prevents a journalist with any integrity from reporting what you have said.

✓ Check it yourself

1 Figure 3.5 is a fictitious press release, but if you have access to the Internet you can see dozens of real ones very easily! The best place to start is with the Government site – http://open.gov.com. Then select one of the major departments, such as the HSE, the Home Office, the Department for Trade and Industry or the Department for Education and Employment, and read what they have recently announced to the press.

2 Find out which events held in your college each year are advertised in the local press. Then see if someone from Marketing will talk to you about the strategies used to try to obtain free publicity about such events.

3 Imagine that your group is planning a presentation on the work of PAs, to give to an invited audience of year 11 pupils from local schools. Your tutor has persuaded an ex-student to return to give a short talk on her work as a PA for a very famous personality (the name of the personality is up to you!) Draft a press release that could be sent to your local paper, informing them of the event. Invent any details you need to add substance to your document.

4 You work for a company that has continuing difficulties between management and workers over flexible working contracts. This resulted in a protest outside the company by union members, which received coverage in the local paper. Today senior managers met with the union leaders and agreement was reached on the terms and conditions of a new contract. The details are complicated but include additional payments in return for more flexible working practices.

Draft a *short* statement for the local press stating the current position.

● Alternatives for events – using modern technology

Whilst everything you have studied so far is relevant to all types of events, there is another consideration for today's PAs to take into account. That is the degree to which modern technology could be used to organise an event in a rather different way. There are three basic choices, all generally known by the term **conference systems** – although they are more often used for holding meetings rather than conferences, so beware of becoming confused!

Telephone conferencing

A telephone conference is one where several people are linked together by telephone, regardless of their location. Most internal (digital) switchboard systems allow for a number of internal line users to talk to each other simultaneously. However, they may be more limited as to the number of *external* lines that can be linked. Alternatives include a private circuit between different branches or offices in a group, or the use of the audioconferencing service offered by major telephone service suppliers, such as BT and Mercury. The services vary, but are likely to include:

- a system coordinator to call up the participants at a pre-arranged time – alternatively, participants are given a special number to call

- unlimited time allocation

- minimal booking and set-up time (often as short as ten minutes)

- the availability of an interpreter on line or the production of a translation of the discussion

- connection to hundreds of locations at one time with no geographical constraints.

No special equipment is required, although special audioconferencing terminals can be purchased. These make it easier for groups of people to participate collectively at each location (rather than share an ordinary loudspeaker phone).

There are several advantages to telephone conferencing:

- travel and accommodation costs are reduced

- time is saved as communications are quicker

- people who might not be able to attend a meeting in person can be available over the telephone

- the discussion can easily be taped and replayed (this is ideal if you are preparing the minutes of the meeting!)

- decisions can be reached more quickly, particularly in critical situations.

The disadvantages relate to the following:

- there is a limit to the number of participants who can useful contribute to a telephone discussion simultaneously – unless there is some obvious order of speaking or a leader appointed to control the session

- the cost can be high – for a long meeting involving several overseas locations, it may run into thousands of pounds

- the only contact is by voice. The lack of face-to-face contact means it may be difficult to 'read' people's feelings. In addition, audioconferencing does not allow for group discussion of documents. For that reason, many meetings are held using video conferencing facilities.

Video conferencing

Video conferencing has changed out of all recognition since it was first introduced – and it is still evolving. Originally, the only way video conferencing could be organised was for people to visit customised conferencing rooms, or studios, which were linked together. Today there are a range of alternatives to choose from:

- the installation of videophones

- TV set-top videophones – which use standard television sets

- PC-based conferencing – better known as **desktop conferencing**

- group conferencing systems.

At present the move is towards desktop conferencing, primarily because of its flexibility, the significantly lower cost and the fact that most executives (and PAs) have a PC on their desks already. However, whilst desktop conferencing is ideal for a 'one-to-one', it is more limited for larger numbers. For that reason, there is still likely to be a need for group systems, even though they are more expensive. In many organisations you are likely to find both systems in operation.

The type of system installed will depend largely upon the current technology used by the organisation. Those with an ISDN line will have a video-conferencing capability as part of the ISDN package. ISDN (Integrated Services Digital Network) is the digital equivalent of an ordinary telephone line (often referred to today as POTS – standing for 'plain old telephone service'). It enables much faster and cleaner links between locations for a vast range of data and information.

In addition, many organisations today operate a system of networked computers, and these can be linked together for video communication as well as the traditional use of e-mail and shared data, given the appropriate hardware and software. Most organisations are less likely to be interested in installing videophones (given that these can only be used if the receiver also has a videophone) and more keen on utilising their current equipment and facilities.

The advantages and drawbacks of desktop systems

To operate a desktop system you need a modern computer (with a Pentium processor), and a video kit – comprising a tiny camera (which often sits on top of the VDU), an audio set and the required software. You can then link with any other user internally and, given an ISDN link, externally on a 'point-to-point' (or one-to-one) basis. This enables you to contact other people, both visually and orally, by simply dialling their number. Equally, you can send files, share and comment on graphics, show a brief presentation or work on a report together.

The drawbacks are the cost of the ISDN line, the fact that your contact must also have an ISDN link, the quality of the video image in some cases and the fact that, although it is not impossible to link more than one computer at a time, it can be difficult to 'manage' the video conference (deciding who to see, who to talk to). This is why, for larger meetings, group systems are usually installed.

The advantages and drawbacks of group systems

Group systems are more sophisticated. They use specialist equipment with a more sophisticated camera that can zoom in on individual speakers, pan and tilt as necessary, as well as large-screen VDUs. Because they are portable they are sometimes called 'rollabouts'. In effect, they provide a video studio wherever they are sited.

From the technological point of view, a multiparty virtual meeting requires a special control unit or server to link the users together in a form of 'daisy chain', and usually relies on the services of one of the major telecommunications suppliers, such as BT or AT&T, to unite the users. Some control units are so sophisticated that they can even 'patch in' to the meeting users without any special equipment, thereby including POTS users with all the others!

The advantages are fairly obvious, given that with some systems several groups of users worldwide can be linked together. Presentations can be given to a large audience by a distant speaker, seminars can be held with speakers 'patched in' from around the globe, meetings can be held either on a group-to-group or multi-group basis. The savings in time and travel costs are tremendous.

The disadvantages all relate to the management of the event – an organisational aspect upon which the technologists are currently focused. In a one-to-one conference it is quite obvious who will speak when, but complications arise when several sites are linked together. Imagine having the facility to see and hear several groups of people, but not simultaneously. Who do you listen to first? Should anyone be in overall control, and how can you indicate to a certain person in a certain group that it is his or her turn to speak?

There have been various efforts to solve these problems through technological advances.

- In a **voice-activated** control system, the software is designed to differentiate between background and primary noises. The person speaking the loudest will therefore be the person viewed on screen. The problem with this system is that chaos ensues if everyone starts to shout simultaneously or if one participant has a particularly loud voice (or a noisy cough).

- A **direct control** system allows an administrator or chairperson to manage the meeting and decide which site should be screened at any one time. This is useful for potentially contentious meetings or for formal, structured sessions (eg a presentation or a question and answer session). It can, however, present problems if the chairperson is also trying to participate in the discussion and is distracted by his or her other duties.

- An **autoscan** system views each site on a timed, rotating basis. This can be irritating as the system does not necessarily focus on the key site or the person speaking. However, between three equal participants or during a straight exchange session, it can be useful.

- **Continuous presence** is the latest development. This system splits the screen into sections, with several sites appearing simultaneously in its different segments. Whilst this is the most realistic option, there are obvious limitations, particularly if only a small screen is being viewed.

You should note that these systems are not mutually exclusive, and therefore a combination can be used. Forecasters envisage a combination of voice-activated with direct control plus continuous presence for a realistic meeting. This may result in many PAs becoming meetings administrators with the key duties of managing the cameras and the system rather than taking minutes – particularly since the whole session can be recorded on video anyway.

The other drawback to such elaborate systems is the cost – which can range from as little as £15 000 to £100 000 or more. In addition, there is the cost of the transmission link. ISDN lines are not cheap (particularly for small businesses) and neither are international telephone calls. For that reason, many small business users are very interested in the development of Internet conferencing.

Internet conferencing

Most people are familiar with the Net as a source of information and as a useful (and cheap) way of sending e-mails. To be 'on the Net' a user simply needs a modern PC, a modem, the communications software, a telephone line and to be registered with a service provider. If you add a camera, microphone and the right software, there is no reason why 'real-time' video pictures cannot be transmitted over the Net in the same way as data and sound.

The main software product on the market at present – free of charge – is Microsoft NetMeeting, which can be downloaded. In addition, users can copy and paste video images into a pasteboard, exchange graphics, transfer files and chat to one another (in text). The huge advantage is that all telephone calls over the Net are charged at local rate – so you could hold a video conference with your brother in Australia for the price of phoning your friend down the road! You could also call from a hotel or any other location using a laptop. The main disadvantage is the speed of transmission if you are using POTS, and the fact that the camera is minuscule, so it is difficult to see more than one person at once.

Cheap links via an electric power point

Each year technology is developing even further in the realms of video conferencing. To date one of the largest conferences ever held was set up in Japan in December 1996. This involved the linking together of over 1 000 terminals to enable the Japanese Prime Minister to talk to school children.

Whilst a major concern for many businesses is that of cost, this may fall dramatically with the latest idea that communication links could be provided by simply plugging into the electricity supply! The 'electric superhighway', as it has been termed, will give Internet access through the electricity mains, with users making a single monthly payment for unlimited use. The other benefit will be speed – researchers predict that Internet access will be at speeds up to 30 times greater than the best achieved today. If you live in the Norweb region you should note that Norweb Communications has plans to offer the service to its customers following a six-month marketing trial starting at the beginning of 1998.

Check it yourself

1 Access the Net yourself and find out about NetMeeting by accessing the Microsoft site on http://www.microsoft.com/products/prodref/113. Print out any pages you find helpful.

2 Find out what video conferencing or Internet conferencing facilities exist in your college and see if your tutor can arrange a demonstration. Critically appraise the session and make your own 'advantages and disadvantages' list.

3 As a group, hold a brainstorming session to consider how classes such as yours might be held in the future if video conferencing equipment and Net access become the norm – not only in schools and colleges but also in everyone's homes.

Review quiz

1 State FOUR advantages of using a checklist.

2 How would you describe the difference between a checklist and a planning schedule to a new member of staff?

3 Identify THREE benefits and TWO limitations of video conferencing.

4 Give FOUR consequences of inadequate preparation for an event.

5 Briefly describe the planning and document-retention systems you would set up if you were asked to organise a conference for the first time.

6 Draft SIX questions you would ask a Catering Manager if you were visiting a local hotel to make the provisional arrangements for a seminar.

7 a Identify TWO major areas of health and safety that would concern you if you were organising an event.
  b State the checks you would make in relation to each area before making a booking at an external venue.

8 Identify THREE aspects of security that would concern you when assessing an external venue.

9 Give THREE examples of the special considerations that must be borne in mind with certain guests.

10 Give examples of FOUR types of visual aids you may be asked to provide at a meeting where there is to be a brief presentation by your advertising agency.

Test yourself

You now know enough to be able to reinforce the theoretical information contained in this book by starting to undertake practical activities yourself. Although you are obviously under no compulsion to do so, it is recommended that you carry out the following tasks to start learning by experience!

1 Your organisation is starting a database that will hold information on different venues under three headings – general information, location and travel, transport facilities. The aim is to create a library of information for event organisers to give the key facts on a variety of hotels.

   Hold a group meeting to decide the information that might be recorded under each heading and check your answers with the key suggested on page 185.

2 Divide into two groups. One group has the task of obtaining information on a venue suitable for a business meeting or small seminar within ten miles of your college. The other has to find out information on a venue suitable for holding a large formal meeting or conference within fifty miles of your college. Useful sources of information include Yellow Pages, your local Tourist Office and the Internet, as well as appropriate journals in your library.

   Each group should obtain information on at least six venues by telephoning or writing to the establishments concerned. Try to ensure you are sent some indication of the charges – as well as advertising leaflets – so that you can compare both prices and facilities. From the information you have available, rank your venues in order of suitability. Discuss your selection with your tutor and be prepared to justify your decisions!

3 Assume you are going to visit the top three venues of each group to assess them personally. Hold a brainstorming session (with a flip chart handy) to decide all the facilities you would check in order to assess suitability under the following headings:

   * accommodation (conference/meetings rooms and sleeping accommodation)

   * furniture and equipment

   * meals and refreshments

   * general facilities and leisure amenities

   * health and safety.

Compare your suggestions with the checklist key on page 186.

4 You have been asked to write an 'impression report' on your return to give your opinions on the venue, the people you met and the service you received. As a group, decide the type of observations you might make and areas upon which it would be appropriate to report. Compare your ideas with the key suggested on page 187.

5 Through your tutor, try to arrange to visit a large hotel or other venue in your locality. Either with a copy of the checklist on page 186, or with your own version produced in the brainstorming session, assess it for suitability *either* for a business meeting *or* for a conference. Each person should then prepare an individual impression report on the visit. You might find it interesting to compare these once they have been written.

Organising and administering a meeting

4

By this stage you should know about the different types of events that may be held, the importance of keeping to a budget, the organisational skills you will require and the type of arrangements you will need to make. It is now a case of continuing to put your skills into practice!

However, whilst there are some similarities between events there are obviously considerable differences – particularly in the way certain events operate. At one extreme is the informal internal meeting called on the spot, at the other is the company AGM. In between are the variety of 'semi-formal' meetings held in every organisation which are formal in the sense that they involve the Board of Directors or committees, and operate according to specific rules, but which are not constrained by formal procedures and terminology.

For that reason, we are going to study meetings in three sub-sections:

a informal, internal meetings

b semi-formal, usually internal meetings

c formal meetings involving external parties, such as shareholders.

In this chapter we are less concerned with why, when and where a meeting is held (which has been discussed previously) but will concentrate upon

- **who** will be involved – and their roles (including your own)

- **what** documentation will be needed

- **how** the meeting will operate (the procedures to be followed).

We will also consider the tasks you must carry out after the meeting has ended.

● Informal meetings

As you saw at the beginning of this section, informal meetings are a common feature of all organisations. However, their informality does not mean that no planning or organisation is required. You may also be expected to prepare the required documentation and to take notes to record what took place.

Who will be involved – the roles of participants

The leader or coordinator of an informal meeting is your key liaison person and he or she will know who must be invited. Your first task is to clarify the main aspects (who, what, where, when) with the coordinator and then to check that each person can attend. This *may* be done by telephone but it is

---

MEMO

TO   Publicity group members
FROM   Joanne Marshall
DATE   23 February 199–

New photographs

The marketing department has arranged for a photographer to visit us on 16 and 17 March to update our publicity material. Many of the photographs we use on displays and in other literature are out of date and we could use his services on those dates to take some new photographs for us.

Obviously, we will need to let him have our ideas beforehand.

I should therefore be grateful if you could attend a short meeting in the seminar room on the ground floor on Tuesday next, 1 March, at 3 pm, so that we can discuss our requirements. I expect the meeting to last about half an hour. Please contact Louise, my PA, if you are unable to attend.

JM

Figure 4.1   A memo inviting staff to a meeting

sensible to send a brief confirmatory memo. E-mail is even better – and much quicker. Normally such documents are worded quite informally. You are unlikely to be asked to produce an official agenda (see pages 119–121) for an informal meeting, although information on the topics to be discussed may be included in body of the memo or e-mail. For an example, see Figure 4.1.

You may find that some people cannot attend at the suggested time or date, particularly if a meeting is called at short notice. This will mean liaising with the coordinator to see whether a different time or day should be scheduled or whether the meeting should go ahead anyway. Much will depend upon the number of people who cannot attend and their relative importance in terms of their individual contributions and expertise.

What documentation will be needed?

It is sensible to check any documents that must be prepared or photocopied in advance with the coordinator. You should already know the quantities required by the number of people who are attending. Bear in mind that two types of **supplementary documents** are required for meetings.

- Those sent out in advance. For a formal meeting such documents are sent with the official notice and agenda (see page 123). These are documents that people will need to read in advance of any discussions, so that they can then make useful comments. Obviously, it is no use issuing a ten-page report to people at a meeting and expecting them to read, understand and comment upon it intelligently there and then!

- Those that are **tabled** at the meeting. In other words, they are given to participants whilst the meeting is in progress. These are shorter papers, often documents produced that day which are relevant to the items being discussed.

It is not good practice to overwhelm participants with reams of paper before a meeting or to drown them in unnecessary detail. A good leader or chairperson selects the supplementary documentation which is required very judiciously.

Absentees are also usually sent any documents that were tabled at the meeting together with any notes of the meeting – so that they know what they missed and can bring themselves up to date for next time.

How it will operate

There are usually no specific procedures to be followed at an informal meeting, so the format can vary. Normally the leader will introduce the reason for calling the meeting and expect participation from the others. This may include you! Be aware therefore that you may be expected to make a positive contribution to some of these sessions. Rather than being overawed, think of it as an opportunity to become involved and to participate in some of the decisions that are made.

However, your major role may be to make brief notes. These are useful, even for an informal meeting, as they remind everyone what was discussed and agreed. A copy is also useful for the file, in case there are any disputes later. Normally, taking notes means that you simply keep a record of action points and decisions made – particularly who promised to do which task. Don't be distracted by long debates or discussions – so long as you record the conclusion. A good leader or chairperson should summarise each item verbally, once a decision has been reached, at which point you can check that your notes make sense.

After the meeting

After the meeting it will be your responsibility to make sure that the room is left tidy, any borrowed equipment is returned, your notes are typed up neatly and accurately and checked by the leader or chairperson, and that all papers are filed safely. You will also be responsible for photocopying and circulating the notes and any other paperwork, to both those who attended and those who did not.

The notes may be circulated in the form of a short report or as part of a memo. As an example, Figure 4.2 shows the communication sent to the publicity group after the meeting referred to in Figure 4.1.

MEMO

TO Publicity group members

FROM Joanne Marshall

DATE 2 March 199–

New photographs

Following our meeting yesterday, please find below a summary of the requirements and action points we agreed.

1 New staff

The staff display board in reception is outdated. Photographs to be taken of the following new members of staff. Katrina Westwell, Zubida Iqbal, Alistair Jones and Danielle Scott.

JB to arrange for above staff to be available in the seminar room at 10 am 16 March.

2 Company literature

No photographs are included for the new customer service facility or the new automated distribution centre. Both would be valuable.

KM to liaise with Customer Service Manager and Distribution Manager to agree best day/time for photographer to visit and provide schedule by 7 March.

3 Product photographs for catalogue

These will be arranged by Simona Franks in Marketing. We will require enlarged and mounted (selected) photographs for our displays.

ML to liaise with Simona to arrange for the publicity group to view photographs on receipt to select those most suitable for enlargement.

4 Staff handbook

JB felt that photographs of key staff – particularly line managers – would be a useful addition. JM to put forward this suggestion at management team meeting on Monday.

JM

Figure 4.2 Memo containing notes on a meeting

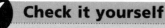

Check it yourself

Not all meetings always run smoothly! Discuss as a group:

a the action you would take in each of the following situations

b the action you would take to try to minimise the possibility of a recurrence.

i A meeting that you have organised overruns and four people scheduled to attend the next meeting are waiting impatiently outside the door.

ii The meeting *before* yours overruns and your people are already arriving.

iii When you open the door you find the tables littered with dirty cups and saucers and screwed up paper on the floor.

iv When you check the OHP, you find that it doesn't work.

v Your boss needed some papers photocopying urgently. When you give out the sets and start to look through your own copy, you notice that one page is missing, another is upside down and some are in the wrong order.

vi Your boss has just started chairing a meeting that her own boss is also attending. She has said that she doesn't want to be disturbed. Immediately you return to your desk you spot a message that her partner phoned ten minutes ago and wants her to ring back immediately.

vii The meeting started at 10 am and you booked coffee for 10.15. It is now 10.25, nothing has arrived, and your boss is getting very edgy.

Test yourself

Organise your own informal meeting to discuss, as a group, how your course is progressing and to identify any *major* items of concern. Note that the object of the exercise is not to hold a 'moans and groans' session but to evaluate your course objectively – and this includes the positive points! As a group, take the following steps.

1 Decide who should lead the meeting. Note that this person must be able to keep everyone focused upon the business in hand, move the discussion onwards to achieve the objectives of the meeting, try to involve everyone equally and keep the peace!

2 Decide on an appropriate date and time, book some suitable accommodation and arrange the seating appropriately. Check with your tutor if you can also arrange for refreshments.

3 Nominate one person to send a memo or e-mail to everyone in the group to confirm the arrangements.

4 Decide upon any documentation you need to produce beforehand and divide this task amongst you.

5 Hold the meeting and nominate one person to produce brief notes afterwards, summarising the main points agreed under clear headings. Circulate a copy to your tutor and to everyone else who attended.

6 After the event, hold a discussion to decide how effective and well-organised it was.

a Was the time and date convenient for most people?
b Did everyone receive notification in time?
c Were the room and seating suitable?
d Were the required facilities well organised?
e Was all the required documentation available?
f Was the general tone and mood of the meeting positive and cooperative, or negative and defensive? Give a reason for your views.
g Did the notes accurately reflect what happened?
h What would/could you do in future to improve the situation?

Semi-formal meetings

Under this category of meeting you are likely to find those held by senior managers, the Board of Directors, most committees and key groupings in commercial organisations. However, if you work for a local authority or a health trust then you may find that your committee documentation is rather more formal, given that it is often published afterwards. Internal committees set up in other types of establishments are less likely to adopt extremely formal procedures or documentation.

Who will be involved – the roles of participants

Semi-formal meetings mainly comprise **internal** participants. However, external people may be invited and many boards of directors also comprise non-executive members (see page 19).

In this type of meeting the participants will be mainly senior or middle managers. The standards of this group of people are likely to be exacting. They are busy people who expect the events they attend to be well organised and to run smoothly. If you intend to reach the top as a PA, you obviously want to impress everyone at this level with your calm efficiency and first-rate organisational skills!

Because of their status, it is quite likely that some participants will receive messages whilst they are involved in the meeting, so it is sensible to make

Tuckman and group formation

The psychology of group formation has been studied by many people. One writer, B W Tuckman, argued that all groups go through a four-stage development process which he called forming, storming, norming and performing. You may like to apply his theory to the development of your own course group.

At the **forming** stage the group is new, and people are unsure of the rules and each other. Dependence upon any leader is very high. Some members may be anxious and apprehensive, and there may be some informal banter or 'ice-breaking.' Everyone needs to know what is likely to happen and when. For this stage, think about your first days in college in a new group. Do you remember what it was like?

At the **storming** stage, members are not sure of their individual roles and there may be some differences of opinion – both between individual members and the leader and amongst members. Different points of view are put forward and there may be some disputes. Some people may be disappointed because the group is not living up to their expectations. In most new college groups you will find that there is some interchange between friendship groups in the early weeks. In addition, one or two members may leave or transfer because the course isn't what they expected. Eventually the group 'shakes down' into one where

individual differences are tolerated to a greater degree and the group is more cohesive and permanent.

At this stage the group enters the **norming** stage, where members become supportive of each other. There is an open exchange of opinions and more camaraderie. Formal and informal roles are allocated (one person may become the 'class wit' or the 'class speaker'). There is a shared responsibility for group activities and harmony amongst members is valued.

Finally, the group reaches the stage when its energies can be focused on task performance rather than individual concerns. This is the **performing** stage, where the group will work together to solve a problem and suggest solutions. This is the major productive period for all groups – and hopefully the one that now exists for your own!

What is the relevance of Tuckman's theory to meetings and events? Quite simply, it is argued that unless members or delegates are given the chance to go through the stages of group development, they will not perform to their maximum potential. For that reason, it is valuable:

- for forming – to allow time at the beginning for informal chat, usually over coffee, and then give an outline of the content of the meeting or event and describe any rules or procedures that must be observed

- for storming – to introduce any controversial topics or difficult tasks that must be achieved

- for norming – to allow the group time to discuss how best to achieve the task

- for performing – to encourage the group to decide jointly what to do.

You will often find this pattern reflected at meetings and at other events, such as seminars, when groups meet over coffee and only later are divided into workshops and asked to undertake different tasks (see page 165).

A final point. Tuckman also considered that groups which later disband go through a **mourning** stage when individuals feel sad at parting, and often agree to meet again in the future. You may remember these words on your last day in college with your current group – even if you hold different views at present!

sure that someone is nominated to receive any calls and take a message. In many cases it is also courteous to inform the switchboard operator and the receptionist, in case there are any general queries regarding a person's whereabouts.

In a semi-formal meeting many of the participants have a distinct role during the meeting – including you, if you are the designated meetings secretary! Your main link will be with the chairperson responsible for the meeting.

The role of the chairperson

A good chairperson makes all the difference to the running of the meeting, the amount of business it gets through, the atmosphere that prevails and the ease with which you can prepare for the meeting. Ideally, a chairperson is nominated because of his or her expertise and skill in managing people. The tasks of a chairperson involve the following.

- To know the rules, regulations and procedures relating to that particular meeting – particularly what is allowable and what is not.

- To start the meeting on time.

- To ensure that all participants know each other and introduce any new members or others invited to attend.

- To follow the agenda (see pages 119–122).

- To explain the topic to be discussed, distribute or refer to relevant papers, give the participants any background information they need and then encourage relevant discussion.

- To insist that all participants **address the chair**, rather than each other – which means that all the remarks are made to the chairperson. This may seem odd, if you are not used to formal meetings, but is extremely sensible. It stops individuals starting to converse amongst themselves, which could rapidly lead to chaos, with different conversations breaking out around the table! It also means that the chairperson is aware of all aspects of the discussion.

- To make sure that everyone has the opportunity to put forward their views, stop anyone from talking too much or overpowering the others, and make each person keep to the point.

- To decide when the topic has been discussed enough, summarise the points made and put forward the decision or action to be taken for general agreement. You should note that a good chairperson will always propose a *positive* action (ie to do something) rather than a *negative* one (ie not to do something).

- To arbitrate when there is disagreement between members. If there is deadlock then the chairperson has the **casting vote**. This means he or she makes the final decision. In this situation, it is normal for a chairperson to preserve the **status quo** (existing state of affairs) rather than to use his or her casting vote to enforce radical change!

- To make certain that everyone is clear on what has been agreed.

- To close the meeting properly so that everyone is clear it has ended. A good chairperson will also close it on time, rather than overrun.

The role of other participants
Even those who attend without an official role have a responsibility to ensure the meeting runs smoothly and that it is productive. Unless each person is prepared to make a positive contribution, and to be interested in the proceedings, then it is better to resign. An effective participant will:

- confirm his or her attendance upon receiving the notice and agenda, or promptly inform the meetings secretary why he or she will be unable to attend

- arrive on time

- remember to bring any paperwork sent out with the notice and agenda

- read the paperwork in advance and be able to contribute knowledgeably to any discussions on the contents

- be able to put his or her point of view clearly and succinctly

- be prepared to listen to different views put forward by other people

- undertake any activities delegated to him or her before the deadline agreed

- support the chairperson (certainly in public!) – a participant who strongly disagrees with an action or decision should discuss the matter in private with the chairperson afterwards.

The role of the secretary

The role of the meetings secretary is to support the chairperson by undertaking all the administrative essentials of running a meeting.

During the meeting your major responsibility will be to take the minutes of the meeting. It is sensible not to offer your services for other duties that might conflict, such as serving coffee! A practical way around this is to arrange for coffee to be available as people arrive – they will often be quite prepared to pour their own cup. This enables early arrivals to start chatting and accords with Tuckman's ideas on group formation (see page 114).

Assuming that you have made all the preparations beforehand and checked everything you need is available and all the equipment is in working order, you can now concentrate on taking your notes.

What documentation will be needed?

It is likely to be your job to prepare and issue both the specialist meetings documentation and any supplementary papers required (either beforehand or to be tabled). Most of the documentation is devised to enable the meeting to run smoothly and to a set formula that everyone knows.

Significant others

Whilst most company meetings will simply have a nominated chair and, possibly (but not always) a nominated meetings secretary, committees representing social, voluntary or charitable organisations often have other nominated roles as well. These may include a treasurer, who is responsible for keeping the accounts and reporting on all financial transactions; a membership secretary, responsible for membership applications and subscriptions; and a social secretary, responsible for social events and fund-raising activities. There may also be a vice-chairperson, nominated to stand in for the chairperson when he or she is absent.

If your memory of the beginning of this section is good, you may remember that the duties of this latter role (and others relating to 'company officers') are usually covered in a company's Articles of Association.

A semi-formal or formal meeting will be called by issuing a **notice**, which gives details of when and where the meeting will be held. The wording varies depending upon the degree of formality of the event. This is followed by a written **agenda** listing the business in the order in which items will be debated. Often the two are combined into one document so that those invited receive a **notice and agenda** which giving them all the information they need prior to the meeting. In some cases, the chairperson may request that a special **chair's agenda** is produced. This is the standard agenda together with reminder points for the chair.

During the meeting, one person – often the meetings secretary – is responsible for taking the **minutes** of the meeting. This is a written record of what occurred. The degree of detail in minutes is quite variable. **Minutes of narration** 'tell the story' of a meeting (albeit concisely) and therefore give rather more information than **minutes of action** – which simply list the conclusions and action agreed. In one company a Production department decided simply to list the action agreed at the meeting, by whom and for when! This was fine for those who attended and who understood the jargon, but much less comprehensible to other people who needed to refer to them. **Minutes of resolution** are those produced for very formal meetings, such as an AGM or EGM (see page 142).

Whilst meetings documents are relatively standard (see below), it is sensible to familiarise yourself with the house style you are expected to use. There should be ample evidence in the files to show you how the organisation sets out notices, agendas and minutes. You should establish which chairpersons like to use a chairperson's agenda and which do not. You also need to check the rules, regulations, standing orders or constitution that applies to that particular type of meeting. These should tell you

- who should be involved
- the length of notice required
- if there is any stipulation about how frequently meetings should be held.

Keep this information close to hand until you know it by heart.

Notice and agenda

A notice of meeting gives details of where and when the meeting will be held. All members eligible to attend must receive a copy – otherwise, for some meetings, you may find that the **validity** of the meeting is threatened. This is the ability of those present to make binding decisions. If you do forget to include someone, your omission may be excused if the rules provide for **waiver** – when those present are allowed to overlook a genuine mistake. It may also happen that a person who should be present is agreed to be 'beyond summoning distance'. This means that he or she is too ill or too far away to be expected to attend.

You need to consider how best to communicate your notice and agenda. In some organisations, semi-formal meetings may be called by memo or e-mail. Don't forget, however, that any external members will expect to be notified through the post – unless you usually communicate with them by e-mail over the Internet. Usually you will find a standard method is used for each particular type of meeting you are asked to organise.

Information in a notice

Key facts to include are:

- the company name and address, if non-executive directors or external people are being invited

- the date, day and time of the meeting

- the place (room and location address, if different from the company address) where the meeting will be held

- the type of meeting, if appropriate

- the date of the notice.

Sometimes, if special business is to be discussed, this is also described. An example of a notice is given in Figure 4.3.

Information in an agenda

The agenda is a vital document for those who are to attend as it gives information about the business to be discussed. It also lists the 'order of

---

NOTICE OF MEETING

Perriman Software plc
Park House
Morley Park Road
HIGHTOWN
HG3 8PN

20 March 199–

The next Board meeting will be held in the Committee Room at 1500 hours on Thursday, 7 April 199–.

Gemma Harrison

Secretary

Figure 4.3 A notice for a meeting

business'. If, for instance, a non-executive director can only attend for a short time for a particular reason, he or she would be able to estimate when a key item of interest – or one to which he or she is expected to make a particular contribution – is likely to be discussed.

In some cases the rules of the meeting prescribe a particular order for the agenda. In other cases, the meetings secretary should order the items logically. The guidelines below should help you to do this.

- **Apologies for absence.** Those who cannot attend a formal meeting are expected to send their apologies in advance. The meetings secretary keeps a list of members who have made contact to say they cannot attend – with reasons. Having this item at the start of the meeting means that the chairperson can quickly check that all those who were expected to arrive have done so and the meeting can commence. The names of those who could not attend are recorded.

- **Minutes of the previous meeting.** This is normally a formality where the chairperson checks that everyone present agrees the minutes are a correct record of what took place. A phrase you may often hear is **taken as read**. This means that the meeting has agreed that the chairperson (or secretary) does not need to read the previous minutes aloud. On the majority of occasions this is agreed and there are no comments. If, however, an inaccuracy is identified, the *previous minutes must not be altered.* Instead, the comments – and the correction – are recorded in the minutes for the *current* meeting.

- **Matters arising.** This item enables members to comment on and/or query any action taken since the last meeting. A good chairperson will not allow discussion, at this time, on any items that are listed as 'specific items' (see below) on the agenda.

- **Correspondence.** If there is no correspondence this item is omitted. Only if a communication is of interest to the meeting as a whole would it be included under this heading.

- **Specific item(s).** This is the main business of the meeting and there may be as many items of specific business as the chairperson requires. However, it is sensible not to overload an agenda, as this reduces time for discussion or means that items at the end of the list are rushed or have to be deferred. It is usual to list specific items in order of importance, in case anyone has to leave early. Sometimes a particular item may occur over several subsequent meetings because there are ongoing developments and discussions about it.

- **Any other business (AOB).** This item is for *minor*, general areas of discussion that are not included on the main agenda or have arisen since the agenda was issued. Important issues can be raised, but the chairperson is likely to indicate that the matter will be included as a specific item in the next agenda.

- **Date and time of next meeting.** Traditionally this is the final agenda item, but this can be inconvenient if one or two people have had to leave the meeting early for some reason. Some chairs therefore prefer to discuss it much earlier in the meeting – even at the beginning!

An example of a *combined* notice and agenda is given in Figure 4.4. Note that this practice is usually followed to save time as well as stationery and postage costs. Even when organisations prefer the two documents to be produced separately, they are usually despatched together unless there has been a delay over the agenda and the notice must be sent out to allow sufficient clear days.

NOTICE AND AGENDA

Perriman Software plc
Park House
Morley Park Road
HIGHTOWN
HG3 8PN

20 March 199–

The next Board meeting will be held in the Committee Room at 1500 hours on Thursday, 7 April 199–.

AGENDA

1 Apologies for absence
2 Minutes of the previous meeting
3 Matters arising
4 Correspondence
5 Finance for new product development
6 Appointment of new marketing director
7 Company representation at IT exhibitions
8 Any other business
9 Date and time of next meeting

Gemma Harrison

Secretary

Figure 4.4 A combined notice and agenda

Devising an agenda

Whereas an agenda may seem a strange document if you are not familiar with a particular meeting, for a practised meetings secretary who organises and attends meetings of a specific group or committee, many of the items are a natural progression from the last meeting, where the chairperson has indicated that a topic will be included in the next agenda.

Routine items comprise the first three items and the last two (apart from the first meeting of a group, which will obviously have no past minutes or matters arising!) Correspondence, as you have seen, is only included if there is a document of interest.

Special items may be forthcoming from:

- the previous set of minutes – where 'ongoing' items or action points have been identified

- suggestions made by the chairperson during the meeting

- suggestions made during AOB, which the chairperson decided should be specific items at the next meeting

- suggestions made by members between one meeting and another (which may arrive in the form of notes, e-mails or telephone calls)

- current events and issues of concern. You can establish these by discussing the items to be included with the chairperson prior to the next agenda being finalised. It is also sensible to consult the chairperson about other suggestions received from members. He or she may have views on what should be included and why.

Information in a chairperson's agenda

Not all chairs will want you to produce a chairperson's agenda – and you will soon learn the preferences of your own line managers and their individual idiosyncrasies in relation to meetings. The idea of such an agenda is to give the chairperson an 'extended' version of the main agenda with useful reminders and comments, in addition to space in which to write notes both before and during the meeting. It is usual to produce this document just before the meeting is held, so that your notes and comments are as up-to-date as possible.

It is sensible to arrange for the chairperson to give you the completed copy of the chair's agenda at the end of the meeting. This enables you to check the minutes against his or her notes. It also enables you to dispose of it once the minutes have been agreed and signed, particularly if it contains ideas that were amended, or adverse comments on suggestions made by participants!

A copy of the prepared chair's agenda to match the notice and agenda in Figure 4.4 is given in Figure 4.5.

Meeting	Board Meeting
Date/time	7 April 199–, 1500 hours
Place	Committee Room, Park House

AGENDA ITEM

NOTES

1 **Apologies for absence**   1
Peter Sharpe in Australia until end of April.

2 **Minutes of previous meeting**   2

3 **Matters arising**   3
Questions may be asked about
- feedback on customer survey – JL has details
- progress with new staff contracts – issue date is 3 May, staff meeting arranged for 26 April.

4 **Correspondence**   4
Request from television company to feature us in programme on IT for the millennium.

5 **Finance for new product development**   5
- focus on software for Windows NT
- NH to table report
- estimated investment £4m.

6 **Appointment of new marketing director**   6
- appointment given to Premier Selection
- shortlist due 12 April
- projected interviews week commencing 15 May.

7 **Company representation at IT exhibition**   7
- NEC 10 June
- PT has full details.

8 **Any other business**   8
Recent approach by Interactive Sales Ltd (summary attached).

9 **Date and time of next meeting**   9
Avoid 6–13 May – US visit.

Figure 4.5 Chairperson's Agenda

Supplementary papers

These were first discussed on page 109. When you are sending out supplementary papers in advance for a semi-formal meeting, it is useful to mark each one with the agenda item to which it refers. It is sensible to make sure that you have spare copies at the meeting to give to people who have forgotten to bring their own copy. Spare copies of the agenda and the last set of minutes never go amiss either, for the same reason!

The day before the meeting you need to check whether the chairperson wishes to table any papers at the meeting, and make sure you have sufficient copies.

The minutes of the meeting

A set of minutes usually includes the following information.

- The name of the organisation.

- The type of meeting held plus the place, date and time of the meeting.

- The names of those present. The chairperson is normally listed first and the meetings secretary last. Others attending are usually listed in alphabetical order, to prevent any status problems. Anyone present for a specific reason is also identified, ie

  - someone invited who is not a member of that committee or group. For instance, the Board of Directors may ask the Health and Safety Officer to attend a meeting if there is discussion on an area at which his or her expertise is required. This type of person is known as a **co-opted member** and it is usual to mark them as **in attendance** in the minutes

  - someone who is entitled to attend by virtue of his or her position in the organisation (but who may not always do so). For instance, your college's Principal may have the right to join the Marketing Committee when it meets each week, but may often be too busy to do so. Such persons are known as **ex officio members**. In other words, by virtue of rank they cannot be excluded from any meeting they choose to attend.

- A numbered list of items discussed, which normally accords with the agenda numbering system. Under each heading is a brief record of what has been discussed and decided. In some organisations each minute item has a separate number and these run on from one meeting to another in a particular year. In this case, minute number 42/99 would be the forty-second minute item recorded for a particular committee in 1999.

- An action column containing the initials of those who have been asked to undertake particular tasks and report back at the next meeting. These are not required by all organisations, nor for all committees, but are becoming much more popular as they focus attention on jobs to be done by each member – reminding them that they will be accountable for progress at the next meeting.

- Space for the chairperson to sign and date the minutes once they have been agreed as correct.

Writing minutes

If you are responsible for taking minutes at a meeting, you need the following attributes and assistance.

- An effective chairperson, who keeps to the agenda, summarises the discussion and is willing to check your draft minutes afterwards.

- Good note taking abilities – or an excellent memory.

- A relatively good mastery of the English language and your word-processing package.

- To be excused from other duties during the course of the meeting (such as serving coffee or participating in discussions).

- A basic understanding of the reason for the meeting, and knowledge of the names and faces of those attending and any technical terms or abbreviations that may be used.

- The ability to summarise.

- Tact, diplomacy and the ability to guess what the chairperson expects you to write!

It is little wonder that most new minute-writers dread the ordeal. Unless you have an excellent relationship with the chairperson (whom you may be reluctant to approach with all your concerns) the secret is to find a 'meetings mentor' – someone who attends the meetings, understands what they are about, appreciates what the chair is trying to achieve and is prepared to give you guidance in your early days. He or she will explain any unusual terms, help you to rephrase or reword difficult points and clarify any queries. Before long you will find you need less and less guidance.

Hints and tips on minute taking

Many good minute takers are not high-speed shorthand writers – so don't let a lack of this skill put you off. However, you obviously need to develop some system of abbreviating common words and expressions in order to write quickly. Interestingly, many high-speed writers struggle because they are tempted to record *too much* information, and then have difficulty deciding what to leave out. The following tips may help to give you some confidence in the early days.

- Try to attend your first few meetings 'shadowing' an experienced meetings secretary. This means that you are not responsible for producing the final set of minutes, unless you volunteer to do so. It also means you can practise typing up your notes and comparing your version with that of an expert.

- Make sure you are well prepared. Note the names of those who attend and their initials, as this is the quickest way of noting who is speaking.

Rovers 1, Notetaker 1

Some years ago a (now) Premier League football club called an EGM. A local businessman had challenged the club chairman and put in a bid to replace him. The result was a meeting held in the local town hall to which club members and the local press were invited. Amongst those present was a young and inexperienced shorthand writer, who had been asked to take the minutes as the usual secretary was on holiday. She had been given the job purely because her own boss was a member of the club's board – and had volunteered her for the task without consultation!

Seated at a vast oak desk in the centre of a large room, she felt isolated, nervous and exposed. Her major worry had been whether she would be able to understand her notes later. When people started to arrive a greater concern arose. All the faces were totally unfamiliar – how would she know who was speaking and to whom to attribute different remarks?

Even the Chair and the members of the Board – bar one – were strangers.

At the last minute she was joined by small, older man. He rapidly introduced himself as the sports columnist for the local paper – he had arrived to cover the event. Here was her salvation. He knew the names of everyone present, but his shorthand was rusty – hers was good, but people's names were unknown to her. Together they devised a scheme. On two overlapping sheets of paper, he scribbled each name whilst she wrote down their comments. Afterwards over a drink in a local pub they pooled their notes. The result was a first-rate newspaper report and an acceptable (if not excellent) set of minutes.

How do I know? Because I was that young shorthand writer! The football club was Blackburn Rovers and the reporter's name was Alf Thornton. My heartfelt thanks still go to him!

Blackburn Rovers football ground

In some organisations today, initials are used in the actual minutes, rather than full names. Collect together your stationery requirements – A4 lined paper is often better than a shorthand notebook as you can write more before turning over. Divide the page into two columns, a narrow one for initials and a wide one for remarks. Some experienced secretaries put a third column on the right for noting amendments made later. Much depends upon the decisiveness of your chairperson!

- The first time you attend on your own, ask if you can have a tape-recorder with you as a back-up. Do not be personally affronted if this is refused, because there may be worries about security if sensitive matters are discussed.

- Look back through previous sets of minutes to establish the level of detail you are expected to record. If all the minutes comprise brief summary points covering one or two pages at most, your chairperson will be extremely surprised to receive in-depth narrative minutes on ten sheets of paper.

- Learn to be selective about what you record. Generally, all the points made in discussions are not recorded, but only a summary statement. For this reason, a phrase used in many minutes is 'after much discussion it was decided that . . . '. Be aware, however, that on occasion people may specifically ask that their objection to a suggestion is minuted.

- Equally, on other occasions, your chairperson may wish to talk 'off the record' and ask you *not* to minute a particular comment. You are obviously expected to accede to such a request!

- If you are worried about something you have written, or didn't understand something that was discussed, make a note in the margin and query it with the chairperson or an understanding participant at the end of the meeting. Unless you are absolutely desperate, it is not a good idea to interrupt a chairperson in full flow to clarify something he or she said ten minutes earlier! If necessary, check what you should record at the end of a discussion, before the chairperson moves on to the next topic. Most chairs are kind and understanding with a new minute writer, and they prefer a few *brief* questions at the time to inaccurate or incomprehensible minutes, or being confronted with a query on a complex discussion point five days later!

- Type up the minutes as soon as possible after the meeting has ended. Word processors mean you can alter and amend your text as necessary.

- In the early days at least, make arrangements for your chairperson to check your draft minutes. This makes it clear that you do not mind if he or she amends items as required (or even improves your English!). In some cases your chairperson will be acutely aware of the wider audience who may read the minutes – and possible reactions to different comments. Until you develop a feel for the politics of an organisation or a meeting it is sensible to let the chairperson have a free hand with your draft.

- Edit the minutes on your word processor. Ask the chairperson to sign and date the minutes and check which other members of the organisation routinely receive a copy. Make a copy for each person who must receive a set. It is useful to highlight each person's name on the attendance list for distribution of each particular copy – this saves you forgetting anyone. For semi-formal and formal meetings, it is usual to put the *original* signed document in a file folder. It is also customary in some cases to number each set of minutes so that it is easy to check that none are missing.

The technique of minute taking

Certain grammatical conventions are observed when writing minutes, and you should know these before writing your first set.

- The third person, past tense, and reported speech are *always* used. You should never, therefore, find yourself writing 'I', 'we' or 'you'! The past tense is employed because the meeting has now ended – everything you are writing about happened in the past. Reported speech is logical, given that you are reporting on what people have said. In practical terms this means that you *never* use quotation marks.

- Slang and colloquial expressions should not feature in your minutes. Neither should strong adjectives, expletives or exaggerated statements! Your reporting should be objective and factual – no matter what was really said at the time.

- Good minute writers avoid repetition. 'Mr Bloggs said that . . . then Mr West said that . . . then Mrs Marshall said that . . .' is boring to write and monotonous to read.

- It goes without saying that the grammatical construction of your sentences, your spelling, punctuation and proof-reading skills must be first rate.

Even people who think they are good at writing in reported speech can have difficulties in certain areas. These including the following.

- **Pronouns.** It is too easy to put a pronoun into a sentence and promptly make it ambiguous, eg

  She said she should go to the meeting.

  In this case, it is not clear to whom the second 'she' relates. Is the speaker talking about herself, or giving an instruction to someone else? The answer is *either* to substitute the person's name or title at a point where there may be ambiguity, *or* to re-emphasise the fact that the speaker was talking about herself.

She thought Ann Brown should go to the meeting.
She thought she should go to the meeting herself.

- **'Always true' statements.** A speaker may make a statement that is true today and will also be true tomorrow. Take an 'unmeetings-like' sentence such as

The world is round.

Although reported speech normally uses the past tense, it would look peculiar if you wrote 'the world was round' – this implies that the world has subsequently become a different shape! In such a case, the present tense of the verb is retained, eg

*Peter Brown commented that the company **is** very adept at selling in that market.*

- **Time and place.** In direct speech it is easy to refer to place and time in the current form, ie

'I will see Jessica today or tomorrow – though I had hoped to see her yesterday. I may meet her here but I would prefer to go there.'

In reported speech the terms referring to days change, and references to places have to be made specific if the term 'there' would prove ambiguous, eg

He said that he would see Jessica on that day or the following day, although he had hoped to see her the previous day. He said he might meet her in his office but he would prefer to go to her office.

Note also that 'now' becomes 'then' and, generally, 'here' becomes 'there', ie

He welcomed all who were there that day.

- **Rhetorical questions.** A rhetorical question is one that expects or requires no reply. It is said for effect, eg

'So what you're telling me is that we're incapable of producing a quotation in time?' said the chairman to the Sales Manager, sarcastically.

This statement has an implied meaning obvious to everyone at the meeting – and this is the meaning that must be conveyed in the minutes. Therefore it would be *incorrect* to write a 'literal' version, eg *The chairman confirmed that the staff were incapable of producing a quotation in time.* Instead, a correct version would be

The chairman stressed that he expected a quotation to be produced in time.

✓ Check it yourself

1   It is good practice to avoid repetition of common verbs in a set of minutes. As a group, identify as many alternatives as you can for each of the following words. If necessary, use a thesaurus to help you.

a asked   **b** said
c urged   **d** told

2   Convert each of the following statements into reported speech. Remember that, for minute taking, conveying the meaning accurately is far more important than the 'literal' technique you perhaps learned in school!

a 'America's a big place,' commented Martin Banks, 'you'll be lucky to get that far in a fortnight.'

b 'Do you honestly think I'm going to put that suggestion to their MD?' asked the Chairman. 'If so, you must think I was born yesterday.'

c 'I think this idea has a lot going for it,' said Martina Malova. 'I, for one, would be prepared to back it.'

d 'I think we can sort it out now,' said Hussain Patel. 'John Brown's train arrives at Waterloo today so I can bring him to the factory tomorrow.'

3   **a** A set of minutes which relate to the notice and agenda in figure 4.5 is shown in figure 4.6. Read them through carefully and check the contents against the information you have read above. Clarify any concerns or queries you have with your tutor.

MINUTES

Minutes of the Board Meeting held in the Committee Room, Park House, at 1500 hours on 7 April 199-.

PRESENT

Barbara Davies	(Chair)
Nasreen Hussain	Finance Director
Jolanta Lindt	Sales Director
John Morrison	Personnel Director
Antonio Parente	Production Director
Petra Taylor	Administration Director
Gemma Harrison	(Secretary)

1   APOLOGIES FOR ABSENCE   ACTION
Apologies were received from Peter Sharpe,
Technical Director, who is currently visiting clients
in Australia.

2   MINUTES OF PREVIOUS MEETING
The minutes of the previous meeting were taken as
read, agreed as a true and correct record and signed
by the Chair.

3   MATTERS ARISING
Jolanta Lindt reported that the results of the
customer survey were very positive and a printed
summary would be sent to all present. She
requested that the item be carried forward to the
next agenda for discussion as a specific item.   JL

The Chair reported that, following a meeting with
the unions, it had been agreed that the new staff
contracts would be issued on 3 May. A full staff
meeting would be held on 26 April to enable any
queries to be answered.

4   CORRESPONDENCE
The Secretary read a request from Planet TV to
feature the company in a programme on 'IT for the
Millennium'. The benefits of such publicity were
discussed against the difficulties of cooperating with
the requirements of the television company. Petra
Taylor to meet with computer section and prepare
report for next meeting when a full discussion of the
request could be held and action agreed.   PT

5   FINANCE FOR NEW PRODUCT DEVELOPMENT
The Chair asked Nasreen Hussain to table a report
projecting a financial investment of £4 million for
the company to achieve its corporate aims of
developing software compatible with Windows NT.
Petra Taylor queried whether further developments
in operating software could mean that Windows NT
would only have a short shelf life. After discussion,
it was agreed to recommend the investment be
reduced to £3 million for the current financial
year.

6   APPOINTMENT OF NEW MARKETING DIRECTOR   ACTION

The Chair reported that the appointment was being
handled by Premier Selection, who were to submit a
shortlist by 12 April. Interviews would be held week
commencing 15 May and all Board members were
asked to be available to meet the candidates. It was
agreed that the most convenient date for this would
be 17 May and John Morrison would circulate the
interview schedule the previous week.   JM

7   COMPANY REPRESENTATION AT IT EXHIBITION

Petra Taylor reported that this year's IT exhibition
would be held at the NEC on 10 June. Jolanta Lindt
commented that the Marketing department had
specifically requested a larger stand area, as last
year the available space had been extremely
crowded. It was agreed that more staff and a larger
stand were required to give a good impression to
visitors. Jolanta Lindt agreed to prepare a report
including costings of new publicity material to
be discussed in full at the next meeting.   JL

8   ANY OTHER BUSINESS

The Chair reported that the company had been
approached by Interactive Sales to represent software
sales in the US. Antonio Parente commented that he
had heard good reports about this company. It was
agreed that further investigations would be undertaken
by Jolanta Lindt and the item would be included for
discussion in next week's agenda.   JL

Antonio Parente reported that Peter Sharpe had sent
a recent report outlining some of the difficulties
being experienced by Australian customers which he
would forward to all Board members. The Chair
agreed this would be a key item for discussion next
week.

9   DATE AND TIME OF NEXT MEETING

It was agreed that the next meeting should be held
at 1500 hours on Thursday, 14 April 199-.

Signed ....(Chairperson) .... (Date)

Figure 4.6   A set of minutes

b Assume that the following week there is no correspondence and the only new items of business given to you by the Chairperson are

  – application for IIP accreditation, and
  – building rewiring schedule.

Prepare the notice and agenda for the following week's meeting. Remember to include all the items that it was agreed would be carried forward from the last meeting.

4 An extract from a college Equal Opportunities Committee discussion is shown in Figure 4.7. Assume you are writing the minutes for this and convert the statements into one or two brief paragraphs to convey the information accurately.

Equal opportunities meeting

Sean Kelly   What provision does the college have for monitoring applications from prospective members of staff?

Gemma Tate   We issue a monitoring form with every application, but it's up to the candidates whether they complete them. There's no compulsion to do so.

Rizwan Malik   More importantly, what does the college do with the findings? We have a high ratio of ethnic minority students, but very few ethnic staff to teach them. Surely we should aim for a better balance?

Gemma Tate   We always include our equal opportunities statement in all our applications. We can hardly be blamed if we don't receive many applications from ethnic minority tutors – we would certainly welcome far more.

Sean Kelly   Ah, but do we know how many applications we actually receive? And can we prove that all applications are dealt with according to the proper procedures? May I suggest that, as a first stage, we monitor how many applications are received from different candidates for a vacancy? I don't just mean from ethnic minorities – but also from women candidates and from the disabled. Then we can decide what to do next. If we receive a wide variety of applications but few minority applicants are ever appointed, that's a different issue than receiving few minority applications.

Gemma Tate	That's an excellent point. In the first case we would need to examine the interview and selection procedures, and in the second we would need to examine our advertising and recruitment strategy.
Rizwan Malik	I agree. I'll arrange for Paula Martel, our Staffing Officer, to produce a breakdown of the applications for the next six vacancies – both teaching and non-teaching – and then we can see if there is any pattern.
Gemma Tate	There are several vacancies in the pipeline at present. You should be able to obtain the information to bring to the next meeting in a month's time. Now, let's move on.

Figure 4.7 Extract from a committee discussion

Check your answers with your tutor.

How it will operate

Generally you can expect people to arrive slightly before the official starting time. It is often easier to have refreshments available at the outset rather than interrupt the meeting part-way through. There is usually a short time for people to talk informally (the 'forming' process) and the chairperson will indicate the start by sitting down (normally at the head of the table, with the secretary to his or her right) and arranging the papers. This is the signal to everyone to be seated!

The chairperson will then *usually* deal with each item of business in the order listed on the agenda – introducing the topic, allowing discussion (where appropriate) and then stating what action will be taken. The order may be varied at the chairperson's discretion. For instance, if someone has to leave before an important item would normally be debated, it can be brought forward.

You will be expected to read the apologies and to pass around any tabled papers as and when required.

At the end of the meeting the chairperson should signal that the proceedings are closed. At this point, members are free to exchange information again and speak informally, rather than address the chair and have their remarks noted for posterity!

After the meeting

Your duties in this case are similar to those identified on page 110, for informal meetings. You need to ensure, however, that the receptionist and switchboard know that the meeting has ended and to ask the catering staff to remove any refreshments. You would also be sensible to remove and destroy any paperwork you do not need for the minutes, particularly if contentious or sensitive issues have been discussed. If you get into the habit of making certain nothing is left around then you will be erring on the side of caution. Check that no-one has left any personal possessions in the room and remove any notices posted on the door, or direction signs for visitors.

Allocate some time for transcribing your notes. Draft your minutes and ask the chairperson to check them for accuracy, then copy them for circulation. If the contents have security implications, you may be expected to put the minutes in envelopes and mark them as confidential.

You may also have the responsibility of checking that the chairperson and other participants undertake promised action before the next meeting – in addition to your own. Your strategies here will depend upon the status of the person concerned – and their reliability factor. In most cases it is sensible to:

- record the dates when actions must be completed in your own diary, the chairperson's diary, and the diaries of the people concerned

- send an e-mail or brief memo the week before, with a polite reminder of the promised action

- highlight any items on members' personal copies of the next agenda on which they will have to report progress.

 Test yourself

Form your own committee, or committees, depending upon how many there are in your group. Between eight and eleven members is ideal in each one. Each committee is given the task of organising a particular event – to be selected by the members. At this stage you are to plan your first meeting.

- Decide where and when the first meeting will be held and make any required bookings.

- Decide whether you will need any particular equipment (you might find a flipchart or whiteboard and pens very useful).

- Ask for a volunteer to be meetings secretary the first time. Note that this duty should revolve around the group each time!

- The meetings secretary should prepare a notice and agenda. The notice will be straightforward. The agenda should be as follows:

1 Apologies
2 Election of chairperson
3 Rota for meetings secretary
4 Selection of event
5 Any other business
6 Time and date of next meeting

- The first item should be undertaken properly – anyone not able to attend *must* give his or her apologies to the meetings secretary beforehand, together with a reason.

- The election of the chairperson can be undertaken using any fair system agreed by your committee as a whole. You may wish to discuss alternative systems with your tutor before the meeting (or read ahead to pages 152–153). Bear in mind the qualities required of a good chairperson – you need someone who is well organised and can lead the group as a whole!

- The rota for the meetings secretary is a straightforward item. Remember, at this point the chairperson will have the casting vote if there are any disputes.

- The event to be selected is the main item of business. As a group, you will be organising and arranging an event at some time in the future. This shouldn't be overly ambitious, nor should it involve much, if any, expenditure (unless you have some good ideas as to how you can raise the money). Ideally, the event should be held in about two to three months' time. Much further away and everyone will lose interest; too soon and you won't have enough time to organise it properly. The following are some suggestions, but you are obviously free to ignore these and substitute a different idea, providing your tutor approves.

  - A one- or two-hour seminar with one or two guest speakers
  - A half-hour presentation on a specialist topic to an invited audience
  - An 'away day' for the group as a whole
  - A mini conference lasting half a day and comprising various activities for the whole group.

  It is useful if any topics you select for your seminar, presentation or conference are useful for your course, rather than fascinating for you, personally! Ideas may include:

  - inviting the manager of a large, local hotel to give you views from the 'other side' on holding conferences

- asking a security expert or a representative of your local police to talk to you about security arrangements
- inviting a VAT official to give you the 'ins and outs' of VAT (or a local accountant to tell you about expenses and expense claims)
- asking someone from the town hall to talk to you about planning applications, appeals and public inquiries
- inviting a professional conference organiser to give you an inside view
- asking a local Environmental Health Officer to talk to you about health and safety in hotels and conference centres
- inviting a past successful student to give you a talk on life as a PA.

The alternative, if you cannot find a speaker, is to organise a presentation yourself. People will often willingly give you information (the VAT office, for instance, will let you borrow an introductory film) even if they haven't the time to visit you personally. Your job will be to organise the information into a presentation.

A mini conference is probably the most ambitious idea. This would involve organising one or two speakers and probably a workshop session for participants. Before you go down this route you may wish to read pages 159–166 of the next chapter and talk through your plans with your tutor.

Finally, *who* you know rather than *what* you know may be your key to making a choice! If one person has a father who is a police inspector and another has a mother who runs a hotel, your decision might be much easier!

- If a decision can't be reached at the first meeting, everyone could be asked to go away to think of other ideas, find out about different options, check information with friends and relatives, etc, and report back at the next meeting. This is what happens at all meetings – some of the business is carried forward – and the continuing items will form your agenda next time.

- Finally, check if anyone has anything to raise under AOB and then decide the time and date of the next meeting.

- The meetings secretary, of course, now has the job of producing the minutes – as promptly as possible, and duly signed by the chairperson. Remember, too, that it is the job of all participants to undertake any agreed action before the next meeting!

Formal meetings

You may never be involved with making the arrangements for a very formal meeting – nor may you ever attend one – particularly if you work for a small firm. However, as a PA (and presumably one who wants to get on in life) it is important that you can adapt your skills to cope with a wide range of situations. Even, therefore, if the information below seems very theoretical in relation to your first job, it will be useful to keep it to hand if you are ever changing jobs or applying for promotion.

Who will be involved – the roles of participants

In a business organisation the most formal meetings are the AGM or an EGM, with the chairperson and Board present, together with shareholders. Members of the press may also attend. Other formal meetings include local government committees (which councillors attend), civil service and some union meetings.

Although some very formal meetings may still be relatively small affairs, they do have the potential to be large gatherings that include a wide range of people, most of whom will be complete strangers to you. This is particularly so in the following cases.

- A public company could be a privatised organisation with very many small shareholders. If they are aggrieved about something, attendance could be high – as British Gas found when their past chairman, Cedric Brown, awarded himself a large pay rise!

- A public company could have been in the news recently and/or stimulated the interest of several pressure groups. Shell's Nigerian policy was criticised by both Greenpeace and Friends of the Earth – both of whom sent protesters to its AGM.

- An association or society may have a large, national membership which is very supportive of its activities.

- A formal committee or grouping may comprise a large number of people with diverse interests.

It is unsurprising that in such cases organisers often have problems, first in deciding how many people may attend and secondly, in handling them all diplomatically once they arrive. The role of the chairperson is also very demanding, particularly if a meeting will be large or contentious issues may be debated. Unflappable support and calm efficiency on the part of a PA is likely to be very welcome indeed in this situation.

Your first requirement is to find out who must be invited, by when and how. The second is to make sure the notices and agendas are despatched promptly with other required documentation, and that any returned proxy forms are carefully logged. You will also be involved in discussions as to who will be on the platform and who will not. The chairperson will be in the centre, and, at a General Meeting, is usually flanked by the directors and other company officers. The Company Secretary has a particularly important role in the organisation of an AGM or EGM, and it is likely that this person will be the one you must consult over organisational details and arrangements for any VIP guests or the press.

It is usual to appoint staff to be on duty at a special reception desk, at which members can register their attendance. In some formal meetings this is a legal requirement. Spare copies of all documents should be available for people who have forgotten to bring their own.

At a large meeting it is usual to nominate at least one member of staff to greet and escort VIPs, another two or three to welcome and direct other arrivals and one or two to be in the main hall to check that everyone is seated without any difficulty.

What documentation will be needed?

There are many similarities with semi-formal meetings in that a notice and agenda is issued and minutes are taken. However, the wording is rather different, as you will see below.

In addition, there are often specific papers to be issued with the notice and agenda. For an AGM these must include:

- the report and accounts
- the auditor's report
- any other documents to be presented at the meeting (such as the chairperson's annual report or the minutes of the last AGM)
- proxy forms.

On the day, an attendance register will be kept to note those who attend, even though only the overall number is recorded in the minutes. Ballot or voting papers will also be required.

For an EGM, the documentation is likely to include a letter from the chairperson giving the reason for the meeting and noting any **resolutions** (see below) that will be proposed. Any financial documents or information relating to the meeting will also be included.

Note that you may also have to prepare a press release before the meeting and a press briefing pack to give to journalists who attend. A press statement may also be issued after the meeting (see pages 96–99).

✓ Check it yourself

The notice and agenda of the 1997 AGM of the Institute of Qualified Private Secretaries Ltd (IQPS) is shown in Figure 4.8 and the minutes of the 1996 meeting, which were circulated with the notice, are shown in Figure 4.9. At this stage, simply note the differences in wording and style of these documents from those prepared for semi-formal meetings. Once you have read the next section, the wording becomes much easier to understand – as does the proxy form illustrated in Figure 4.10.

NOTICE OF MEETING

NOTICE IS HEREBY GIVEN THAT THE THIRTY-SIXTH Annual General Meeting of the Institute of Qualified Private Secretaries Limited will be held at Redworth Hall Hotel, Newton Aycliffe, Co Durham, on Saturday 4 October 1997.

AGENDA

1. To receive the MINUTES of the Annual General Meeting of the Institute of Qualified Private Secretaries Limited held on 5 October 1996.

2. Matters Arising Therefrom.

3. To receive and consider the CHAIRMAN'S REPORT for the year ended 31 March 1997.

4. To receive and adopt the FINANCIAL STATEMENTS, REPORT OF THE COUNCIL, and REPORT OF THE AUDITORS for the year ended 31 March 1997.

5. To elect the following members of Council who retire by rotation according to Article 47 of the Articles of Association, but who are eligible for re-election:

   MRS JANE SMITH
   MISS MARY JONES
   MRS JOAN WHITE

6. To elect the following to Council:

   MRS ANN BLACK

7. To re-elect the following as CHAIRMAN of the Institute:

   MISS ELIZABETH SMAJE

8.   To elect the following as VICE CHAIRMAN of the Institute:

        MS JACQUELINE GRANT

9.   To elect the following as COMPANY SECRETARY of the Institute:

        MISS JANET GREEN

10.   To elect the following as TREASURER of the Institute:

        MRS LINDA SMITH

11.   To propose the appointment of Mr R Smith, FCA ATII of R Smith & Partners, 111 High Street, London SW1E 4JA, as Auditor for the ensuing year at a fee to be agreed with Council.

BY ORDER OF THE COUNCIL

JACQUELINE A GRANT
Company Secretary   August 1997

Figure 4.8   Notice of a meeting for AGM of IQPS

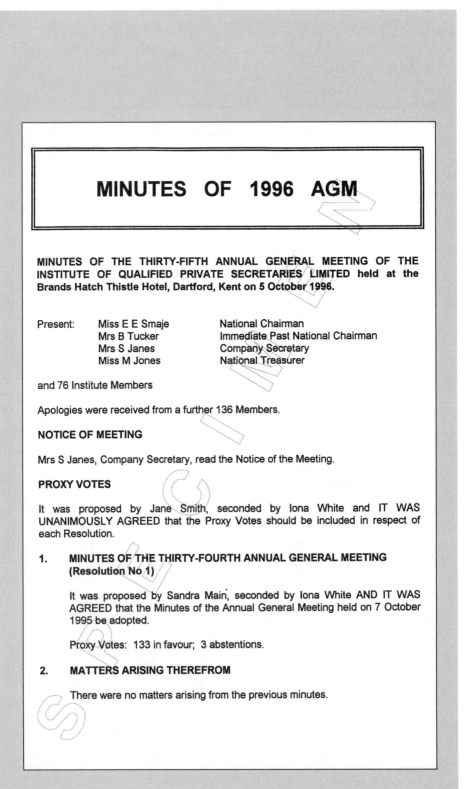

MINUTES OF 1996 AGM

MINUTES OF THE THIRTY-FIFTH ANNUAL GENERAL MEETING OF THE INSTITUTE OF QUALIFIED PRIVATE SECRETARIES LIMITED held at the Brands Hatch Thistle Hotel, Dartford, Kent on 5 October 1996.

Present:　　Miss E E Smaje　　　National Chairman
　　　　　　Mrs B Tucker　　　　Immediate Past National Chairman
　　　　　　Mrs S Janes　　　　 Company Secretary
　　　　　　Miss M Jones　　　　National Treasurer

and 76 Institute Members

Apologies were received from a further 136 Members.

NOTICE OF MEETING

Mrs S Janes, Company Secretary, read the Notice of the Meeting.

PROXY VOTES

It was proposed by Jane Smith, seconded by Iona White and IT WAS UNANIMOUSLY AGREED that the Proxy Votes should be included in respect of each Resolution.

1.　**MINUTES OF THE THIRTY-FOURTH ANNUAL GENERAL MEETING (Resolution No 1)**

　　It was proposed by Sandra Main, seconded by Iona White AND IT WAS AGREED that the Minutes of the Annual General Meeting held on 7 October 1995 be adopted.

　　Proxy Votes: 133 in favour; 3 abstentions.

2.　**MATTERS ARISING THEREFROM**

　　There were no matters arising from the previous minutes.

3. **CHAIRMAN'S REPORT FOR THE YEAR ENDED 31 MARCH 1996**
   (Resolution No 2)

   It was proposed by Tricia McKenzie, seconded by Eve Ross AND IT WAS AGREED that the Chairman's Report for the year ended 31 March 1996, be and is hereby adopted.

   Proxy Votes: 136 in favour.

4. **FINANCIAL STATEMENTS, REPORT OF THE COUNCIL AND REPORT OF THE AUDITORS FOR THE YEAR ENDED 31 MARCH 1996**
   (Resolution No 3)

   It was proposed by Eve Ross, seconded by Jane Arrowsmith AND IT WAS AGREED that the Financial Statements, Report of the Council and Report of the Auditors for the year ended 31 March 1996, be and are hereby adopted.

   Proxy Votes: 135 in favour, 1 abstention.

5. **ELECTION OF COUNCIL MEMBERS**
   (Resolution No 4)

   It was proposed by Ann Black, seconded by Lillian Prout AND IT WAS AGREED that MISS JANET GREEN, who stands down from Council and offers herself for re-election, be and is hereby re-elected.

   Proxy Votes: 135 in favour, 1 against.

   (Resolution No 5)
   It was proposed by Betty Wilson, seconded by Tricia McKenzie AND IT WAS AGREED that MRS JANE GRANT, who stands down from Council and offers herself for re-election, be and is hereby re-elected.

   Proxy Votes: 135 in favour, 1 against.

   (Resolution No 6)
   It was proposed by Iona White, seconded by Lorna Booth AND IT WAS AGREED that MRS SUE JANES, who stands down from Council and offers herself for re-election, be and is hereby re-elected.

   Proxy Votes: 135 in favour, 1 abstention.

   (Resolution No 7)
   It was proposed by Sheila Lawson, seconded by Susan Frost AND IT WAS AGREED that MRS LORNA BOOTH, who offers herself for election to Council, be and is hereby elected.

   Proxy Votes: 133 in favour; 1 against; 2 abstentions.

(Resolution No 8)

It was proposed by Nina Hughes, seconded by Alison Platt AND IT WAS AGREED that MRS JOAN WHITE, who offers herself for election to Council, be and is hereby elected.

Proxy Votes: 135 in favour, 1 abstention.

(Resolution No 9)

It was proposed by Sandra Main, seconded by Janet Green AND IT WAS AGREED that MRS LINDA SMITH, who offers herself for election to Council, be and is hereby elected.

Proxy Votes: 133 in favour; 2 against; 1 abstention.

6. **RE-ELECTION OF CHAIRMAN OF THE INSTITUTE**
   (Resolution No 10)

It was proposed by Jane Smith, seconded by Janet Richardson AND IT WAS AGREED that MISS ELIZABETH SMAJE, who offers herself for re-election as Chairman, be and is hereby re-elected.

Proxy Votes: 136 in favour.

7. **ELECTION OF COMPANY SECRETARY OF THE INSTITUTE**
   (Resolution No 11)

It was proposed by Janet Richardson, seconded by Tricia McKenzie AND IT WAS AGREED that MRS JACQUELINE WALTON, who offers herself for election as Company Secretary, be and is hereby elected.

Proxy Votes: 134 in favour; 1 against; 1 abstention.

8. **RE-ELECTION OF TREASURER OF THE INSTITUTE**
   (Resolution No 12)

It was proposed by Briony Tucker, seconded by Jane Smith AND IT WAS AGREED that MISS MARY JONES, who offers herself for re-election as Treasurer, be and is hereby re-elected.

Proxy Votes: 135 in favour, 1 abstention.

9. **APPOINTMENT OF AUDITOR**
   (Resolution No 13)

It was proposed by Mary Jones, seconded by Briony Tucker AND IT WAS AGREED that MR R S SMITH, FCA ATII, of R Smith & Partners, 111 High Street, London SW1E 4JA, be appointed Auditor for the ensuing year at a fee to be agreed with Council.

Proxy Votes: 136 in favour.

10. **SPECIAL RESOLUTION NO 1**

It was proposed by Jane Smith, seconded by Jane Grant AND IT WAS AGREED that the full annual subscription to the Institute be increased to £35 per annum with effect from 1 April 1997.

Proxy votes: 118 in favour, 18 against.

Figure 4.9 Minutes of meeting for AGM

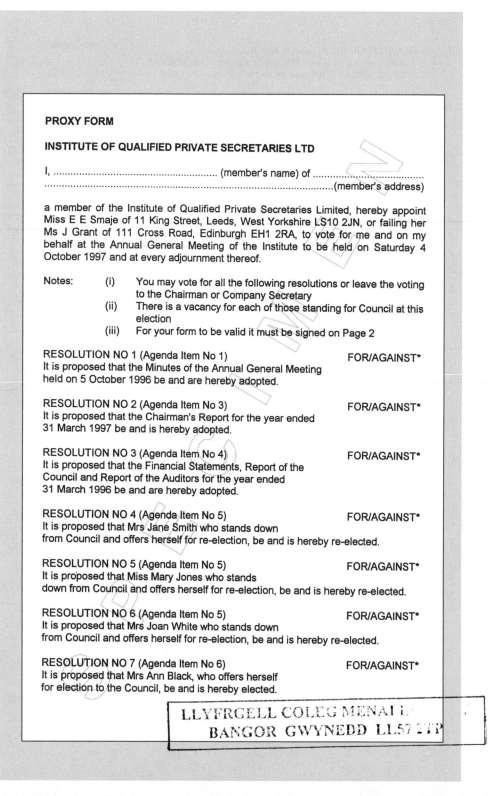

PROXY FORM

INSTITUTE OF QUALIFIED PRIVATE SECRETARIES LTD

I, ... (member's name) of ....
....(member's address)

a member of the Institute of Qualified Private Secretaries Limited, hereby appoint Miss E E Smaje of 11 King Street, Leeds, West Yorkshire LS10 2JN, or failing her Ms J Grant of 111 Cross Road, Edinburgh EH1 2RA, to vote for me and on my behalf at the Annual General Meeting of the Institute to be held on Saturday 4 October 1997 and at every adjournment thereof.

Notes: (i)   You may vote for all the following resolutions or leave the voting to the Chairman or Company Secretary

          (ii)   There is a vacancy for each of those standing for Council at this election

          (iii)   For your form to be valid it must be signed on Page 2

RESOLUTION NO 1 (Agenda Item No 1)   FOR/AGAINST*
It is proposed that the Minutes of the Annual General Meeting held on 5 October 1996 be and are hereby adopted.

RESOLUTION NO 2 (Agenda Item No 3)   FOR/AGAINST*
It is proposed that the Chairman's Report for the year ended 31 March 1997 be and is hereby adopted.

RESOLUTION NO 3 (Agenda Item No 4)   FOR/AGAINST*
It is proposed that the Financial Statements, Report of the Council and Report of the Auditors for the year ended 31 March 1996 be and are hereby adopted.

RESOLUTION NO 4 (Agenda Item No 5)   FOR/AGAINST*
It is proposed that Mrs Jane Smith who stands down from Council and offers herself for re-election, be and is hereby re-elected.

RESOLUTION NO 5 (Agenda Item No 5)   FOR/AGAINST*
It is proposed that Miss Mary Jones who stands down from Council and offers herself for re-election, be and is hereby re-elected.

RESOLUTION NO 6 (Agenda Item No 5)   FOR/AGAINST*
It is proposed that Mrs Joan White who stands down from Council and offers herself for re-election, be and is hereby re-elected.

RESOLUTION NO 7 (Agenda Item No 6)   FOR/AGAINST*
It is proposed that Mrs Ann Black, who offers herself for election to the Council, be and is hereby elected.

RESOLUTION NO 8 (Agenda Item No 7)
It is proposed that Miss Elizabeth Smaje, who offers herself
for re-election as Chairman, be and is hereby re-elected.

FOR/AGAINST*

RESOLUTION NO 9 (Agenda Item No 8)
It is proposed that Ms Jacqueline Grant, who offers herself
for election as Vice Chairman, be and is hereby elected.

FOR/AGAINST*

RESOLUTION NO 10 (Agenda Item No 9)
It is proposed that Miss Janet Green, who offers herself
for election as Company Secretary, be and is hereby elected.

FOR/AGAINST*

RESOLUTION NO 11 (Agenda Item No 10)
It is proposed that Mrs Linda Smith, who offers herself
for election as Treasurer, be and is hereby elected.

FOR/AGAINST*

RESOLUTION NO 12 (Agenda Item No 11)
It is proposed that Mr R Smith FCA ATII of
R Smith & Partners, 111 High Street, London,
SW1E 4JA, be and is hereby appointed
Auditor for the ensuing year at a fee to be agreed with Council.

FOR/AGAINST*

Given by hand this .... day of ....1997......
                     (date)   (month)

Member's signature ....

Category of membership of IQPS: ....

* please delete as necessary

This form MUST BE RECEIVED BY the Company Secretary, Institute of Qualified Private Secretaries Limited, 111 Cross Road, Edinburgh EH1 2RA, by NOT LATER THAN NOON on Friday 26 September 1997.

Unless otherwise instructed, the proxy will vote as she thinks fit. A proxy MUST be a member of the Institute.

Figure 4.10 Proxy form

How will it operate

Formal meetings usually have the following characteristics:

- There are specified rules and requirements (eg in the Articles of Association or a committee's standing orders) which *must* be followed precisely, often for legal reasons.

- There must be a quorum at the outset and this must usually be maintained throughout the meeting.

- There is a set procedure to be followed, often known as the **order of business**.

- **Rules of debate** usually apply, which regulate the way in which proposals and questions are dealt with.

- The wording of the notice and agenda is very formal.

- Minutes of resolution are taken.

- The minutes and other details of the meeting (good and bad!) are often publicised.

You are advised to attend one of these meetings yourself before you have an active part in organising or recording one. The first time, you may find certain parts difficult to follow, and it is useful if someone can guide you through what is happening. However, it obviously helps if you have some previous knowledge of the terms and style of discussion you are likely to hear – which is the aim of the next section.

Check it yourself

Read the script below, taken from a union meeting. At the first reading, try to get an idea of what is happening and check your understanding with the questions below. Then read the section on formal meeting conventions that follows. Return to the script and read it again. By now, it should be much easier to follow. (In some cases, it might be more effective to distribute roles to individual class members and act out the script, rather than read it individually.)

Chair   The next item of business before this meeting is the proposal by management to introduce a system of teleworking for computer operatives in the company. Selected operatives will retain full employment rights but will work from home.

The motion put to this meeting, proposed by John Grey and seconded by Barry White, is as follows

THAT the members require full details of the scheme before it is agreed by the membership, to include sight of a teleworker's contract of employment, information on payment of expenses incurred through home working and confirmation that the employer is still liable for the health and safety of staff working at home.

John Grey will now speak for the motion.

Grey   *(Stands)* Mr Chairman. Many members present will have heard about teleworking, the system of working on computer equipment in the home. Such employment saves many costs for employers but can leave the workers themselves isolated, lonely and with few employment rights. For these reasons, I consider it is essential that this membership obtains full details on the proposed scheme before it can make any recommendations for acceptance or rejection. *(Sits)*

Chair   Mr White, do you now formally second the motion?

White   *(Stands)* I do, Mr Chairman. I think it is essential that we obtain further details to protect the interests of our members who may be selected for teleworking. *(Sits)*

Chair   *(Responding to raised hand)* Miss Barry.

Barry   *(Stands)* Thank you, Mr Chairman. Whilst I appreciate the concerns of my fellow members, may I point out that many employees in the organisation would welcome the opportunity to have more flexible terms and conditions. In particular, it would enable those employees with families to cope more easily and reduce their travel expenses. Many members would not like to see the company withdraw the suggestion because of rigid conditions made by this membership. *(Sits)*

(The discussion continues, through the Chair, for some time with different members speaking either for or against the motion. Eventually, one member, Sally Smith, is given leave to speak by the Chair)

Smith   *(Stands)* Mr Chairman, I feel that many issues would be resolved if an addendum could be added to the motion as follows 'THAT any selection for teleworking is undertaken on a voluntary basis.' I therefore propose that this addendum be incorporated. *(Sits)*

Chair	Is there a seconder for this amendment? *(Acknowledges raised hand)* Miss Thomas.
Thomas	*(Stands)* I formally second the amendment. May I also add, Mr Chairman, that we should state that all overtime agreements should also be voluntary, not just teleworking.
White	*(Stands)* Point of order, Mr Chairman. This meeting was convened to discuss the teleworking proposal, not overtime. *(Both sit)*
Chair	Accepted. I propose that we continue by putting the amendment to the vote. All those in favour? *(Tellers count raised hands)* All those against? *(Tellers again count and give result to Chair).* 65 votes in favour, 10 votes against, 5 abstentions.
	We will now put the substantive motion to the vote. *(Re-reads the original motion plus the addendum for the benefit of the audience)* Mr Grey, you have the right of reply to the arguments put forward against the motion. Do you wish to exercise this right?
Grey	*(Stands and briefly recaps his main argument)*
Chair	*(Responding to another raised hand)* Mr Tomlins?

(Jack Tomlins stands and proceeds to give a long speech relating to the pros and cons of teleworking. At a pause, the Chair responds to another raised hand – that of Jo Dixon)

Dixon	*(Stands)* Mr Chairman, I feel I speak for most people when I say that I consider that the discussions have gone on long enough. I would therefore move THAT the question be now put. *(Sits)*
Chair	Seconded?
Watkins	*(Stands)* I second the motion, Mr Chairman. *(Sits)*
Chair	The motion that the question be now put is carried. We will therefore vote on the substantive motion. All those in favour? *(Tellers count raised hands)* All those against? *(Tellers count again)*
	Those in favour 70, no votes against, 10 abstentions. The motion is carried nem con and the resolution agreed will be duly recorded in the minutes of this meeting.

Check your understanding with the questions below.

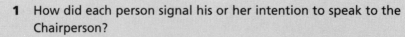

1 How did each person signal his or her intention to speak to the Chairperson?

2 How did each person respond when **given the floor** (ie the opportunity to speak)?

3 Did the members address each other or the Chair? What evidence is there to validate your answer?

4 If one person proposes a motion, what else is needed before the issue can be debated?

5 What phrase was used, when a member thought another person was introducing an irrelevant point?

6 How did a member curtail discussion when she felt it was going on too long?

7 Could discussion have been curtailed if everyone else had wanted to continue the debate? If not, why not?

8 If members want to change the wording of a motion which is under discussion, how is this done?

9 How many times can the proposer of a motion speak in the debate?

10 How did the members vote? What other methods of voting do you think could have been used?

11 What is the name given to someone who counts votes at an official meeting?

12 What is the phrase used when there are no votes against a motion, even though there may be some abstentions?

13 What is an abstention?

14 What new word is used to describe a motion that has been put to the vote and carried?

Meeting conventions

Formal committees and other groups are often governed by **standing orders** which were discussed on page 22. In particular, these may include **rules of debate** which prescribe:

a how motions are to be proposed and seconded
b that the speaker must stand and address the chair at the meeting
c the length of time for which people may speak

d the number of times individuals may speak

e how improper conduct should be handled.

It is the duty of the chairperson to be familiar with the rules that apply and to follow these rigorously to ensure that the meeting is conducted in an equitable manner.

The chair will usually open the meeting by reading the notice (or asking the secretary to read it). He or she will then check that the minutes of the previous meeting can be taken as read, and agreed as a true and correct record of what occurred.

The main business of the meeting is then discussed. This is usually concerned with various proposals or **motions** that have been put before the meeting. In some cases these must be submitted in writing before the meeting, together with the names of the **proposer** and **seconder** and their signatures. A motion must be positive and declare an opinion or propose a course of action – or both. Ones that are phrased negatively must be rejected by the chair. All motions (and the resolutions that follow them) must start with the word 'THAT'. A motion with only a proposer and no seconder cannot proceed – so it is usual for proposers to find a seconder before the meeting commences.

Each motion is then discussed. Normally no second speeches are allowed to any individual except the proposer of the original motion, who has the right of reply. At most meetings, advocates and opposers speak alternately – sometimes for a limited time.

The chairperson is responsible for calling members to speak and, to preserve order, it is often the case that members signal their request by raising a hand. To prevent confusion, the chairperson will signal who is to speak next by announcing the person's name. A good chairperson should be impartial, enable all views to be represented and refuse to allow any member to become disruptive, talk for too long, insult other members or interrupt a speaker. However, any member can also raise a **point of order** or objection to another person's behaviour. The chair's decision on points of order is final.

When a motion has been discussed it is put to the vote. However, during the discussion, a member may propose an **amendment** or **addendum** to the motion. In the first case, a member is suggesting that words be omitted or amended in some way, in the second a member is suggesting that words be added to the motion. Any such suggestions must be seconded and put to the vote. If several amendments are suggested, each one must be dealt with separately and in a logical order. If the proposal to amend a motion is carried, the motion now becomes a **substantive motion** and the vote will be taken on this new version. If the motion is carried it becomes a **resolution.**

You should note that even resolutions can be amended by changing the wording. In this case the amendment is known as a **rider**.

Procedural motions

These types of motion are used by experienced participants to influence the debate. There are six types of procedural motion.

1 THAT the question be now put. Referred to as **closure**, this motion is put to bring discussion to an end. If it is successful the vote must be taken immediately. However, in most cases it is at the chairperson's discretion whether to accept such a motion and it should refused if it is being employed tactically to prevent people from putting their views.

2 THAT the question be not now put. Known as **the previous question,** this motion is more powerful than closure, as it proposes that the motion be dropped completely. If this fails the motion must then be put to the vote immediately. In either way, debate is immediately ended on the issue.

3 THAT the meeting proceed to the next business. This motion is similar to the above in that it aims to end discussion and move on to the next item on the agenda. However, if the motion is not carried then discussion resumes on the topic under debate (unlike **the previous question**).

4 THAT the recommendation be referred back. **Reference back** occurs when the meeting is deliberating a report or recommendation made by a committee and requires further details or information before making a decision. It therefore refers back the issue to the committee, usually for further clarification.

5 THAT the debate be adjourned. If this motion is proposed then the mover of the original motion being debated is usually allowed the right of reply. It is often proposed when further information is required before a decision can be reached and the debate may be adjourned until this is to hand. If the motion is carried, the debate can still be resumed either later in the same meeting or at a future meeting.

6 THAT the meeting be adjourned. This motion may be proposed at the end of a speech, or at any time in the meeting if time is short or if there is another good reason to defer continuance of the meeting until another time. The mover of the motion currently being debated would be allowed the right of reply before the motion is put to the vote. If it is carried then it is usual to agree a date and time for the continuance of the meeting. Otherwise the meeting is said to be adjourned **sine die** (without a date being arranged).

Voting

The permissible methods of voting at a meeting are usually specified in the standing orders. These may include the following.

- **By voice.** This is normally only appropriate in very small meetings or where there is virtual unanimity amongst the voters. After reading the motion the chairperson asks those who agree to say 'Aye', and listens to the volume of responses. Those against then say 'No' and again the volume is assessed. He or she will then announce 'The ayes (or the noes) have it.' If the majority view cannot be established by this method it is usual for members present to be able to demand a vote by show of hands.

- **By show of hands.** Each person has one vote and holds up a hand to establish his or her view. If there is any challenge to the counting of the vote then a second show of hands may be demanded.

- **By poll.** In this case each person eligible to vote marks a voting paper. In some cases members may have more than one vote (eg shareholders have one vote for each share they hold). The votes are then counted.

- **By division.** This is the traditional procedure in Parliament, where members go into separate rooms according to whether they are for or against the motion. In Parliament, this procedure is marked by the ringing of the division bell. The members file past tellers and are counted as they enter each room.

- **By ballot.** A secret ballot is one where the name of the person voting is not put on the slip. The paper is then put into a box which is opened afterwards and the votes are counted. This is the method used in general and local elections.

Voters have a choice of three options when casting their votes. They can vote for or against a motion – or they can choose to abstain (not vote at all). Depending upon the majority required, this can affect the result. For instance, if a motion requires a two-thirds majority *of those present*, if 100 are present and 65 vote for, 32 against and three people abstain the motion will be lost. Note that for most votes there must be a **clear majority**, and for some meetings, particularly General Meetings, those entitled to vote can nominate a proxy if they are unable to attend in person (see page 14).

Declaring the result
The chairperson is responsible for declaring the result of the vote in clear, unambiguous terms. The phrase 'the motion is carried' means that the proposal has now been agreed and has now become a formal resolution. The motion may be carried **unanimously** (everyone voted in favour) or **nem con** (no-one voted against, but there were some abstentions). Alternatively, of course, the chairperson may announce the 'the motion is lost', which means it has been rejected by the members.

Check it yourself

1 Look back at the script on pages 147–149 and read it again. Check that you now follow the discussion.

2 Make out your own dictionary of meetings terms from the highlighted words in this section and check your definitions with your tutor.

3 All meetings must have at least two tellers. Why do you think that one teller is not permissible?

Formal procedures at general business meetings

At a company AGM or EGM you may find some variations in the debating procedures outlined above. The first difference is that the rules and regulations are contained in the Articles of Association, rather than in any standing orders. This includes information on voting rights and regulations, the quorum, the chairperson and other details as given on page 14. The second difference is that, under the terms of the Companies Act 1985 (as amended by the Companies Act 1989) different types of resolutions may be put forward.

- An **ordinary resolution** is a resolution relating to the normal business the company is authorised to undertake at a general meeting, under the terms of its Articles of Association.

- If an **extraordinary resolution** is to be put before members, this must be clearly stated in the notice of the meeting and a three-quarters majority of votes is required.

- a **special resolution** also requires a three-quarters majority, and will normally require 21 days' notice to members. Again, the notice must clearly specify the type of resolution.

The difference between an extraordinary and a special resolution is very technical and outside the scope of this book. Suffice it to say that this is the remit of the Company Secretary, not the meetings secretary or organiser!

Public inquiries and the PA's role

The role of the PA at a formal public inquiry is likely to be restricted to checking the regulations and procedure to be followed, making sure that all forms are submitted by the due date, collecting and copying all the evidence to substantiate the appeal, liaising with the company solicitor or other legal representative, liaising with the case officer nominated by the Planning Inspectorate and ensuring that all records are carefully labelled and filed. Unless, of course, you are specifically employed to organise and record the inquiry.

If there is a hearing or local inquiry – particularly if you are competent at shorthand or taking notes quickly – you might be asked to attend by your boss to keep an informal written record of the proceedings for future reference. Such a record may be useful if your boss later wants to prepare a report to the directors about the inquiry.

✓ Check it yourself

1 Look back at the formal meetings documents illustrated in Figures 4.8–4.10 and check whether they have become more intelligible! If you have any queries, ask your tutor. You may like to note that the Institute of Qualified Private Secretaries welcomes eligible student members in addition to fully qualified PAs. If you are interested, contact the Membership Secretary for details at The Institute of Qualified Private Secretaries Ltd, First Floor, 6 Bridge Avenue, MAIDENHEAD SL6 1RR (telephone 01628 625007, fax 01628 624990). You will be eligible to attend their AGMs yourself!

2 Hold your own class debate, either on one of the following topics or a subject of your own choosing. Nominate a chairperson and hold the debate according to the formal rules of debate given on

page 151. Remember that you will need a proposer and seconder and speakers for and against each motion. Decide, too, on the voting system you will use. Agree beforehand how much time each speaker should be allowed and time him or her accordingly! The audience can ask questions (through the Chair) but it is sensible to limit the number. At the end of the debate the Chair should sum up the arguments for and against and put the motion to the vote. After the tellers have counted the votes, they should pass the result to the Chair, who officially announces the result. Ask your tutor to adjudicate if there are any disputes about procedure!

a   All drivers should retake their test every five years.
b   Women make better managers than men.
c   Private car usage should be restricted to safeguard the environment.
d   Private firework parties should be banned.
e   There should be a legal minimum wage.
f   Formal procedures are essential to keep order at meetings where contentious issues are debated.

Review quiz

1   Briefly explain the difference between minutes of narration and minutes of resolution.

2   List FOUR tips you would give a PA about to take minutes for the first time.

3   Identify FOUR documents that you, as meetings secretary, might take into a Board meeting.

4   Explain the difference between a committee meeting and an Annual General Meeting in relation to the type of people who would attend and the type of business that would be conducted.

5   List the routine items of business contained in an agenda.

6 Explain each of the following terms:

  a resolution
  b point of order
  c sine die
  d casting vote.

7 Explain the term 'addressing the Chair'. State TWO benefits of following this procedure at a meeting.

8 Describe THREE duties of a meetings secretary.

9 State FOUR duties or responsibilities of a chairperson.

10 Explain each of the following terms:

  a nem con
  b show of hands
  c motion
  d rider.

11 Identify FOUR tasks you would carry out before a meeting.

12 The chairperson of a committee has asked you to ensure that members undertake the action they promised at the meeting. Describe THREE strategies you would use to do this.

Test yourself

1 You should now be in a position to summarise the duties of a PA before, during and after any type of meeting in a checklist. Rather than undertake this task individually, hold a brainstorming session for the whole group. Alternatively, divide into three groups, each to concentrate on one type of meeting (informal, semi-formal and formal). This will provide useful revision and you can exchange your checklists afterwards.

You can also check you have included all the main items by referring to the key on pages 188–190.

2 Check that you are still on target with your own committee meetings for holding an event. Remember that a key role of the chairperson and meetings secretary is to ensure that planned meetings are actually held! You will need to have completed your outline plans by the time you move on to the final chapter in this section of the book.

Organising and administering an event

5

In the final chapter of this section we will turn our attention to the other types of events you may be asked to organise – specifically presentations, seminars and conferences. In most cases, presentations and seminars are held and completed in a day or a few hours, whereas a conference may last several days. For that reason this chapter considers making arrangements under two headings:

a non-residential events
b residential events.

Again we will concentrate on

- **who** will be involved – and their roles

- **what** documentation will be needed

- **how** the event will operate

in addition to the tasks you must carry out after the event.

● Non-residential events

Each type of event discussed in this chapter can be held on a non-residential basis – one-day conferences are certainly not unknown. With a non-residential event there is no requirement for block bookings of accommodation, although you may need to reserve rooms and organise transport for visiting speakers or other important guests travelling from a distance to attend.

Presentations

The reason for holding presentations was discussed in Chapter 1 (page 26). The main aim may be to sell a product, service or even an image or idea – but this cannot be achieved unless the presentation is organised professionally. Otherwise your words may say one thing but your message will be totally different!

Who will be involved – the roles of participants

The main reason for holding a presentation is to give a message to a particular audience – either to update, inform or persuade them. Although presentations are often held with a sales objective in mind, other departments and sections of an organisation may also be involved. Internal presentations may be made by an individual section or department to other staff or to the directors.

The audience for a commercial presentation usually comprises potential customers or clients. However, members of an institution or professional body may be invited to attend a presentation on planned future changes or on a specialist topic.

Specialist speakers or experts in an area may be invited to take part. However, you should note that if several presentations are made, one after another, then the event rapidly turns into a mini-conference! Generally, a presentation is just one session, even if various speakers take part.

What documentation will be needed?

There are two types of materials you may be asked to produce for a presentation. The first are those to be used by the presenter(s), the second are the documents to be given to the guests. Sometimes the two are identical, which is ideal with a computerised presentation package. You then create the documents, import them into the presentation package and copy them out on a colour printer – on OHTs and/or as hard (paper) copies. Equally, you can save the presentation to disk for a presenter to use in a laptop.

Needless to say, the quality and accuracy of the documents must be second to none. In addition, the print size on any transparencies or for any computer-generated graphics *must* be large enough for the audience to read without difficulty. Spreadsheets are probably the most difficult documents to show in a presentation, as the figures are usually too small to read. Ideally, you should test the projection of any documents you create, with the presenter, using the same equipment in the same setting. This is obviously easier said than done if the setting is an external venue with unknown equipment. In this case, it is sensible to have a test pack of documents that you can try out to establish what works (and what doesn't!) when you visit the venue to look round.

The documentation to be given to those invited may range from one page of information to a full pack of documentation with drawings, photographs and technical details. The reason for giving documentation is to provide the audience with a summary of the main points of the presentation, so that these can be referred to afterwards. No-one can remember everything said at a presentation and it is not usual to expect an important client or potential customer to take notes (though some may). You should remember, too, that some modern equipment is designed to enable any notes made by the presenter to be printed out for guests (see copyboards, Figure 3.4, page 93). Usually, the type and quantity of documentation will depend upon the reason for the presentation and the audience. For example:

- if prospective students and their parents are invited to your College for a presentation about particular courses, they would probably receive a prospectus and course leaflets on the areas in which they are interested

- if parents of A-level students attend a presentation on the UCAS system and how to apply for HE courses, they would receive an information pack under such headings as 'How to apply', 'Funding', 'Alternatives to HE', 'Information for parents', 'Information for students', etc

- prospective clients interested in buying an expensive piece of equipment or machinery would expect to receive a folder containing all the technical information as well as the key features outlined in the sales presentation and details of the cost and any financing arrangements. The proposal can then be discussed in more detail over the next few days or weeks. If the client is from abroad, it is normal to arrange for the information in the pack to be translated into his or her native language.

You may be asked to produce and copy any documents needed and to collate these into packs before the presentation takes place. For a complex presentation, you may be coordinating the receipt of information from different people or departments, making sure that this is all produced according to your house style and bound together in special folders (see below).

To Russia with love

One PA had her work cut out when she was given three weeks notice to produce a set of documents for shipment to Russia, to link with a presentation being given by the sales team during a business trip. Her task involved visiting a supplier and taking notes on a variety of different textile machines, arranging for a draughtsman to prepare drawings on each one, obtaining the technical specifications and samples of fabrics produced on each machine, arranging for a photographer to take pictures of each machine and assembling all the information in ten lever arch files for the Russian committee who were to make the purchasing decision. Also to be included were the terms and conditions of sale, the quotations and details of the financing packages available. Finally, the whole package had to be translated into Russian, typed in Cyrillic script and shipped to Russia in time to be collected by one of the sales representatives on arrival.

To help, her boss put a company car and a team of administrative staff at her disposal. Later, when the deal was agreed and the contract signed, he treated her and her team to lunch as a reward!

Note that if a presentation is being made overseas you may have the job of packing the documentation and checking whether the presentation team can carry everything or if it can be airfreighted to the destination (or to an overseas branch office) and collected by the team on arrival.

How it will operate

The basic format at presentation events can vary considerably, but usually includes the following:

* refreshments on arrival

* the presentation

* question and answer session (if a small group) or break into smaller groups, each with a leader, to discuss the details and answer any questions.

Your role will usually involve checking that the refreshments are delivered on time, greeting guests on arrival, checking all the equipment is functioning and any presentation packs are to hand, and helping to clear up afterwards. If a large group is dividing into smaller units and there are room changes involved, you might be asked to escort some groups to their new rooms.

You may also be asked to give out presentation packs to those who attend. However, if a large number of people are expected, a more professional and streamlined approach is to place a pack on each chair before the presentation starts. This prevents having to ask your guests to pass the packs along each row!

Check it yourself

1 Look through an office equipment catalogue and note the different types of document presentation products on the market today which would help you to create a perfectly bound and professional looking presentation pack. In particular, note the difference between plastic comb, wire binding and thermoplastic binders and the different types and sizes of folders that can be purchased.

2 Re-read question 3 on page 99. Assume your group are planning the content of the presentation and the documents required. Decide the information you would include, the equipment you would need and the type of documents that would be appropriate for your audience. Check your answers with your tutor.

3 As a group, list the duties you consider a PA would have to undertake before, during and after a presentation. Check your answers with the key on page 191.

Seminars

As you saw in Chapter 1, the term 'seminar' is normally used when people will attend an event to learn about a topic. Much as you might do every day – though you might never have thought of yourself as attending a series of seminars! It may be helpful to think of a seminar as a very short course, usually lasting just one day or half a day. There may be one or two speakers, or several. Generally, in contrast with a presentation – where the audience just listens – a seminar is a more interactive occasion and for that reason the numbers are often restricted. If you can organise a meeting and a presentation, a seminar should present few problems.

Who will be involved – the roles of participants

The audience is likely to comprise people with a common interest in a particular topic – although the number can be variable. Some seminars are open to anyone and are advertised in the national or trade press. Others are only held for members of a particular association or profession. Many are run by professional organisations for profit, and the fees for attendance can be quite considerable. Because the number of people expected will determine the size of the venue, and because the venue must be reserved in advance, it is usual to ask people who wish to attend a seminar to reserve a place or complete a booking form (and often, pay in advance).

The speakers are usually specialists in their own area, each of whom can contribute on a different aspect of the topic.

What documentation will be needed?

The type of documentation required will depend upon the speakers. Some will prepare their own visual aids and material and copy it – leaving you nothing to do at all! Others will produce their own material but ask you to copy it – and perhaps to produce one or two visual aids. Another group may simply draft something in writing and ask you to type it and produce the visual aids or other presentation materials as well! Depending upon the type of organisation you work for and the seminars it holds, you will need to check the amount and type of work you are expected to carry out in this regard. It may *not* be part of your job to produce reams of paperwork for outside speakers who are being paid a fee to attend.

However, it may be your responsibility to prepare any advertisements or leaflets to publicise the seminar, to prepare the programme, type out a menu and prepare any notices, posters or directional signs that are required. An example of a press advertisement for a free seminar – which was of interest to PAs – is shown in Figure 5.1.

How it will operate

Normally, a seminar is a series of informative sessions on a particular topic, during which those present are given the opportunity to interact through

Figure 5.1 Advertisement for a seminar

question and answer forums, workshops or problem-solving sessions, giving feedback on their own conclusions to the presenter(s). However, this model can vary. At an exhibition, for instance, you may see short seminar sessions advertised which last thirty minutes, or an hour, at which you could find out more about a particular topic of interest. At other seminars, there may be role-play or practical activities to reinforce the theoretical aspects.

Usually, because of the interactive nature of the event, a large number of people will be sub-divided into smaller groups for much of the time – although the organisers may rearrange the groups in different formations throughout the day, depending upon the degree to which this would facilitate the objectives of the event.

Check it yourself

Figure 5.2 illustrates the programme for a one-day seminar on appraisals. Note how the activities are varied to include the different aspects of the topic and to retain the interest and involvement of those who attend.

THE A–Z OF APPRAISALS FOR PAs

A ONE–DAY SEMINAR

BRANTWOOD LODGE HOTEL

TUESDAY, 24 MARCH 199-

PROGRAMME

9.15 am	Registration and coffee
9.30 am	Introduction to Appraisals – Sarah Jones – Employment Adviser, PSI Recruitment Ltd
10.00 am	The value of appraisals for appraiser and appraisee – Richard Bryant, Human Resources Manager, J B Enterprises plc
10.30 am	Coffee
10.45 am	Preparing for an appraisal – Sarah Jones
11.15 am	The do's and don't's of an appraisal interview – Richard Bryant
12.00 noon	Lunch
1.00 pm	'An objective appraisal' – video – followed by discussion session on appraisal experiences
2.00 pm	The art of giving and receiving negative feedback – Pamela Jenkins, Communications Consultant
2.30 pm	Coffee
3.00 pm	Appraisal role-play exercises
4.00 pm	Feedback from role-play
4.30 pm	Plenary session
4.45 pm	Close

Figure 5.2 Programme for a one-day seminar

1 In groups of three or four, select one of the following topics as the basis for a one-day seminar for PAs and decide upon the programme you would suggest. Note that the sessions must be linked and progressive throughout the day.

   a Business writing skills
   b Communication skills

    c Time management
    d Listening and memory skills
    e Assertiveness training
    f Stress management
    g Team building
    h Organising business travel

    Check your ideas with your tutor.

2 Assuming you were the PA responsible for organising the seminar illustrated in Figure 5.1, list the duties you think you would have to carry out before, during and after the event to ensure everything ran smoothly. Check your answers with the key on page 192.

3 As a group, choose one of the above topics (or a similar one of mutual interest) and organise *your own* seminar (as a change from your normal classes). Bear in mind that one of your first tasks may be to find good speakers who will make the day interesting and memorable. Your tutor may be able to suggest one or two colleagues – if they can be persuaded to help! If you devise an interesting programme, and your facilities are suitable, you may be able to invite members of other groups to attend.

● Residential events

Although the occasional seminar may be run over several days, with the participants staying in accommodation on site or nearby, the main type of residential event with which you are likely to be involved is the conference.

Conferences can vary considerably – from a one- or two-day event involving twenty organisational staff, to an international convention lasting a week, held abroad, and with a delegate list running into thousands! For simplicity, we will call these 'internal' and 'external' conferences. For large external conferences either a conference team or committee is established years in advance – or the whole task is given to a professional conference organiser. In some cases professional organisations and institutions that run several conferences a year employ a full-time, experienced conference organiser.

As a PA with a range of administrative responsibilities, it is unlikely that you would ever be expected to organise such a prestigious event on your own or to take on such a responsibility without forfeiting some of your other duties. In general, the main type of conferences organised by PAs are internal, or small to mid-range external events such as the following:

- Conferences for staff who are brought together for a few days. For instance, most organisations hold sales conferences at regular intervals, which all sales representatives attend. This gives them a useful opportunity to discuss important issues as a group, since the representatives are usually travelling around the country – or even around the world.

- Two- or three-day conferences organised by professional bodies and institutions where the total delegate list is not likely to be more than 100. Even then, it is likely you would be a member (or leader) of a team organising the event rather than expected to do it on your own.

For these reasons, this section does not contain the type of in-depth information that would be needed by a professional conference planner – such as organising finance, letting exhibition space and arranging international travel. Instead, it concentrates on the type of duties you as organiser and/or team leader would be expected to carry out as an integral part of your PA duties.

Who will be involved – the roles of participants

If the conference is internal, you can expect to liaise with the line manager responsible for the event in addition to any managers or other PAs who will have an influence in planning or assisting with the arrangements. Expect, too, to liaise with other departments or personnel who can provide specialist services or undertake a specific role – such as Reprographics, Accounts and Finance.

For an external conference you are more likely to liaise with your publicity, marketing or PR people as well as those who will take a role in its organisation. Broadly speaking, for a small team, the duties can be sub-divided into the following areas:

- general administration – including budget management, venue selection, preparation of all documentation and material, organising insurance, publicity and delegate registration

- accommodation and travel – including booking hotel rooms according to requirements (eg smoking/non-smoking, size of room, facilities etc), arranging transport for equipment, important guests and speakers

- conference programme and format – including devising and agreeing the programme, deciding topics, arranging speakers, obtaining papers and biographies from speakers, organising AVA equipment, deciding stage presentation and any special themes

- social events – including arranging alternative activities (such as sightseeing excursions and shopping trips) for off-duty delegates and their partners, organising all catering requirements including the opening reception and the banquet or dinner held on the last night

- other duties – depending on the type of conference being organised. For instance, if there is to be a small exhibition or display area then stands must be organised and hired to interested parties and the opening times agreed (normally from coffee break in the morning to the end of the tea break in the afternoon). Alternatively (or additionally) if publicity is a major item, this may be delegated to a particular person instead of being part of general administration.

The first task is normally to get everyone together to decide the overall object of the event, who will undertake each role and how any potential overlaps should be resolved (eg whether the person in charge of social events should arrange transport for trips, or the accommodation and travel person).

At this stage the budget and the financing should be considered – as this will directly influence the scale of the event and the type of venue selected (see Chapter 2). If several people are involved with the arrangements it is important that expenditure levels are either set in advance and delegated within those constraints, or that all projected expenditure is sanctioned by a person in charge of the overall budget.

An internal conference held for staff will involve specific participants and speakers, depending upon the aim of the event. An external conference is likely to involve:

- the delegates and their guests
- the speakers
- any sponsors, exhibitors or providers of display materials
- temporary staff required for the event (eg security or clerical staff)
- significant others (eg any local dignitaries or VIPs invited to open the event or attend the last dinner).

It is worth considering at the outset the type of people who are likely to attend and their possible needs. Will there be any VIPs? Will there be anyone who is likely to need an interpreter? Will there be any groups whose diet will be constrained by religious considerations? Will there be any groups who have a particular requirement or who suffer from a particular disability? If these factors are considered at the beginning, then arrangements can be drawn up to reflect them from the outset – which generally makes life much easier.

Finally – if this is not an automatic role for a particular person, the decision needs to be made as to who will chair the conference (eg to introduce speakers, act as anchor person on the platform, officiate at any functions, chair question panels, and officially close the conference). Usually this is the most senior person in the organisation who will be attending, or the currently elected chairperson in an association or society.

What documentation will be needed?

For some conferences, special stationery is designed on which all correspondence is written and all materials are prepared. In most other cases standard company headed paper will usually suffice.

It is often easier to think of an internal conference as a series of presentations and discussion sessions – each of which will require the preparation of certain visual aids and the photocopying of documentation for those attending. The sensible route is to start a folder *for each session* (which may, in some cases, become a box file!). This prevents you confusing one person's papers or visual aids with another's. You will also need to prepare a programme listing all the sessions that will take place and showing the times allocated for meals, refreshments and 'comfort' breaks.

For an external, more formal conference, the type of documents with which you may be involved include:

- general publicity materials – including advertisements, leaflets and press releases

- speakers' papers, summaries and biographies

- delegate publicity information

- delegate packs issued upon registration

- press kits including a background to the conference, speaker biographies, outlines of talks plus press statements after the event.

For any conference, there will also be a considerable amount of correspondence. Before the event all arrangements and supplies must be confirmed in writing – either by letter or fax. After the event, thank you letters need to be sent to all external speakers, any sponsors and all those who have helped in any way. Even for an internal event, it is a nice touch to send those staff who have worked above and beyond their normal duties a 'thank you' note from you or your boss.

Publicity documents

A conference may be promoted in the press, through sending leaflets to potential delegates, or both. Any advertisement must include all the key information (dates, location, cost) as well as outlining the main features and attractions of the event, such as:

- the reputation of the speakers

- the variety of the sessions

- the additional activities available

- the facilities at the venue.

An advertisement must also tell potential delegates what to do next if they are interested, by giving a contact number or address to which they should write for further information.

An example of such an advertisement for college staff and students is shown in Figure 5.3, showing all the essential information designed to attract delegates. Perhaps you should ask your tutor if he or she attended this conference!

Speakers' papers, summaries and biographies

The biographies are the first items you will need from speakers, so that you can write a short feature article about each of the speakers for your programme. If each guest speaker also includes a photograph these can be used to illustrate the programme. If you obtain this information soon enough, it is a simple matter to draw up a special page to add to your publicity materials – as well-known or interesting speakers are a key attraction.

Figure 5.3 Advertisement for Association of Colleges Annual Conference

At certain types of conferences, the papers are copied and available (sometimes for a fee) to delegates. The summaries are useful if you are going to prepare a press release after the event or to write any articles for a newsletter to be sent to members of an association or members of staff. They enable you to give a brief résumé of each talk very accurately. However, some guidance to speakers about the length of their summary is usually appreciated – and saves you from having to cut it dramatically.

Delegate publicity materials

All members of an association will usually be notified of a forthcoming conference in writing. This may be by letter or leaflet, and more detailed information can be given than could be included in a general advertisement. Often a draft programme is included in addition to a booking form. This will give the various options available, eg:

- participation in the full event (which may be over several days) plus accommodation

- participation for selected days

- attendance for only one day or evening

- non-residential attendance (eg for people living locally).

In each case it should be absolutely clear what facilities are offered and for what price (see also Chapter 2). The booking form should also ask delegates to specify any special requirements, as in the illustration in Figure 5.4.

Delegate packs

A delegate pack is usually issued to each person upon registration. The pack' comprises a variety of documents in a special folder. It is sensible to keep small items, such as name badges, separate as these are prone to get lost in a large folder. Rather than ask delegates to mill around a large table to find their own badge, it is more professional to have small items in separate, named envelopes to be given along with the folder.

The pack is likely to include:

- an information sheet on the guest speakers (taken from their biographies)

- the official programme

- a list of participants (for information and making contacts)

- a pack of notepaper

- a pencil or pen

- any tickets required to special functions or external activities

- details of any additional activities or facilities available.

MANAGEMENT SKILLS FOR PAs

14–16 MARCH 199–

PARK VIEW HOTEL, HIGHTOWN

CONFERENCE APPLICATION FORM

DELEGATE
First name ....Title .... Surname .... Tel ....

PARTNER
First name ....Title .... Surname .... Tel ....

Contact address ....

Company name .... **Town or city** ....

Type of accommodation preferred (single/double/twin) ....

I would/would not be prepared to share accommodation

I require smoking/non-smoking accommodation

Special dietary requirements ....

Other special requirements ....

My company will/will not be paying the fee   **I do/do not require a receipt**

OPTIONS	Delegate fee	Partner fee*
Full package – 2 nights' accommodation, bed/breakfast, lunch (3 days), dinner Wed, conference dinner Thurs, full conference programme, optional visit Thurs pm, individual profile session and career counselling Fri am	£250	£200
Alternative package – 2 nights' accommodation, bed/breakfast, lunch (Wed/Thur), dinner Wed, conference dinner Thurs, full conference programme Wed/ Thurs	£200	£160
Non-residential package – lunch (Wed/Thur), dinner Wed, conference dinner Thurs, full conference programme Wed/Thurs	£120	N/A

* excludes conference sessions, optional visit, profile and counselling sessions

Please complete and send with cheque payable to PA Events Ltd, 15 Riverside Walk, Hightown, HG3 6KD no later than 12 February 199-

1   No refunds can be issued for cancellations received within 7 days of the Conference
2   Confirmation of registration will be sent in acknowledgement, together with hotel brochure and location map.

Figure 5.4 A conference booking form

The official programme itemises every session in date and time order for the whole period of the conference. If alternative sessions are available at certain times, the room may be stated, or the information must be posted on a central noticeboard.

Press kits

A press kit is prepared to provide the most important information about the conference, to save time for any journalists who attend. The usual items include:

- background notes to the conference

- biographies of the speakers

- a copy of the official programme

- copies of the keynote speech

- summaries of other speeches and talks

- any press releases on other items of interest.

Where is your tutor next Easter?

Every Easter the Society of Teachers in Business Education (STBE) holds its annual conference, with a varied programme of speakers, workshops and visits – all of interest to teachers and lecturers of Business, Secretarial Studies and Administration. The conference is open to both members and non-members and each year it is organised by a different regional branch of the Society and held in a different part of the country. This way, no-one can grumble that they always have a long way to travel to attend! In 1998 it is the turn of the East Midlands Region to organise the conference, and they have chosen Nottingham as their venue. As an example of the information sent to members, read the leaflet illustrated in

Figure 5.5 and the programme shown in Figure 5.6. This will give you a better appreciation of the type of sessions organised for these events and the way in which the conferences themselves are promoted – and are useful models for conference documents you may have to prepare.

If your tutor is interested in joining the Society, or finding out more about its activities, the Membership Secretary would be very happy to provide more information. The Registered Office of the Society is at 88 Springfield Road, Millhouses, Sheffield S7 2GF, telephone 0114 236 3659, e-mail address gensec@stbe.demon.co.uk.

Society of Teachers in Business Education

1998 CONFERENCE

PREPARING FOR THE NEW MILLENNIUM

Learning Technologies for the 21st Century

hosted by

EAST MIDLANDS REGION

16 - 18 April 1998

to be held at

The Rutland Square Hotel
by The Castle
Nottingham

- Multimedia
- Latest IT innovations and solutions for Special Needs
- Examination Boards - latest updates
- Remote Learning
- Stands and exhibitions

- IT in the Curriculum
- Speakers from Education and Industry
- Funding in Schools and Colleges
- Demonstrations - latest equipment
- Internet/Intranet and Powerpoint Seminars

The above are a selection of topics which will be addressed
at the Conference and will be of interest for all in Schools and Colleges.

Then, at your leisure, look around the famous Nottingham Castle or Tales of Robin Hood.
Visit 'Ye Olde Trip To Jerusalem'(the oldest pub in England)
or even just Shop 'Til you Drop in the city with 2 indoor shopping centres!

Another option may be to visit Newstead Abbey, home of Lord Byron.
Spend time viewing the spectacular stately home and gardens.

For further information contact:
Sue Tidbury, Conference Secretary on 01623 793020

Figure 5.5   STBE conference leaflet

Figure 5.6   STBE conference programme

Thursday 16 April 1998

1200   **Conference Registration for residential and day delegates**

Exhibition of books, equipment and examining boards

1300   **Lunch**
(Council meeting and working lunch)

1400   **Welcome**
Chair, East Midlands Region - Janice Crookes

Presidential Address
Val Bell, President and National Chair of
The Society of Teachers in Business Education

1415   **Keynote Address**
Robert Valentine, Director of Education,
Nottinghamshire County Council

1450   **Curriculum Opportunities for The Millennium**
Hilde McNeil, FEFC Registered Inspector

1530   **Tea/coffee**

Exhibition of books, equipment and examining boards

1600   **New NVQ Initiative - Rigour without Rigidity**
Speaker to be arranged

1645   *Exhibition of books, equipment and examining boards*

1800   **Reception at 'Tales of Robin Hood'**
Welcome by Lord Mayor of Nottingham and
Michael Williams, Director of Leisure and Community
Services, Nottingham

1930   **Dinner and entertainment**
Strolling minstrels

Friday 17 April 1998

0900	**Registration - Day delegates**
0930	**New Learning Technologies in Schools and Colleges** Pat Morgan-Webb, Principal, Clarendon College, Nottingham
1015	**Tea/coffee**

Exhibition of books, equipment and examining boards

1045-1130 1130-1215 1215-1300	**Seminars** Each seminar to be run 3 times between 1045 and 1300 and delegates to choose 3 out of 4 of the following:

A	**Internet/Intranet - Teri Browett Training**
B	**Microsoft PowerPoint - Christine Price, Portland College**
C	**Learning technologies for students with additional requirements - The Computability Centre**
D	**Computerised photography - Kodak demonstration**

1300	**Lunch**
1400	**Business Education 14-19: An Update From QCA** Liz Francis, Principal Officer, QCA
1500	**IT and Communications, East Midlands Airport** John Spooner, Managing Director
1545	**Tea/coffee**

Exhibition of books, equipment and examining boards

1615	**Annual General Meeting (Members only)**
1715	**STBE Council Meeting**
1930	**President's Reception** Sponsored by Addison Wesley Longman
2000	**Conference Dinner** followed by light piano music

Saturday 18 April 1998

0930	**Funding in Colleges and Schools** Trefor Davies, Independent Consultant

1015	**Tea/coffee**

Exhibition of books, equipment and examining boards

1045	**A Company's Approach to Using Learning Technologies** Mabyn Thomas, Education and Development Manager, Experian Ltd - Global Information Services Organisation

1130	**Open Forum**

1230	**Close of Conference**

There are many places of interest in the City of Nottingham within easy walking distance of the Rutland Square Hotel and full details of these will be supplied in an information leaflet you will receive on booking your place on the conference. They include:

The Tales of Robin Hood
Nottingham Castle Museum and Art Gallery
The Lace Centre
The Robin Hood Statue
The Museum of Costume and Textiles
Ye Olde Trip to Jerusalem
Canal Museum
Condemned - at the Galleries of Justice

If you like shopping there are over 800 shops in the city centre:

Victoria Shopping Centre
Broad Marsh Shopping Centre
Flying Horse Walk and Exchange Arcade
Hockley

There are also other places of interest a car or bus journey away:

Green's Mill and Science Centre
Newstead Abbey (home of Lord Byron)
Wollaton Hall (Natural History and Industrial Museums)
Clumber Park
Sherwood Forest
Brewhouse Yard

✓ Check it yourself

1 Assume your tutor is a member of the STBE and has been asked to devise a booking form for the Nottingham conference. From the information given in Figures 5.5 and 5.6, and the rates shown in Figure 5.7, design a booking form that you think would be appropriate. Incorporate a section where those attending can select their first, second and third choice of seminar events (see Figure 5.6). Ask your tutor for comments when you have completed it.

Conference Charges

Residential (inc all refreshments)		Member	Non-member	Non-delegate (inc breakfast/eve meal only)
Full conference (fully inclusive)		£220	£250	£150
Friday (including dinner and Sat. breakfast)		£175	£195	£90
Non-residential (fully inclusive)				
Full conference		£110	£145	
Thursday	1200–1800	£30	£35	
Friday	0900–1715	£60	£80	
Thursday	Evening meal	£25	£25	£25
Friday	Conference dinner	£30	£30	£30
Saturday	0900–1230	£20	£25	
	Total cost:			

Figure 5.7 STBE conference rates – 1998

2 Those who agree to speak at a conference (especially free of charge) will expect to receive three or four letters.

- One letter will request their attendance (although this is often done by telephone to save time).
- Another letter confirms they have agreed to attend, with outline details giving the date, time, venue, length of their session and suggested topic. Usually this letter also asks the speaker to let the organiser have a summary of the talk about four weeks before the event, together with a biography (and sometimes a recent photograph) for publicity purposes. It also

asks the speaker to confirm whether he or she will require any particular transport facilities, will need accommodation, will be staying for meals, depending upon the session time, and to state the AVAs required and whether he or she will be bringing a partner. This letter also states whether a full rehearsal will be undertaken the previous day.

- A letter will confirm all final arrangements about two weeks before the conference.
- A letter of thanks will go to the speaker after the event. This is usually personalised and refers to some of the points made by the speaker, commenting favourably upon the relevance of the presentation for delegates – rather than being a standardised and therefore impersonal letter.

Assume you wish to approach your tutor to speak at a conference you are organising. Select the topic of interest yourself and invent all other relevant details for the conference.

a Write the first letter asking him or her to speak for a one-hour session. Use phrases that will make your tutor feel really needed and wanted! Refer to his or her expertise in a particular area and stress how beneficial you think his or her talk would be for delegates!

b Assume your tutor has agreed by telephone and has asked you to send more details. Write the second letter (bearing in mind the content above) inventing all relevant details in relation to time, date, location and so on.
   Write that you will expect your tutor to telephone you to confirm travel and AVA requirements, etc.

c You have now received the summary and the biography plus a photograph. Write to thank your tutor and to confirm the final arrangements you have made on his or her behalf.

d The event is now over and your tutor's session went very well indeed. Many delegates remarked how interesting and informative they found it. Write a thank you letter to your tutor passing on these compliments.

How it will operate

The format of different conferences varies, depending upon various factors:

- the length and style of the event
- whether it is an internal or external event
- the number and type of fringe activities or partner programmes on offer.

Usually, at least an hour is allowed for people to arrive and register, even for an internal event. For a large conference to which people are travelling from all over the country, you may have registration staff on duty all morning or afternoon prior to the conference start. If single-day delegates are a feature of the conference, then registration facilities will also open early each morning, often whilst residential delegates are having breakfast.

A senior official of the organisation – such as the chair or MD – usually opens the event. Alternatively, at an important conference a local dignitary may be invited to do this and welcome all delegates. The first speeches normally involve important officials or those making a keynote address. Throughout the rest of the day the sessions and activities may vary to include seminars, workshops, open forums and discussion groups. During breaks for refreshments (and often throughout the day), relevant exhibitions of materials and/or equipment may be displayed in adjacent areas. Each evening there is usually a dinner or visit, possibly with some entertainment. One night is usually set aside for the main conference dinner or banquet, often preceded by a sherry or champagne reception.

Rather than let a conference drift towards a close, experienced organisers make certain that a variety of interesting and informative sessions are scheduled for the final day so that the audience will still be largely intact when the chairperson or another official brings the proceedings to a close. It is normal to end the event at lunchtime or during the early part of the afternoon, to allow people time to travel home before nightfall. Do bear in mind, however, that there may be less latitude allowed for an internal event, which people are attending during working hours!

Review quiz

1   Identify FOUR items of equipment that might be required for a presentation. How would you ensure that these were well maintained and always ready for use?

2   State THREE tasks you may be expected to undertake during a presentation and THREE tasks you would have to do afterwards.

3   How would you describe the objectives of a seminar to a new member of staff?

4 Identify SIX key items of information you would include in an advertisement for a seminar.

5 State FOUR factors that would influence your choice of room layout for an event.

6 Identify THREE types of insurance you might take out for a conference and state why each might be required.

7 Describe SIX activities you would undertake if you were planning a sales conference for staff.

8 Identify TWO ways in which a conference may be publicised and state the advantages and disadvantages of each.

9 Describe FOUR items you would include in a delegate kit.

10 Identify FIVE factors which would influence your choice of venue for a conference.

11 Briefly explain the strategies you would employ to ensure that the registration of a large number of delegates took place as efficiently as possible.

Test yourself

1 You have just organised your first conference for internal staff and think it went well. However, you want to check their reactions – both to the programme and to the venue.

Design a short questionnaire that could be issued to everyone on their last day to find out their views.

2 Hold a brainstorming session to determine the main duties a PA would have to undertake before, during and after a conference. Check your answers with the key on page 193.

3 By now, your committee meetings to plan your own event should have reached some sort of result. If they have, now is the time to run an event yourselves – and evaluate its success afterwards. If you have let this opportunity lapse, then carry out task 4 instead!

4 As a group, you have been given the responsibility of organising a two-day conference for all the secretarial and administration students in your section or department.

a Hold a brainstorming session to decide what topics you think would be of interest to your audience and, from this, decide the theme of your conference. (Some of the sessions outlined in the programme in Figure 5.6 might prompt some ideas – as may suggestions from your tutor).

b Decide the length of each session and appropriate guest speakers (invent details here, if necessary).

c Divide into three groups.

- Group one should prepare a publicity leaflet.
- Group two should design and prepare the programme.
- Group three should prepare at least two appropriate items for the press kit.

Copy and circulate your final documents.

However, do remember that nothing helps you to learn more than the real thing! If you have not already done so, why not organise and run your own event, before it's too late!

Section 1 – Keys

● Key to conference terms on page 30

Registration – the term is used in two contexts, first referring to registration by people who wish to attend the event (ie by completing a registration or booking form), and secondly to registration on arrival. It is usual for arriving delegates to give their names at a special registration desk and be supplied with a delegate pack of information and name badge. This also enables the organisers to check that all expected delegates have arrived.

Keynote address – a short speech on an important topic of interest to participants, regarded as a key part of the proceedings.

Workshop – an interactive session where participants and leaders come together to consider a particular problem or undertake a practical activity.

Simultaneous translation – a system through which interpreters listening to a speech and, sitting in a separate booth, simultaneously speak a translation of what they hear for foreign delegates. The translation is relayed by means of earphones.

Open forum – a session in which participants or delegates may ask questions, often to a panel of experts.

Fringe programme – activities of secondary interest which may be of interest to delegates or participants at a large event, offered as an alternative to the main programme.

Plenary session – the final session which reviews and summarises the event as a whole.

● Key to Check it Yourself on page 40

a £170   **b** £200

● Key to Check it Yourself on page 47

a London hotel bill for accommodation of three sales consultants attending a national conference on corporate planning – *allowable*

b Air ticket for the MD to give keynote address at a major conference in New York – *allowable*

c Lunch for staff hosting a seminar at a hotel for local business people – *allowable*

d Bottles of wine given as gifts to all those who attend a seminar – *not allowable*

e A new outfit for the MD's PA who is accompanying staff to New York – *not allowable*

f Air ticket for the MD's wife who is accompanying him to New York – *not allowable*

g Hotel bill for rooms booked during a firm's AGM – *allowable*

h Postage costs for sending out the AGM notice and agenda and the company report and accounts – *allowable*

i Stationery costs for all documents required for an AGM – *allowable*

j Drinks and nibbles for journalists at a press conference – *not allowable*

k Cost of producing slides and a video for a major sales presentation – *allowable*

l Insurance premium paid against the non-appearance of a famous American management guru at a forthcoming conference – *allowable*

m The American guru's speaker fee – *allowable*

n Drinks party given by MD at his own home for overseas visitors – *not allowable*

o Cost of Institute of Directors' membership fees for the Board of Directors – *allowable*

p Printing of conference kits for 500 delegates at a forthcoming conference – *allowable*

q Your own travel to the conference venue 150 miles away – *allowable*

r Your own travel to a conference venue that is nearer to your home than your employer's premises – *not allowable*

● Keys to Check it Yourself on page 83

a Check general cleanliness and tidiness.

Check the heating and ventilation in any rooms you may hire.

Ask if they will supply any presentation equipment you need and check it has been safety tested.

Ask to see the fire certificate – decide if fire equipment is both plentiful and regularly inspected (the last date is marked on the extinguisher).

Ask how the alarm is sounded, how often it is tested and a fire drill undertaken.

Ask what would happen if a fire started in the middle of the night.

Check if they have a Public Entertainments Licence, which means they are subject to further restrictions and requirements.

Find out the number of people they can legally accommodate both in sleeping accommodation and public room accommodation.

Check there are plenty of exit and fire safety signs and good emergency lighting.

Ask about cleaning policies and any likely maintenance work. You don't want delegates falling over vacuum cleaner wires on their way down to breakfast or trying to listen to a debate over the roar of a pneumatic drill!

Find out about first aid facilities and what would happen in the event of a medical or other emergency.

The score given to each establishment by the Environmental Health Officer is not public information, therefore your only guidance in relation to the quality of food prepared and serviced would be if the hotel had won any catering awards (such as Michelin stars). In addition, some local councils operate 'gold', 'silver' and 'bronze' schemes for catering excellence. The general manager may, of course, offer to take you on a tour of the kitchen areas but if not, there is little you can do.

b Read the fire notice inside your room.

Find the fire exit nearest to your room.

Check the exit door is not locked and opens easily.

Check that the window in your room opens easily.

Look for a balcony or ledge you could use in an emergency and estimate the distance to the ground.

● Keys to Test Yourself on page 106

1 General information
Name, address, postcode, telephone and fax numbers
Name of general manager
Name of event contact(s) (eg conference organiser)
Name of hotel chain (if any)
Tel/fax number of head office (if applicable)
Rating (Tourist Board, AA, RAC, etc)
Other awards (eg Michelin stars or local catering awards)

Location and travel
Type of location (city/town centre, village, rural, seaside resort)
Type of building (modern, Victorian, historic, listed, country house, etc)
Nearest motorway and distance

Nearest main road and distance
Distance from your organisation
Distance from your other offices/main contacts
Nearest railway station and distance
Nearest airport and distance
Nearest underground station and distance (if applicable)

Transport facilities
Car parking spaces available
Nearest public parking and spaces available
Minibus or chauffeur service available
Helicopter landing pad/area available

3 Accommodation

Conference / meetings rooms
Number of conference rooms, size and capacity
Number of meeting/syndicate/workshop rooms, size and capacity
Types of possible layout (classroom/theatre/boardroom/horseshoe)
Location in hotel (front/rear, floor level)
Distance between conference/syndicate rooms
Exhibition space available
Registration space available
General facilities (daylight/artificial light, air conditioning, private bar, sound-proofing)

Sleeping accommodation
Number and type of rooms (single, double, twin, executive, suites)
Availability of smoking/non-smoking rooms
Bedrooms for disabled guests
Private facilities (en suite, bath and/or shower, no private facilities)
Room facilities (telephone, alarm, radio, television (and number of channels), 24-hour room service, tea/coffee making facilities, mini safe, mini bar, trouser press, hairdryer, laundry service, bathrobes, heating, air conditioning)

Furniture and equipment
Conference facilities – chairs with arms, PA system, platform, lectern, projection/AVA system, fixed screen, OHP, video and monitor, controllable access (eg through ante-room)
Syndicate/meeting room facilities – chairs, tables, whiteboard, OHP, screen, flip charts, video and monitor

Meals and refreshments
Number/type/size of restaurants
Banqueting facilities
Range of menus (vegetarian, vegan, special diets, slimmers' meals)
Type of meals (à la carte, table d'hôte, carvery, buffet)

Flexibility of meal-times
Flexibility of menus
Flexibility of refreshment times
Price range of meals
Cost of refreshments

General facilities and leisure amenities

Night porter/24-hour access/late night coffee shop/other shops/ daily newspapers
Security staff/surveillance cameras
Access/facilities for disabled
Swimming pool (indoor/outdoor), other sports facilities (eg golf, snooker, squash/tennis courts), games room, beauty/hair salon, gymnasium/keep fit centre, sauna, number of bars, nightclub
Public entertainment licence

Health and safety

Separate loading/unloading area
Marked parking/traffic areas
No ongoing maintenance work
Cleaning programme flexible around conference schedule
Appropriate fire equipment (smoke alarms/detectors, extinguishers etc) currently maintained
Emergency lighting
Current fire certificate
High standard of cleanliness
Appropriate and variable heating/ventilation/air conditioning
Good signs for fire routes, etc
Portable electrical equipment policy
Catering award
First aiders/medical emergency policy

4 Impression report

Ease of finding/clear signposting, etc
Appearance of hotel and grounds
Appearance and cleanliness of foyer
Number of staff on duty
Time taken to receive attention on arrival
Appearance and cleanliness of other areas (public/meeting rooms, bedrooms, restaurants, leisure areas)
Attitude/appearance of manager/receptionist/other staff
Standard of service
Standard of equipment
Standard of any meals, drinks or refreshments taken
Suitability of rooms for purpose
Availability of information and costs (printed and verbal)

● Key to Test Yourself on page 157

PA duties at meetings – summary

	Informal	Semi-formal/ internal	Formal/external
Before the meeting	Check participants' availability Establish venue Book room (allow time + 20 per cent) Book refreshments Confirm meeting to participants Prepare and send supplementary papers Check and book equipment Book parking spaces for externals	Check and book usual venue (allow time + 20 per cent) Check and organise seating (if necessary) Book refreshments Check requests for agenda items Prepare notice and agenda and agree with chairperson Prepare supplementary papers Send paperwork to all eligible to attend (usually also includes previous Minutes) Remind participants (tactfully!) of action or documents they have promised for next meeting Book parking spaces for externals Check and book equipment Keep record of apologies and other notes from absentees Prepare chairperson's agenda Inform reception and switchboard Nominate person to take messages Prepare name cards/seating plan if required Prepare spare copies of all documentation	Agree details of meeting – format, budget, participants, press coverage, special requirements (eg security) Check and select external venue (allow time + 50 per cent) Agree seating and parking arrangements, and type of refreshments with venue Confirm ancillary rooms required Confirm additional requirements (microphone, flowers, tables on platform, drapes for table, publicity displays, lectern, water and glasses, direction signs, name cards, etc) Prepare Notice of Meeting and Agenda Prepare other required documentation (eg proxy forms, voting papers, report and accounts) Arrange printing of documentation Arrange circulation of paperwork within prescribed clear days Check/agree staffing requirements Check/agree staff uniform/badge requirements Prepare attendance register Check/agree VIP requirements (eg transport/accommodation) Check/agree press coverage/requirements Prepare seating plan for platform party Check supply of pens, paper on platform and on reception Log proxy forms received Prepare chairperson's agenda Prepare spare copies of all documentation Confirm any special requirements with venue (diet, disabled access, etc) Prepare press release (if required)

PA duties at meetings – summary

	Informal	Semi-formal/ internal	Formal/external
On the day and at the meeting	Check cleanliness of room Check heating/ lighting Check blinds (if OHP used) Welcome participants Take notes if requested	Check chairperson has his/her agenda Remind switchboard and reception Remind message-taker Check accommodation, equipment and seating Take relevant papers, files and spare documentation to the room Place notice on door (if required) Arrange name plates (if used) Arrange drinking water and glasses (if used) Check there is clear area for refreshments to be sited Arrange paper, pencils and pens Welcome participants Serve refreshments (if not self-service) Sit next to chairperson to pass papers and give information (eg on absentees) Take minutes of meeting Discreetly remind chairperson if meeting overrunning	Arrive early to 'walk' venue and check all arrangements/facilities Check all equipment (and microphones) operational Ensure staff are briefed on individual roles and responsibilities Arrange for venue switchboard or member of own staff to take messages for directors, VIPs, etc whilst meeting in progress Set out reception area with attendance register and required documentation Greet arrivals – register and direct them to cloakrooms/refreshments or main hall as appropriate Greet VIPs and arrange escort to VIP room Greet press and direct to press area. If delegated to do so, distribute press release Check number attended for inclusion in minutes If taking minutes, check names of all proposers and seconders (often written down beforehand) and record all resolutions If counting votes, check correct figures recorded both 'for' and 'against' the motion, as well as total number of abstentions

PA duties at meetings – summary

	Informal	Semi-formal/internal	Formal/external
After the meeting	Type up notes Check with coordinator Circulate notes Check any action promised by self or boss Enter next meeting date in own diary and boss's diary	Check all messages are passed to correct recipient Remove notice from door Notify switchboard/reception/catering staff that meeting has ended Remove surplus papers and tidy room Check notes for urgent action promised by self or chairperson Draft minutes and check with chairperson Print out and photocopy minutes Circulate minutes (unless kept until next agenda sent out) File all papers Prepare any required correspondence Enter date of next meeting in own diary and chairperson's diary Enter any action dates in relevant diaries	Clear away any surplus papers left by the platform party Collect all voting slips and the attendance register/registration forms Collect any other important or relevant paperwork Ensure all publicity displays or company equipment removed from venue Draft minutes and check with chairperson Draft any press statements required and check with chairperson Arrange printing and distribution of minutes and other required documentation Arrange circulation of press statement to agencies and media Prepare any correspondence required (eg to thank a guest speaker or VIP invited for a particular reason) File all paperwork Hold review meeting with staff to evaluate success of event and recommend improvements

● Key to Check it Yourself on page 162

PA duties for a presentation

Before the event	Attend meeting with presenters to decide date, time, theme and outline requirements Draft invitation list and/or advertisements and/or draft confirmatory letter to customer(s) Agree timings with presenters Decide and book venue and specify layout Decide and book AVA equipment and other aids Book refreshments and confirm timings Reserve car parking and arrange visitor passes (if required) Inform reception Draft and check documentation, OHTs and other aids Photocopy sufficient copies of documentation or handouts Check availability of printed literature Collate and bind any packs required Arrange transport of all material to room or venue
Immediately before/on the day	Check room and layout, quantity of seating, equipment, visual aids Put up any posters or marketing materials Post any direction signs required Check reception staff are aware of location for guests and availability of presenters Greet guests on arrival and escort/direct to room Assist with refreshments Distribute presentation packs
After the event	Collect spare documentation and folders Notify catering staff to collect crockery Prepare any follow-up correspondence Prepare any press statements File all related documents Return printed material to storage Check any invoices/internal accounts and make/sanction payments

● Key to Check it Yourself on page 166

PA duties for a seminar

Before the event	Attend planning meeting to decide date, time, theme, length of event, speakers and outline requirements Visit/select venue Contact/book speakers and check AVA requirements Agree order of speakers and timings Agree method of advertising (letter, press advert, press release, etc) Prepare advertising material required Prepare booking forms and issue Log completed forms and note special requirements Confirm refreshments/menus, equipment needs and seating plans with venue Prepare event materials as required Arrange transportation of materials and equipment to venue Arrange insurance for same
Immediately before/on the day	Visit venue to check all requirements met Organise reception area Greet and check in arrivals against list Give out information packs including programme Operate help desk all day Act as liaison between venue service providers and seminar leader
After the event	Collect spare documentation and folders Check any AVAs not belonging to the venue are transported back Prepare any follow-up correspondence to speakers File all related documents Check invoices and make payments

● Key to Test Yourself on page 181

PA duties for a conference

Before the event	Set up event file and hold planning meeting to establish budget; decide team roles Prepare checklist or schedule to cover responsibility for each job Prepare draft programme and list all requirements Establish/approach speakers Decide advertising/prepare press release Visit/select venue, negotiate cost of requirements for all rooms, catering, sleeping accommodation, AVA equipment, etc Decide room layouts Arrange insurance for any equipment to be transported Plan conference activities/tours Confirm speakers, obtain biographies, check AVA needs Check/update budget – check weekly. Finalise/print programme Prepare delegate information and send out with registration/booking forms Log received booking forms and special requirements Confirm accommodation/menus/seating/other requirements with venue Send programme to speakers, confirm timings and request copies of papers to be presented (or summaries) Prepare delegate packs and press kits. Book photographer Organise and brief staff for registration, security, etc Make/confirm transport requirements Update delegate list as required and check details Inform all suppliers of last minute amendments Supervise transport of documentation, equipment, etc
Immediately before/on the day	Post signs in venue and check equipment in place Check stage set, banners and other theme materials Brief team for last time and give out staff badges Set up registration area and display welcome notices Check platform area and microphones/room layouts/AVA equipment Greet delegates on arrival, check names on master list, issue delegate kits Greet speakers on arrival and give final briefing about schedule Monitor and assist at help desk to answer ongoing queries Check refreshment times – liaise with venue if sessions under/over running

	Greet press (if appropriate) and escort to press room Arrange daily briefing sessions for all staff and that day's speakers
Penultimate/ last day	Issue review questionnaire to delegates
After the event	Send thank you letters to speakers and others who have assisted Prepare report on conference for any relevant journals Prepare press release or statement – send out with photographs Check and pay accounts as received Prepare final income and expenditure account File documentation for future reference Hold meeting to review event Type up planning notes to assist organiser of next event, using completed questionaires to assist

SECTION 2 – Travel organisation

● Introduction

Business travel is big business – for travel companies, tourist offices, booking agents, airline carriers, hotels, car rental companies and all the other service providers. In 1997 an American Express survey of the business travel market in the US and Europe calculated it to be worth approximately $US 297 billion – a not inconsiderable sum of money in anyone's language! What is more, business is booming. A greater number of people travel on business every year – despite technological advances such as video and computer conferencing. As more and more organisations operate on a global basis or market their goods worldwide, the need for business executives to meet face to face appears to be ever more important.

Another survey, undertaken by the magazine *Business Traveller*, found that whilst the majority of executives prefer to choose their own travel route and accommodation, less than 50 per cent actually make their own bookings. Most pass on the responsibility for finalising the arrangements to their PA, secretary or travel agent. In some cases business travellers do not have a PA or secretary and therefore have to do most of the work – and make the bookings – themselves. In other cases, executives might not have PAs who are knowledgeable enough to do the job, or may be concerned that their PAs cannot be trusted to plan and organise a complex business trip, make the travel arrangements and consider all the important facets of the journey as efficiently as they would themselves. This is a pity, as organising travel is often one of the most interesting parts of a PA's job role.

Paradoxically, the responsibility for undertaking this work is more common among PAs who work for middle-sized organisations – and even some very small enterprises – than it is among those employed by very large organisations, which often have their own central travel department or appoint a travel broker or specialist travel agent to undertake all the work for them. Even in that case, however, there is a role for an astute PA who knows the individual preferences and idiosyncrasies of his or her boss and can be alert to alternatives and variations from the normal travel pattern which would provide greater flexibility or considerable cost savings. In a small business, economy and flexibility are essential – and the need for them is becoming more pronounced. Today even large, highly profitable organisations are keen to keep costs to a minimum, of course. If nothing else, a PA who is fully conversant with the ins and outs of business travel does much to keep the service providers on their toes!

The chapters in this section are designed to give you all the information you need to start to make informed choices about travel for your boss. In addition to the theory, practical activities are included to help you to reinforce your learning. Obviously, this is one area where actually undertaking the activity is infinitely preferable to merely planning it, which is why it is an important perk for many PAs to travel with their executives on certain trips, rather than just make the arrangements! For the same reason, some practical projects are suggested in the following chapters, which should be costed out and researched carefully. It should be within the means of your group to undertake one of these trips, on a fact-finding basis, to add practical experience to your store of knowledge.

Special note

The chapters that follow contain several examples of prices, intended to illustrate the comparative costs of different methods and standards of travel. While all prices were correct at the time of writing, they are subject to modification by service providers, and therefore should not be used for costing purposes. Current prices can be obtained from the travel organisation direct or through your local travel agent.

Preliminary arrangements

6

This chapter is concerned with the background information you need before you can start to make any sort of travel arrangements. Although it may seem much easier to ring the local travel agent and ask your contact there to solve all your problems, quite often there are many other aspects to consider and a considerable amount of preparatory work must be done before you even consider lifting up the telephone. In addition, several of the issues that arise when planning a trip may be better referred to other types of travel specialists, as you will see later in this chapter.

All business travel involves consideration of each of the following factors:

- the method and form of travel
- the type of accommodation required
- the cost of the trip and the budget allowed.

If the trip is outside the UK, then additional factors include

- necessary travel documentation
- health and safety matters
- monetary issues
- insurance cover
- customs and excise regulations
- other considerations – such as climate, business customs, public holidays and so on.

In this chapter, we will consider each of these issues in more detail.

● Methods of travel

There are four basic options when considering travel.

- Road
- Rail
- Air
- Sea

The final destination obviously affects the choice – and it is doubtful whether all these options are feasible on most trips! Generally your choice will be determined by:

- the distance involved

- the amount of time available
- the reason for the trip
- the budget available
- company policies
- the preferences of your boss.

Within the British mainland the options are road, rail or air. Between the British mainland and Europe the choice is usually road/sea, rail or air. Beyond Europe the usual choice is air travel. You should also note that *within* different countries, optimum choices may vary. In and between smaller countries, road or rail links may be very good and, in some cases, much more convenient than air travel. In large countries, such as the USA and Australia, the opposite applies – in these countries air travel is the natural means of internal transport because of the vast distances involved.

Broadly, all the choices you have to make can be considered under two headings – cost and convenience.

The cost of travel

The days have long since gone when business trips could be planned with little consideration for cost. Today, most organisations operate a strict travel budget and will have policies covering the type and class of travel that is permitted, the type and classification of hotel accommodation allowed and the amount of money that can be allocated for daily subsistence – in other words, basic daily needs such as food, taxis, tips and so on.

The policies may allow for the classifications of travel and accommodation to be varied in different situations. Normally, the main criterion used is the seniority of the member of staff involved. Sometimes the length of the trip may also be a deciding factor.

Travel, accommodation and cost classifications

The first point to note is that different types of tickets can be purchased for various types of journeys and different types of accommodation can be reserved – or different grades of hotel.

- **Air travellers** usually fly internationally on a First Class, Business Class or Economy ticket. The first is the most expensive, the latter is the cheapest. Within Europe, First Class travel is often not an option.

- **Rail travellers** within Britain can travel First Class or Standard – however, a wide range of tickets are available (see page 202). The main options for business use are First, First Apex, Standard, Saver and Supersaver. To Europe on Eurostar (see page 247) the choice is usually Premium First, Normal First, Standard Plus or Standard.

- **Ferry travellers** are offered Club or Executive Class on popular short business routes, such as Dover–Calais and Portsmouth–Le Havre, by some ferry companies (eg P&O). On longer journeys where accommodation is reserved, the type of cabin will also affect the price.

- **Road travellers** will pay to hire a car if they are not taking their own vehicle, and will be charged more for a long journey in a 'black cab' than in an ordinary taxi or even more for a chauffeur-driven service.

- **Hotels** are graded in most countries, with 5-star being the most expensive (luxury) category. Within any hotel, however, there is likely to be a choice between a room (or even types of room) and a suite. Today virtually all hotels used by business executives have en-suite facilities in their rooms.

How does this work in practice? Often it is a simple matter of checking your organisation's ruling, which may allocate different classifications of travel and accommodation to different levels of employee. For instance, a technician travelling on a long-distance flight may have to fly Economy, the Sales Manager may be allowed to travel Business Class, while the MD or Chairman would be issued a First Class ticket. However, on short haul flights, where the best grade may be Business Class, this may be restricted to senior executives only. Similar restrictions may apply to rail travel. Accommodation may be affected in the same way, with a technician staying in a 3-star hotel, the senior managers in a 4-star hotel and the MD or Chairman in a 5-star hotel. However, these rules are extremely variable between organisations and you would need to check which apply in your own place of work. In some cases, no-one travels First Class or stays in 5-star hotels, no matter how important!

The organisation may also restrict the airline, hotel or car-hire choices available to take advantage of loyalty schemes such as Frequent Flyer Programmes (FFPs) with airlines or Honoured Guest schemes with hotels, which allow points to be collected for using specific service suppliers. Further details of such schemes are given in Chapter 7.

Subsistence allowances may also vary for different employees, and the daily allowance for UK travel will usually be less than for foreign trips. In some cases the allowance also varies from one country to another, as daily necessities are far more expensive in some countries than others. Senior executives may be allocated a relatively flexible expense allowance, particularly if they entertain foreign clients in the hope of obtaining business. You may need to complete a form to claim any advance allowance your boss requires, and arrange for this to be paid in the appropriate foreign currency and/or as travellers cheques. Alternatively, many executives charge most of their expenses to a corporate credit card and submit their expense claim detailing these amounts at the end of the trip. Further details of monetary considerations are given on pages 227–232.

Tips on airfares

Airfares are an extremely complex matter and studying exactly how to get the best deal for a business trip is beyond the scope of this book. The price paid depends on many factors – the date of travel, time to be spent away, amount of advance notice given, days of the week for journeys outward and inward, the time of day, the popularity of the flight and so on. However, it is worth noting some basic considerations that are always useful to introduce into a conversation with your travel agent!

- Many air fares have 'hidden extras', such as air travel taxes (almost everywhere), airport improvement fees (in Canada), customs and immigration clearance fees (in the US), security fees (with Virgin airlines). Always check that any quoted price includes the extras.

- National carriers are the airlines with the dominant share of the market in a particular country (such as British Airways in the UK). They set the benchmark price, which is usually the highest. Travelling by a different carrier can reduce the cost considerably. As an example, in November 1997 the BA price for a Business Class return flight from London–New York was £2,814, whereas Continental Airlines were quoting £1,559 and Kuwait Airlines only £550! All flights were direct and non-stop.

- For similar reasons, the cheapest flights around Europe are those offered by non-European airlines. This is often described by the term **fifth freedom** – which refers to a passenger being transported between two countries by an airline from a third. As an example, travelling from Manchester to Zurich could cost up to £396 with Swissair but would cost only about £160 with Emirates. The problem for business trips may be that 'fifth freedom' flights only operate on certain days at certain times, and there may be delays if the flight has originated somewhere else. However, for many small businesses, such savings can be crucial.

- Another consideration is a factor known as **yield management**. On each flight a certain number of seats are available at each of several different prices, ranging from cheap, discounted fares to high fares. As an example, on a BA flight from London to Paris there are up to eight different price codes – currently ranging from £88 to £392! At a busy time, an airline is likely to allocate only a few cheap seats to each flight because experience has told it that passengers will pay more to fly at that time. It can therefore charge more and make more profit. When your travel agent selects a flight, he or she can tell you how many seats are available at each different price and – more importantly – whether or not they have been taken!

- Most people have heard of the term **Apex** in connection with fares. This stands for Advance Purchase Excursion, and is normally the lowest fare available. However, various conditions are attached to an Apex fare, including making the purchase a fixed number of days in advance (normally between seven and fourteen) and minimum/maximum stay restrictions. Lack of flexibility means that the Apex air fares – and other cheap options such as Pex and Excursion fares – are not usually a feasible option for business travel.

The 'no frills' approach

A relatively recent innovation in air travel, made possible by airline deregulation in Europe from 1 April 1997, has been the introduction of 'no frills' flights with fares at considerably below the standard economy rate. These flights depart from regional airports (such as Luton and Liverpool) and do not include in-flight refreshments. They may not be scheduled during peak times. Initially it was believed that these flights would be used mainly by holidaymakers visiting European cities for a cheap break. However, EasyJet, Ryanair and Debonair – all major players in this market – have proved that their cut-price flights to major cities in the UK and Europe are very attractive to small businesses –

who would rather pay £78 for a return ticket to Barcelona than the £184 BA Economy Fare, or £150 to Nice rather than BA's Club Europe price of £660. A recent Ryanair innovation has been flights to Ireland from £19 plus tax! To counter the threat to its business, British Airways has set up its own offshoot company, Go, to operate no frills flights from Stansted to various European capitals at bargain fares from 1998. The aim is to offer a BA alternative to anyone who would prefer to forfeit the in-flight drinks and refreshments to save money. Virgin has already entered this market and its Belgian-based offshoot Virgin Express offers low-priced flights between Rome and Madrid.

Tips on rail fares

The airlines are now not the only carriers to offer Apex fares. Most train operating companies (TOCs) such as Virgin, GNER and Midland have introduced Apex First and Apex (Standard) rail fares – giving hugely discounted prices to those who book return tickets in advance. As an example, the Virgin Apex return fare from London to Glasgow is £25, compared with a Supersaver fare of £64. From Preston to London the Apex fare is £17.50, compared with a standard open fare of £102.50! The Apex First option enables travellers who book at least seven days in advance to use First Class carriages at a discounted rate. Midland charge an executive travelling from Nottingham to London only £31 for this, compared with £92 for a normal First Class ticket. The problem is that peak-time trains or day returns cannot be used, and the tickets are limited in number.

Calculating the cost of rail travel has become much more complicated since the privatisation of the railways, which resulted in the formation of 25 different TOCs in the UK. Indeed, the situation is so complex that concern has been expressed that rail travellers are often given incorrect information about rail fares, times and routes when they telephone for assistance. Certain points, however, can help you to find your way through the maze more easily and assist your boss in keeping costs down.

- The railways use a system of yield management or price discrimination, so that fewer cheaper tickets are usually available on popular routes and at popular times. Early morning InterCity trains to London and Friday afternoon trains out of London are those that attract the highest fares.

- Three types of ticket can be bought on the day of travel. A Supersaver is the cheapest, a Saver is about 25 per cent more expensive and a Standard Open is about double the Saver fare. This is the most expensive unless your boss is travelling First Class. The type of ticket available is usually determined by the time and day of departure, and differs from one station to another.

- The best way to find out about fares and services is to ring the National Rail Enquiry Service on 02345–484950. However, given the accusations that have been made about inaccurate information, it may be sensible to check your quotation by ringing the TOC direct. The appropriate TOC will depend upon the route (see Chapter 7).

- Travelling at a non-peak time saves a considerable amount of money – it may therefore be cheaper to travel for an early morning meeting the day before, even though this would mean that overnight accommodation is also required and the cost of this would have to be taken into account.

- If your boss travels regularly in and out of London from a distance it is possible to reduce the cost substantially by reversing the ticketing for outward and return journeys! This is because, for virtually all ticket types, the outward journey must be made on the date shown on the ticket, but the return journey can be any time in the following thirty days. In this case you could, depending on timings,

- purchase a Standard open return for journey one (outward to London) – but only use the outward portion

- purchase a Supersaver return ticket for the interim journeys, which your boss uses to return home and then go back to London again

- ask your boss to use the return portion of his or her Standard open return for the last journey. However, bear in mind that this 'last' journey must take place within thirty days of the first outward journey.

The savings are considerable – for only two journeys to London up to £100 can be saved, depending on the distance travelled.

- Booking in advance helps you save money on many routes – particularly if you can take advantage of Apex First fares.

- If the trip is not definite, eg for a meeting that has not yet been confirmed, you can often still save money by booking in advance. However, do check the booking conditions attached to the type of ticket purchased. On some tickets a full refund will be given, less a small administration fee, if the trip is cancelled at the last minute.

The convenience factor

Unfortunately for the company accountant, the main criterion for selecting options when travelling is often the 'convenience factor'. Frequently times and routes of travel will be dictated by business appointments, which must fit with the requirements and schedules of customers and clients. For that reason, even if you know several ways to save money, it may not be possible to use them. In addition, no organisation wants key executives to be weary when they arrive to undertake critical business negotiations that could involve millions of pounds. For that reason you are likely to find that the convenience factor plays a key role in your thinking and planning.

Convenience will affect:

- the method of travel (air, rail, road, sea)

- the grade and classification of travel

- the grade and classification of accommodation.

In many cases, given that an executive's time is worth money to the organisation, major considerations will be speed and comfort.

- For **air travel** this will mean selecting a reliable carrier with a reputation for regularly arriving on time, from a local airport, with

departure/arrival gates near the main terminal, executive departure lounges and a range of on-board facilities to minimise fatigue (particularly for long journeys).

- For **rail travel** critical factors will be departure and arrival times, a direct route wherever possible to minimise the duration of the trip and the inconvenience of changing trains, restaurant facilities or seat service (rather than just a buffet bar) and the availability of advance seat booking.

- With **road travel** an executive will not be expected to drive a company car a long distance or to drive to a client in a busy city centre where parking would be very problematic. Coach travel is not normally a business option because of the length of time and inconvenience involved.

- **Sea travel** is mainly used by executives who need to take their cars to Europe or Ireland, and is likely to be chosen only if it is a practical alternative to air travel and car hire (see page 265).

The fundamental advantages and disadvantages of each method of travel are summarised in Figure 6.1 on the next page.

The Premier Service class

A new marketing campaign to attract business travellers was unveiled with the announcement by Midland Main Line (MML) that it intends to introduce a new Business Class service from January 1998. Passengers will be able to use First Class lounges in railway stations, travel in special carriages with more space between seats, read a complimentary newspaper and have at-seat service of food and drinks. All this is in addition to a zone 1 London underground ticket and free parking at the base station. The price? A mere £116 return from London to Sheffield (as compared to the current Standard Open fare of £78).

MML are not the only train operating company to be contemplating such a service. Richard Branson intends to introduce new tilting trains with airplane-type service including massages and video games on the West Coast Virgin route and GNER has plans to revive its Motorail service, complete with trolley service and cinema-style screens. All at a price, of course!

Method	Advantages	Disadvantages
Road Private car/ hire car	Flexible – for time of departure and route taken Door-to-door Relatively inexpensive Unlimited stop-offs possible	Tiring if long journey Delays possible through traffic congestion, road works Unreliable in bad weather Parking difficulties
Taxi	Flexible timings Door-to-door in city centres Assistance in finding location	Expensive for long journeys Traffic delays increase cost Difficulty obtaining taxi during peak times
Rail	City centre to city centre Frequent service Pre-bookable seats Space to work, move and/or relax Reliable in most weathers No restrictions on laptops or mobile phones Refreshments/meals available Additional business services available	May be crowded in all but First Class carriages Peak times expensive May have to change trains on some routes May be delays Difficult to store much luggage
Air	Fastest type of travel Good facilities at most airports Refreshments/meals and other services en route Minimal (or zero) check-in time for some domestic flights	Expensive Airports may be several miles from city centre Long check-in time required for some flights May be delays in bad weather Some connecting flights mean long walks between departure gates Baggage weight limitations
Sea	Reasonably priced Modern vessels have reduced sailing times, including hovercraft option Regular sailing times on popular routes Sleeping accommodation and other facilities on board Cars allowed on most vessels	Slower than air travel Crowded in peak season Ferryports not usually near city centres Delays or cancellations in bad weather Boarding and disembarkation may be slow Rough journeys unpleasant

Figure 6.1 Travel comparison chart

● Planning and checklists

There are several steps you need to undertake when planning and organising travel for a particular trip.

1 Obtain exact details of the requirements and open a specific **travel file** for all the information you will compile relating to the trip. If it is your own boss who is making the trip, mark the proposed dates in pencil in all relevant diaries to avoid double bookings.

2 Make out a checklist of all the jobs you have to undertake.

3 Obtain all the information needed on the various travel options available and all the other aspects of the trip that are your responsibility. Make clear and detailed notes on all the information you obtain.

4 Find out comparative costings of the travel options available (where appropriate).

5 Agree the final choice of travel (and timings) with your boss together with his or her preferences on other related matters, such as accommodation, car hire, etc.

6 Make and confirm all bookings and reservations. Write up the diary entries in ink for the appropriate dates.

7 Prepare and check all documentation and undertake other relevant tasks to prepare for your boss's departure.

Travel is one area when good planning and organisation are absolutely essential – otherwise the consequences can be disastrous, with missed appointments, long delays or unsuitable accommodation. An effective PA is therefore highly skilled at considering all the factors relating to a business trip before making any arrangements or bookings at all.

Obtaining details of requirements

As you have already seen, in different circumstances a variety of travel options may be considered appropriate. Much depends upon the Kipling factors you first met in Section 1 (see page 61) – in other words – *what, why, when, how, where,* and *who.*

When you are planning travel, you need to consider:

- **what** are the organisational and budgetary rules that apply, and what are the travellers' preferences?

- **why** is the trip being made?

- **when** will travel take place?

- **how** can transport and accommodation be arranged most appropriately?

- **where** is the destination?

- **who** is involved – how many people, and what is their status in the organisation?

All these factors will influence your choices and the tasks you have to undertake. Clear, unambiguous information on all these points is essential before you start to make any arrangements. It has been known for people to be booked to travel to Bolivia instead of Bulgaria, and Oman instead of Amman! Making sure you understand the *exact* request is absolutely critical.

In many organisations a specific form is used for executives to give details of any forthcoming trips, together with their preferences or requirements. An example of such a form is shown in Figure 6.2. The contents of the form are invaluable, as it should provide:

- personal information on those travelling, to enable you to give sufficient information to your travel agent for ticketing purposes

- information on individual preferences to save you from having to ask about minor details

- information on other requirements associated with the trip (such as visas, vaccinations, etc) to enable you to make out a comprehensive checklist.

Each form should also act as the basis of a specific travel file for that particular trip. It is sensible to open a new travel file immediately you receive a request, so that you have a home for all the documents and information you are likely to amass in the course of your planning.

Many PAs who arrange travel for their executives are simply told verbally about a forthcoming visit, possibly at a meeting where a trip is being planned or in a short informal working session or even over the telephone. In some cases an executive away on one trip will ring with a request for his PA to organise the next one! Whenever you receive instructions verbally it is very important that you make clear notes from which you can prepare your checklist. During this process you will immediately notice any gaps in your information and questions that you will need to refer back to your boss. As you become more experienced in planning and arranging travel, you will become more expert at asking the right questions immediately you receive the initial request.

Making out a checklist

A checklist is simply a list of jobs you have to do. It is always easier to follow if you list all the items under clear headings, so that you can use your checklist as your 'master sheet' when obtaining information on different options. If there is room you can make notes on the checklist itself. However,

TRAVEL REQUEST FORM

Name ...RICHARD.. .EVANS.... Department MARKETING

PASSENGER DETAILS

Title	Surname	First name(s)	DOB
MR	Evans	Richard John	5.5.58
Ms	Docherty	Paula	7.4.59
MR	McCormack	Jack	11.10.64

TRAVEL/ACCOMMODATION DETAILS

Departure date MON, 25 FEB Place of departure GLASGOW

Cities to be visited	Dates of stay	Accommodation
SYDNEY	26-28 FEB	4-star - singles
MELBOURNE	1-7 MARCH	" "

Type of travel req'd ..AiR.... Preferred carrier(s) .BA. or .Qantas

Preferred class of travel ...Club................

OTHER REQUIREMENTS

Visa check   Y/N̸   Vaccinations check Y̸/N

Transport Taxi to/from Glasgow airport. Car hire both cities — collect at airports.

Currency ..Details to follow..

Other (please specify) Please check Australian driving regs.
I may also be going to Hobart for a day or two — will advise you later.

Signed ..R.Evans...............   Date ..7 January..

Figure 6.2 An executive's travel request form

it is often preferable to prepare a separate information sheet (see below). Many PAs clip the checklist to the front of the relevant travel file – this is invaluable if you are organising several trips simultaneously. In this case, it is also sensible to keep all your travel files in a separate drawer, in date order of travel.

It is important to consult each checklist daily to make sure that you are on schedule and that nothing important is still outstanding. Arranging travel is one job that must not be delayed – particularly if your boss wants a reservation on a busy day at a peak time. Forgetting to make a reservation promptly can result in having to pay more money, or having to accept an indirect travel route or a less convenient time option. Forgetting to make it altogether would be catastrophic!

A checklist for a straightforward, domestic journey is relatively easy to compile. One for a group of people visiting several foreign countries, which includes matters such as vaccinations, visas and currency, is obviously more complex – but will become easier to follow when you have progressed further through this book.

Check it yourself

1 An example of a checklist for a visit to Australia, which matches the request form in Figure 6.2 is shown in Figure 6.3. Look through this now and note the items which are listed and the type of headings used. If you are not sure about any of the locations (including Hobart) check these in an atlas.

Checklist for Richard Evans – Proposed visit to Australia, 25 Feb to 8 March

Travel

Glasgow to Sydney – Mon 25 Feb
Sydney–Melbourne – Fri 1 March
Melbourne–Glasgow – Thurs 7 March

Check available BA/Qantas flights and book 3 × Club class

Accommodation

3 × single rooms (en-suite) 4-star

Sydney – 26–28 Feb inclusive
Melbourne – 1–6 March inclusive

Obtain information on suitable hotels and make reservations

Transport

Taxi
• to Glasgow airport 25 Feb
• collect Glasgow airport on return

(NB check home addresses of travellers for collection + check-in times and book taxis)

Car hire
• Sydney airport collect/return 26 Feb–1 March
• Melbourne airport collect/return 1–7 March

Make car hire reservations – check size/model of car preferred

Currency
Information to follow

Other

Obtain visas for trip
Check driving regulations

Figure 6.3   Checklist for a trip to Australia

2   Your boss Joanne Bretherton has recently called in to tell you about a forthcoming trip she will be making from your office in Chester to Dublin. She has decided to go by ferry from Holyhead and to take her car, as she also wants to drive to a firm in Galway during her visit. She wants to leave on Monday, 26 March, stay in Dublin on Monday and Tuesday night, travel to Galway on Wednesday, return to Dublin and stay there on Thursday, and travel back on Friday, 30 March. She will require a single room with en-suite facilities and £200 in Irish currency. She has also asked you to check the mileage and the route she should take to drive from Dublin to Galway.

Make out a checklist from this information and check your finished work with the key on page 300.

Obtaining and recording information

There are three main ways in which you can find out any information you need:

- through contacting your local travel agent or another travel organisation (such as an airline or ferry operator)
- by using a reference book or timetables
- through a computer network – mainly the Internet.

Each of these options is discussed in more detail in the next section.

A key organisational skill connected with finding out information is the making of clear notes to put into the travel file – rather than scribbled bits of paper! Most efficient PAs prepare a specific information sheet for each trip, on which they record all the details relating to items on their checklist. A useful tip is not to throw any information away until your boss has actually departed! Experienced PAs could list several occasions when plans have had to be altered at the last minute and they have suddenly required information on a travel option that was rejected earlier. If you had thrown away your notes then you would have to start obtaining the details all over again.

Practice on preparing information sheets will be given as you progress through these chapters.

Comparative costings

In some cases, the reason for the trip, the distance, the time allowed and/or the status of the person travelling will determine the type and class of travel and accommodation. In other cases, the first step may be to cost out the various possible forms of travel and to compare the results with the allocated budget. In some cases there may be a valid reason for exceeding the projected budget amount (such as an urgent and important business meeting), but this deviation from normal practice would have to be agreed before any bookings were made.

When undertaking any costing exercise it is important to consider all the requirements, the various alternatives and the company regulations simultaneously. As an example, an executive travelling from London to Manchester could travel by train, road or air and the option chosen will depend upon all the Kipling factors mentioned earlier. However, with some alternatives extra costs such as, taxi or tube fares and/or an additional night's accommodation may be required, and these (together with any inconvenience factors) must be taken into consideration.

Check it yourself

1 The following options are available for an executive wanting to travel from Edinburgh to London (return).

- by air – Economy fare £280, Club Class £512, no-frills flight to Luton £80
- by train – First Class Open £205, Standard Open £139, Supersaver (not valid during peak hours or on Fridays) £64, Apex (not valid during peak hours or for a day return) £48
- by road – coach £30, car 413 miles *each way*.

a Calculate the expense claim that would be submitted by an executive who drove in both directions, assuming that the petrol allowance was 30p per mile.

b As a group, decide the additional costs (and inconvenience) involved in booking a no-frills flight to Luton if the reason for the trip was to attend a meeting in central London starting at 9.30 am and ending at 5 pm.

c Which of the above travel options would you recommend in each of the following situations? Where appropriate, also state the class of travel you think would be most suitable.

   i A sales representative wants to call on several customers en route to London.

   ii Your boss, the Marketing Manager, is going on a three-day visit to your head office in central London. Her first appointment there is for 2 pm on Monday afternoon.

   iii Your MD's presence has been requested at an emergency meeting at head office on Tuesday afternoon. He must be back in Edinburgh for an important appointment the following morning.

   iv Your brother has just started his own business and is trying to keep costs to a minimum. He needs to attend a two-day exhibition in central London next month.

2 An executive travelling from London to Brussels has the choice of flying from London Heathrow or travelling on Eurostar from London Waterloo. The cost of the return journey would be

- air – £120 Economy, £372 Business Class
- Eurostar – £188 Standard Plus and £269 First Class.

a Under what circumstances do you think each travel option would be preferable? Use the information in Figure 6.1 to help you.

b Discuss as a group the circumstances under which an organisation is less interested in the price paid than in the executive's comfort – and vice versa!

3 What alternative method of travel could you suggest for Joanne Bretherton's visit to Eire if she was prepared to hire a car on arrival? What do you consider would be the advantages and disadvantages of both types of travel?

Discuss your answers and suggestions with your tutor.

Agreeing the final choice

Your boss's approval of the particular method of travel, the time of departure, the route, accommodation and other matters will all be required before you can make any reservations. A short trip, with few alternatives, can take just a few moments to agree with your boss and you can quickly proceed to finalising the arrangements. The situation is likely to be rather different if several executives will be involved, the trip will be long or complex, and it will involve several visits and appointments to be scheduled and linked to the overall travel plan. Indeed, requests to change appointment dates and times from customers and clients can be a major contributory factor to last-minute alterations. For that reason, many PAs try to ensure that all the visits to be made have been confirmed before the final travel arrangements are agreed. It is at this point that your comprehensive information sheet is invaluable, as you can help to inform any decisions by discussing the various options. Experienced PAs are apt to develop 'second sight' when it comes to thinking of possibilities that may be useful to note down, particularly after working for an executive for some time!

If the arrangements have been agreed in a meeting where various options have been discussed, it is sensible to spend a few minutes reviewing the complete list to make certain that you have noted all preferences and requirements accurately. A rapid way of marking the selected options is to highlight or underline each one with a red pen or with clear ticks and comments. This is much quicker in a discussion than trying to write out a neat list.

Making the bookings and reservations is discussed in Chapter 7.

Checking and compiling the documentation is covered in Chapter 8.

● Information and reference sources

Obtaining accurate and up-to-date information is crucial for good planning – and in the travel business there are a host of different organisations to

provide information and advice, as mentioned earlier. Your options usually include

- contacting a travel agent
- contacting a different type of travel organisation
- using a reference book or printed timetable
- using a computer network. — Uniform

It is sensible to compile a list of organisations that can provide useful information and to include both their telephone and fax numbers and their URLs (Unique Resource Locators) – the official term for the address line identifying them on the Internet. You can also sensibly keep an information file including timetables, fares and other reference material. However, this file *must* be kept up to date on a very regular basis, otherwise you will be in danger of giving wrong or misleading information.

Travel agents

Most people are familiar with the role of travel agents in booking a package holiday. They may be less familiar with the full range of business services that may be offered both by some of the larger travel agents and by those with special business travel divisions. These include:

- scheduled air and ferry reservations and tickets
- hotel reservations and voucher system
- instant travel information and booking confirmation (sometimes on a 24-hour basis)
- foreign exchange services
- global assistance for clients
- chauffeur-driven transport and parking at airports
- airport representation (sometimes known as 'meet and greet')
- airtaxi or charter bookings
- car hire
- passport and visa service
- provision of interpreters or guide service
- ticket delivery service
- mobile phone hire
- advice on VAT-reclaimable expenses
- group bookings service (for meetings and conferences abroad)

- travel insurance

- theatre tickets (in most major capitals of the world)

- advice on safety aspects in relation to the place being visited.

Some agencies will take a budget management role, and link their rates to the value of the travel portfolio they are managing for a company. An organisation with a £1 million travel budget would therefore pay less for its travel services than one with £50,000 worth of travel business a year. Many large organisations expect the travel agent to manage their travel requirements within a predetermined budget for the year and advise on cost savings that may be possible both overall and for each particular trip. In addition, the travel agent will use his or her knowledge, expertise and contacts to suggest appropriate travel and accommodation options.

The major advantages of using a travel agent, rather than trying to make the bookings yourself, are the obvious benefits of their experience and contacts in helping you to plan the trip. In addition, if anything goes wrong because they make a mistake or otherwise misinform you or your boss then your organisation will have a claim against them. This means that you are not personally responsible – providing, of course, you make sure that you obtain details in writing and pass on information promptly and accurately every time!

Travel organisations

Although a travel agent will provide a comprehensive service, there may be occasions when you need to contact other organisations directly – often for information on particular aspects of a business trip. Examples include the following types of information:

- **on travel** – airlines and airports, ferry and hovercraft companies, train operating companies, National Rail Enquiry Line, car hire companies, AA and/or RAC, Met centre (for weather forecasts)

- **on accommodation** – known/frequently used hotels in UK, central hotel chain booking numbers, hotel booking agencies

- **on travel insurance** – banks, travel agents, insurance companies, motoring organisations, such as the AA, RAC, Europ Assistance

- **on health** – travel agent, local doctor or health centre, the Department of Health, MASTA (the Medical Advisory Service for Travellers Abroad)

- **on money** – banks, travel agents, credit and charge card companies (eg American Express)

- **on passports and visas** – Passport Offices, travel agents, foreign embassies and consulates

- **on imports/exports** – HM Customs and Excise, Department of Trade and Industry, foreign embassies and consulates, London Chamber of Commerce and Industry

- **on countries** – tourist agencies, embassies and consulates, general reference books.

Reference books and timetables

It is always useful to have some basic reference books and leaflets to hand – as this saves you from having to make repeat telephone enquiries on the same subject. For example

- World flight information for all airlines is contained in the *ABC World Airways Guide*. In addition, you may keep a copy of the international timetables for your boss's preferred airline(s).

- Railtrack publish the GB Passenger Railway Timetable, which you can buy from W H Smith's for about £9, or by subscription from Railtrack in York. This contains all train timetables for Great Britain. In addition, train operating companies publish their own timetables in booklet form,

Information at your fingertips – courtesy of Royal Mail

An extremely useful addition to the PA's reference library is the Royal Mail International Business Travel Guide, compiled with the assistance of various tourist offices, embassies, consulates, airlines and other organisations. It provides a wealth of information, country by country, including details on business contact addresses, general geographical information, information on communications, import regulations, passport and visa requirements, money and currency, public holidays, travel (to and within each country), accommodation, business protocol and social conventions, climate and a brief political history. There are useful maps and information on time zones, religious beliefs, weather and health.

Details can be obtained from the Royal Mail Sales Centre on 23345 950 950. Ask your tutor to lobby your College library to obtain at least one copy for your group's reference purposes.

and a small card is obtainable from mainline stations for InterCity services, which is useful for a traveller to carry for reference.

- Ferry companies issue timetables and booklets containing information on their services.

- The *AA* and *RAC Handbook* and *Hotels and Restaurants in Great Britain* provide information for those requiring accommodation in the UK. The former also include maps and useful information for planning routes, including journey distances.

- The *World Travel Guide* and the *Royal Mail International Business Travel Guide* give extremely useful information on different countries (see previous page).

- Various magazines and other publications are produced specifically for the travel trade or for business executives who frequently travel on business, such as *Business Travel World*, *Business Traveller* and *Executive Travel* (all published monthly).

- Thomas Cook sell a wide range of travel guides and reference books, including European rail timetables and driving guides for different countries, maps and the *International Air Travel Handbook* – all of which can be obtaining from Thomas Cook Publishing, PO Box 227, Thorpe Wood, Peterborough PE3 6PU, telephone 01733–503571/2.

Computer networks

At one time, the only computer links available for travel were those installed by travel agents, who each use a computer reservations system (CRS). These are specialist computer networks such as Galileo, Sabre, Worldspan and Socrates which link travel agents to airlines, hotels and rail companies, enabling them to make on-line bookings and reservations. In your own office, you would have been restricted to a range of reference books and printed timetables. Today, however, many PAs can access a wide variety of information through their computers, undertake travel planning with the help of a CD-ROM and both find information and make bookings, in some cases, through the Internet.

Travel is one area where the Internet comes into its own – and if you regularly use key travel sites it is sensible to bookmark them so that you can return to them again and again for current information. To take one example of the usefulness of an Internet link, consider the following possibilities if you regularly book rail travel for your boss.

- Railtrack operates a computerised timetable system on its site (http://www.railtrack.co.uk/travel/).

- Many train operating companies have their own sites giving details of their services and fares, such as Midland (http://mml.rail.co.uk/).

- A list of rail operating companies can be obtained by accessing any of the following sites (http://www.rail.co.uk/, http://crowsnest.co.uk/north/train/htm and http://geocities.com/TheTropics/Shores/4745/. However, the easiest way to find your way around is through the rail regulator's site at http://open.gov.uk/orr/links.htm – which has links to all the main railway information sites.

- There is a European Railway Server called Mercurio which can be accessed via Crowsnest (above).

- Le Shuttle can be accessed on http://www.le-shuttle.com/ and Eurostar is also accessible from this site or directly on http://eurostar.com.

- The latest innovation is a real-time train information page, being piloted by North West Trains. This can be accessed direct (http://nwt.rail.co.uk) or via the Crowsnest site (see above). You choose the station you want to check and current train departures are listed – with notes as to whether they are expected to leave on time or, if not, how long the delay will be. Even though only departures are listed and not arrivals, this could still be useful if you were meeting someone and wished to check that the train departed on time from an earlier station (and should, therefore, arrive on time).

The best way to find your way around the Internet is through a central information site with links to other travel sites. A very useful site is Travel World, which has direct links to all the European airlines, ferry operators,

hotel chains and other organisations of interest to those involved in organising travel from Europe, on http://travel.world.co.uk/index.htm. Another useful general site is http://city.net/countries – where you can find useful information on specific countries or move to business travel interests pages, which provide a number of useful links as well as business travel news. There is also a wide variety of information on hotel accommodation worldwide (see Chapter 7, page 273).

A range of other relevant travel information can be accessed through other sites – two of which are linked to the main government site on http:/open.gov.uk. The Department of Health provides useful information on health risks abroad as well as health advice for travellers. The Foreign Office gives updates on areas you are not advised to visit and other issues of topical interest to business travellers (see page 236).

Using a search engine

The range of travel information on the Internet is so vast that there is a great danger you will be distracted from your enquiry to read dozens of pages of extremely interesting but only marginally relevant information! The other frustration you may sometimes encounter is not being able to find the exact type of information you require. The best way to find out what is available on the Internet is to use a search engine – such as Alta Vista, Yahoo or Infoseek – which enables you to key in the information you require. Internet sites are then listed in order of likely usefulness. The problem for new users is defining their requests and using the search engine effectively – to avoid being drowned by lists of thousands of irrelevant sites!

Start by finding your way around *one* search engine and read the help files carefully. Some allow you to specify that you are only looking for English language documents. Others enable you to put names or phrases in inverted commas so that the words are searched for together, rather than separately (such as 'New South Wales'). Others enable you to add plus and minus signs to refine your requirements.

Try to be as precise as possible when framing your request – a general phrase such as 'health abroad' will give millions of sources, whereas 'vaccinations for Japan' would give a much more specific result. Often the letters 'UK' help to narrow the search. Note that many search engines are 'case sensitive' – so if you are looking for a specific place name do remember to include an initial capital. Grammar is normally irrelevant – you should put the most important word first. Finally, don't be put off by the number of suggestions made – usually only the first 20 or so will be of any use.

If you have a computer with a CD-ROM drive then you can undertake travel planning on your pc. The AA issues route planners called *AA Milemaster* in disk or CD-ROM format to cover Britain, Britain and Ireland, and Britain and Europe. In addition they produce an *AA Streetmaster* for London. The value of planning on computer is that recommended routes are suggested, and driving times between places are given together with the costs. A print-out can be obtained for the driver to take on the journey. PAs wanting to undertake flight planning on pc may subscribe to the Official Airline Guide's FlightDisk, issued by Reed Travel Group, or use a program called TravelPlan, sold through Practical Concepts at Croydon. Whereas the first gives flight information only, the latter provides a schedule of both air and rail travel plus information on hotels in Europe, and foreign currency. The information is updated monthly. You simply select the combination you want and the software will provide a flight timetable, hotel suggestions, costs and estimated journey times.

✓ Check it yourself

1 The best way to find out about the Internet is to use it! However, simply accessing pages at random is not normally as productive as having a specific brief. As a group, either on your own or in pairs, try to find out the following information:

   a services provided by *at least two* travel agents on the Net
   b information given by one UK airline – eg British Airways, British Midland or Virgin
   c current rates for car hire and different types of cars that may be hired in the US or Germany
   d names of ferry and hovercraft companies and the routes they operate
   e information on *at least three* international hotel chains
   f the countries the Foreign Office recommends should *not* be visited at the present time and other useful information for travellers on this site
   g details of the passport/visa requirements for Tokyo, and the usual business hours and holiday dates in Japan
   h suitable train times for an executive travelling tomorrow morning from Oxford to London for a meeting at 10 am
   i as much as you can about form E111
   j the type of assistance and information for travellers given by embassies and consulates. The best site to try is that belonging to the US embassy – find the URL yourself by using a search engine!

   Prepare a brief, clear summary of your information – using appropriate headings – for the rest of the group.

2 Refresh your memory about Joanne Bretherton's trip to Eire by looking back to question 2, page 210.

a State THREE sources of information you could use to find out travel information on car ferries to Dublin.

b Explain how you could find a suitable hotel in Dublin *without* asking a travel agent to help.

c Visit a local travel agent yourself and obtain a brochure which gives details of a city break to Dublin. Select one that might be appropriate for Joanne if she is prepared to fly to Dublin. Under what circumstances do you think choosing this type of booking might be cost effective for a business person – and easier to arrange for the PA?

• Travel documentation

Virtually all business trips require the collation and checking of various types of documents – and, in some cases, their production.

Passports

All UK nationals travelling outside the United Kingdom need a valid passport – which lasts for ten years. Business travellers who regularly go abroad can obtain a jumbo version (48 pages) instead of the normal 32-page passport. Application forms can be obtained from the Post Office or many travel agents, as well as from passport offices in London, Liverpool, Glasgow, Peterborough, Belfast and Newport (Gwent).

It is important that you make a note of when your boss's passport is due for renewal – and allow sufficient time, particularly during the spring and summer months. In an emergency, a new or replacement passport can be obtained immediately by visiting the local Passport Agency. However, to avoid this situation (and to cope with renewal in general) many executives hold two passports so they can travel on one whilst the other is being renewed. This has an additional benefit, as visa stamps for certain countries prevent the bearer from being admitted to some other countries. Those containing an Israeli stamp, for instance, cannot be used in most Arab countries. Having two passports means that this situation can be avoided.

It is sensible to keep a note of the number of your boss's passport and the date and place of issue, and to register the details with a 'card safe' company. If the passport is lost or stolen in the UK you should notify the card safe company, the police and the passport office. If it is missing abroad then your boss should notify the police and contact the nearest British

Embassy or Consulate, who will arrange for the necessary emergency travel documents to be issued for the return journey.

Visas

For entry into certain countries a visa or permit is needed. Usually these are just a formality and are issued by the embassy or consulate of the country concerned. Either the staff there or your travel agent will give you details of the cost, how to apply, the length of time for which the visa is valid and how long it usually takes for one to be issued. Again, in an emergency, it is possible to apply in person.

Normally, obtaining a visa is done for you by your travel agent. You hand over the passport of the visitor and a page is stamped which states the name of the country, type of visa issued and the date of expiry. Again, if your boss is a frequent visitor to countries where visas are essential it is important that you keep a note of the expiry date of each so that you reduce the number of possible emergencies to a minimum!

Insurance

Most organisations where executives are frequent travellers have annual insurance policies to cover the risks of travel. These are available from banks, insurance brokers, building societies and insurance companies – as well as from travel agents. Executives travelling by air or rail will only need **personal** cover. Anyone driving abroad would have to ensure that they also possess valid **vehicle** cover which may not be available on a standard car insurance policy.

Personal cover

A good insurance policy for business travellers will include cover against all of the following.

- **Medical expenses and emergencies** up to £250,000 in Europe and £1 million in the rest of the world. This will include medical treatment (including hospitalisation), a special air ambulance home, an ambulance to and from the airport in both countries and, in many cases, access to a 24-hour emergency helpline.

- **Personal liability** up to £2 million, to cover accidental injury to people or property.

- **Cancellation or early return** insurance should cover the full cost of the trip. Acceptable reasons should include illness or death of self or business associate/fellow traveller, redundancy, disasters at home/work (eg fire) and jury service.

- **Belongings and luggage** insurance for personal items and company equipment or samples taken abroad. The policy should also give compensation so that essential items can be replaced if luggage is delayed en route.

- **Money** – cover should be for travellers' cheques, tickets and passport as well as for cash.

- **Delayed departure** – if the delay is more than 24 hours, through bad weather, strikes or transport failure, then the full cost of the trip should be covered.

Other benefits can include cover for expenses incurred in obtaining a duplicate passport and for legal expenses. The best are 'nil excess' policies, which means the full amount of any claim will be paid, without any deduction.

Vehicle cover

Most travel insurance policies do *not* cover driving a vehicle abroad. Hire car companies issue their own policies (see page 240). People taking their own cars cannot assume that their normal vehicle insurance will cover driving abroad and the type of risks they may face. In this case, cover should be obtained for:

- **pre-departure protection** – if the vehicle is stolen or involved in an accident immediately prior to departure, this cover ensures that a replacement vehicle is provided

- **roadside assistance and recovery** – to help in the case of an emergency breakdown

- **vehicle out of use** – to provide a substitute vehicle or additional hotel expenses if the owner's car is not repairable in the next 24 hours

- **repatriation of vehicle and passengers** – in the case of an unrepairable car this will be transported back to the UK; if a vehicle is stolen abroad or the driver is taken ill the costs of returning home by another means of transport are covered

- **emergency repairs** following a break-in or attempted theft

- **a Bail Bond in Spain** (see page 240).

A business person who regularly takes his or her vehicle abroad can obtain comprehensive cover, which includes personal as well as vehicle cover. This type of insurance is available from several sources, including specialist motoring organisations such as the AA, RAC and Europ Assistance. An insurance broker would also be able to advise you.

The PA's guide to insurance

You should note that it is not simply a case of taking out insurance and then forgetting all about it! Both you and your boss need to be aware of the correct procedure to be followed in case of a claim – otherwise you may find that it is invalid. The main points to note are as follows.

- Ideally your boss should take the insurance document on the trip. Otherwise photocopy the policy and include it in the set of travel documents for the trip plus the number of the 24-hour helpline, if there is one.

- You should both be aware of the exclusion clauses – particularly the limited amounts for any individual valuables and the type of items that can be classed as valuables.

- If your boss has a charge card or gold card, then business travel insurance may be included automatically. However, it is important to check that the cover is sufficient, particularly for visits outside the EU.

- If the trip has to be cancelled and you intend to make a claim, your travel agent must issue you with a cancellation invoice. In addition, you will need to provide written proof as to the reason for the cancellation.

- All bills and receipts for additional travel, medical and accommodation costs relating to a claim must be kept safely.

- Make sure your boss is aware which events which must be reported to the police before a claim can be made. He or she will require written confirmation that this report was made.

- In some cases, medical treatment cannot be started until specific agreement is given – in this case there will be an emergency number to ring. Make sure you copy this clearly and put it in an obvious place in the file.

- If baggage is lost your boss must complete a Property Irregularity Report immediately, which is obtainable from the airline, ferry or train company.

Check it yourself

As a group, obtain information on travel insurance from local banks, insurance companies and/or travel agents. Then check the terms of each policy in the following circumstances.

1 You have a boss who is pregnant. She wants to attend a conference in New York and her baby is due in 10 weeks' time.

2 Your boss loses his passport.

3 The taxi taking your boss to the airport breaks down and she misses her flight.

4 Your boss has his laptop computer stolen at the airport.

- Make sure that your insurers are aware of any ongoing medical condition affecting the health of a business traveller for whom they are providing cover, in case this will mean loss of cover in certain circumstances.

Itineraries

An itinerary is the main document you will prepare once all the bookings have been made and confirmed. It is a brief summary of all the arrangements made, in strict date and time order. In some cases you may find that your boss requires two itineraries:

a a brief summary, preferably on a card, which can be kept in a pocket for ease of reference – alternatively, staple or clip this itinerary to the front of the travel folder

b a longer document including details of events, functions being attended, contact names, relevant documents and other notes for the traveller.

Both types of itineraries are covered in full in Chapter 8.

Other documentation

This is likely to include:

- tickets for the trip
- current vaccination certificates (which should be attached to the back cover of the passport with an elastic band)
- letters and faxes of confirmation for hotels and car hire
- reports, presentation materials and other business documents relevant to the visit
- names, addresses and telephone numbers of emergency contacts, alternative hotels, the British Embassy or Consulate
- list of travellers' cheques and currency receipt plus emergency numbers for the credit card and travellers' cheque companies.

The collation and checking of this information prior to the trip is covered in Chapter 8.

● Health and safety

There are health risks associated with any type of travel to foreign places, although the level and type of risk can vary considerably. Obviously, travelling to countries such as Australia, the United States and France is less hazardous than to third world countries where there may be poor sanitation and a much greater risk of disease.

Large organisations often insist that frequent travellers have regular health checks with the company doctor. Anyone who is travelling can visit their own doctor for information and advice. However, many organisations, such as the World Health Organisation and the Department of Health issue guidelines for travellers and many organisations – and some innovative GP practices – run their own travel clinics. There are several British Airways Travel Clinics around the UK, and the Hospital for Tropical Diseases and Trailfinders run travel clinics in London. MASTA (the Medical Advisory Service for Travellers Abroad) operates a 24-hour travellers' healthline. Executives or PAs can telephone 0891 224100 with details of the trip and receive a specialist report for their particular destination(s). Specialist advice can also be obtained from the Malaria Information Line on 0891 600350. Ideally, all executives should be briefed beforehand on any health dangers endemic to the area they are visiting, with the overall aim that prevention is better than cure.

Vaccinations

Illness abroad can cause havoc to an important schedule, distress to the person concerned and considerable worry for relatives. Nearly 2000 people return to the UK each year with malaria, while others contract diseases such as hepatitis, typhoid and even AIDS. Vaccinations are either required by law in certain countries before entry or recommended by the World Health Organisation. In other situations, vaccinations may be advisable in particular circumstances. Much depends upon the individual traveller, his or her basic state of health and current immunity, the length and type of travel and the time available. However, all travellers are recommended to be immunised against diphtheria, polio and tetanus as a routine precaution. In most cases vaccinations must be undertaken several weeks before travel in order to be effective and, in the case of frequent travellers, must be kept up to date for immunity to continue. Information on the requirements for any country should be readily obtainable from your doctor or local health centre. Alternatively, contact the Department of Health, your travel agent, the embassy or consulate of the country concerned or any of the specialist organisations mentioned above.

The EU and E111

Visitors within the European Union obtain free or reduced-cost medical treatment in an emergency, but must carry with them a form E111 to prove that they are entitled to this service. You should note that an E111 is only issued to UK residents.

The application form can be obtained from any main post office. It is contained in an excellent booklet issued by the Department of Health entitled *Health Advice for Travellers*. The form must be completed with the traveller's details, signed and taken to the post office to be stamped. It should then be fastened inside a passport (with any vaccination forms). The form must be made available if medical attention is required. If, as sometimes happens, a charge is levied for medical assistance within the EU and the person concerned is unable to obtain a refund whilst abroad, a copy of the E111 and the medical receipts must be sent to the Overseas Benefits Directorate in Newcastle-upon-Tyne for repayment to be made.

You should note that an E111 is valid indefinitely; therefore, once your boss has obtained one there is no need for you to worry about a replacement unless it is mislaid or retained by someone abroad giving medical help.

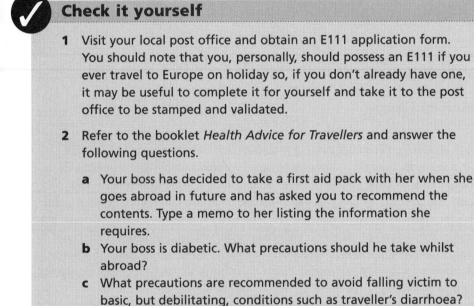

✓ Check it yourself

1   Visit your local post office and obtain an E111 application form. You should note that you, personally, should possess an E111 if you ever travel to Europe on holiday so, if you don't already have one, it may be useful to complete it for yourself and take it to the post office to be stamped and validated.

2   Refer to the booklet *Health Advice for Travellers* and answer the following questions.

   a   Your boss has decided to take a first aid pack with her when she goes abroad in future and has asked you to recommend the contents. Type a memo to her listing the information she requires.

   b   Your boss is diabetic. What precautions should he take whilst abroad?

   c   What precautions are recommended to avoid falling victim to basic, but debilitating, conditions such as traveller's diarrhoea?

   d   Your boss is travelling to Zaire and will need a vaccination against yellow fever. He has heard that this cannot be obtained from his own doctor. Is this true? If so, what arrangements would you make?

   e   What recommendations are made in relation to health insurance for visitors to countries bordering the EU, and why? (Note that health insurance was covered on page 222.)

● Currency

All travellers abroad need money in one form or another to pay for routine expenses. Even if the executive holds a company credit card, cash will be needed for day-to-day requirements, such as a cup of coffee or to tip a hotel porter or taxi driver. Generally, however, the rule should be to keep cash to a minimum in case of loss or theft. Alternatives to cash include Eurocheques, travellers' cheques and credit cards. A survey by American Express in 1997 showed that travellers' cheques accounted for 37 per cent of overseas

spending, credit cards for 33 per cent, local currency for 24 per cent and Eurocheques for 6 per cent.

Foreign currency

Foreign currency can be obtained from a bank or a travel agent with a foreign exchange facility. In many organisations the company's Finance department will organise this centrally and obtain your requirements from the bank. In this case you will have to complete a form and specify the amount required. It is usually much easier to name the amount you need in sterling – but it is important to be aware of the exchange rate when you are ordering (see below) as this will determine the amount of foreign currency received. Do allow sufficient time for your order to be processed, particularly if you need an unusual currency which your bank or travel agent is unlikely to keep in stock.

Two other points should be noted. First, some countries will not permit their currency to be taken out of the country, such as Morocco or Tunisia. In this case your boss will have to obtain any foreign currency required at the airport or hotel, as it is not obtainable in the UK. Secondly, when currency is received you will find that only notes are issued. If these are of a large denomination it can be difficult for your executive to cope with small items (and tips) on arrival. One solution used by many companies and PAs is to ask executives to hand in small change on their return and to keep this, stored by currency, for issuing to executives going to the same country at a later date.

Travellers' cheques

Travellers' cheques are available from banks in sterling, dollars and several other currencies. Sterling and dollars are the most widely used as these are readily acceptable in most countries abroad, whereas specific currency cheques may not be. It is sensible to obtain cheques for a variety of denominations (eg £100, £50 and £20), so that the traveller requiring cash can easily vary the amount and does not need to cash more than is necessary. In theory, on receipt of the cheques the traveller should sign each one in view of the bank cashier. In practice, most banks do not insist on this. However, you should ensure that the cheques are signed before the traveller leaves and a separate note is kept of the number and value of each cheque in case of loss or theft. When the cheques are cashed, the holder must produce his or her passport and sign the cheque again in the space indicated. If the cheques are lost or stolen a refund can be obtained – virtually immediately if there is a 'link' bank in the vicinity. Any unused cheques can be retained for future use but only by the person to whom they were issued.

A major disadvantage with travellers' cheques is that, in many countries, it is difficult to obtain currency on public holidays and weekends when the banks are closed. In this situation it will help your executive if you provide a brief list of the currency regulations relating to the country being visited, together with local banking hours and notes on any public holidays that take place during the trip.

Eurocheques

Eurocheques are only used in European and Mediterranean countries, and the holder must also possess a Eurocheque card which guarantees the cheques – up to £100 or more. If the holder also has a Personal Identity Number, the card can also be used to obtain currency from cash dispensers displaying the red and blue EU logo, and information on these can be obtained from your bank. It normally takes up to ten days to obtain a Eurocheque book and card and, as commission is payable on all cheques issued, this method is rapidly declining in popularity in favour of credit and debit cards.

Credit cards, charge cards and debit cards

Taking 'plastic' abroad has long been the most popular choice with business travellers – and is certainly the most economic. Today, most holidaymakers prefer this method – a survey by American Express showed that UK visitors abroad in 1996 made 82 million 'plastic' transactions – double the 1991 figure. Credit cards and charge cards made up the majority of the transactions, with debit cards rapidly rising in popularity as a method of immediately obtaining local currency from cash machines at a much cheaper rate than with a credit card (where the borrower is charged interest from the day of the transaction).

The main credit cards in use are Mastercard and Visa, and both usually offer better rates of exchange than the local tourist rate. The main problem for business travellers is likely to be the credit limit, especially in countries such as the USA where hotels protect themselves by asking for the card on arrival and then process it for a large amount in case the guest runs up a tremendous bill or causes any damage. The charge is adjusted to the correct amount on departure, but in the meantime the card may be virtually unusable. For that reason most business travellers take two cards with them, so that more credit is always available, or supplement their credit card with a charge card.

The most well-known charge cards are American Express (Amex) and Diners Club. A charge card differs from a credit card in that the full amount must be paid at the end of a pre-set period (between 45 and 60 days) or a late payment penalty is charged. There is no pre-set spending limit so a charge card is ideal for an executive who may have to extend his or her trip at the last minute and purchase additional air tickets and accommodation. Corporate cards can be purchased and issued under the name of the company, which receives a breakdown account for each separate card so that expenses can be checked.

Debit cards are carried by many individuals and are often used to pay for goods (rather than writing a cheque) as well as to obtain cash in automatic teller machines (ATMs). The international network of ATMs is extending each year – so that you could use your debit card to obtain local currency in places as diverse as Swindon and Sydney, Manchester and Montreal.

The next step? Electronic travellers' cheques

Many authorities predict that the next payment option to become available will be an electronic cash card carrying a chip denoting the amount of cash with which it has been credited. The card and a PIN number are obtained from the issuing bank, which programs the card with the required amount (between £100 and £5000). Every time the card is processed at an ATM for cash, the amount on the chip decreases. When the money has run out, the card is thrown away.

In the meantime, if your boss runs out of money abroad or has his or her trip extended in an emergency, it is useful to know the options available. Most banks will send money express to their 'link' bank in any of the major capitals abroad. A new alternative, offered by Thomas Cook, is the MoneyGram. You simply visit your local Thomas Cook shop with some identification, complete a form and pay a small fee. You will be given a reference number to pass on to your executive who simply quotes this at the local MoneyGram agency, proves his or her identity and completes a receipt form. This method is both cheaper and faster than using the banking system – as well as being available at a wider range of destinations.

However, there are still many areas of the world where ATMs may be non-existent, and plastic cards not widely acceptable. It is for this reason that a range of payment options is still recommended for most travellers.

As a PA it is sensible to keep a list of the numbers of any cards your executive regularly takes abroad – in case they are lost or stolen – together with the contact number for reporting the problem. Most executives take advantage of the services of a card protection agency with which all the cards are registered.

You should note the expiry date of each card and check that they are unlikely to expire during a long visit abroad. If they are, you can contact the card company to ask them to expedite the replacement card before the trip.

The cost of foreign currency

All banks, travel agents and other foreign exchange dealers usually charge a commission for exchanging money or issuing travellers' cheques. In many cases there is a set fee to pay regardless of the amount changed. In this case it is better to buy in bulk for a few trips and to keep spare funds in the office safe until they are required. It is useful to check the amount you will be charged and to shop around for an economical source. It is certainly unwise to buy currency at an airport or train station, where the charges are normally very high. You should note that if your boss overestimates the amount required and you need to change it back into sterling you will also pay a second fee. For that reason it is better to err on the side of conservatism – particularly if cash funds will be supplemented with travellers' cheques and plastic.

The other important factor to bear in mind when ordering currency is the exchange rate. This is the rate at which you will convert sterling into foreign currency. In 1996, the pound was weak and UK travellers abroad received much less foreign currency per £1 spent than in 1997, when the pound had strengthened. A traveller to France, for example, would have obtained about 7.5 francs for each pound in 1996, but 9.25 francs in 1997. This may not seem very much of a difference, until you multiply it by 100 and examine the difference between 750 francs and 925 francs – which is quite considerable!

Remember to consider the buying power of the pound when you are deciding on the amount to exchange. In 1996, had your boss been visiting Paris and asked for £300 in currency you would have received 2250 francs. In 1997 you would have received 2775. On the first occasion he might have been short of cash, on the second he might have received too much – and yet you requested the same amount each time!

As a point of note, credit card transactions are determined by the money market exchange rate and not by tourist rates. Because of this, items bought using them are normally a better buy.

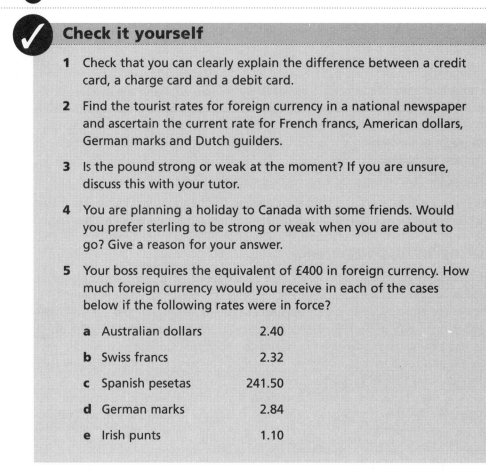

● Custom and excise requirements

Many business travellers take more than paperwork with them when they travel abroad on business. They may take other personal items, such as a laptop computer, and commercial goods, such as samples of the goods they wish to show a customer or client. In these circumstances, an executive is exporting the items out of the UK on departure, importing them into another country on arrival, and re-exporting them on the return home to finally re-import them into this country.

Most people are well aware that there are restrictions on goods that can be brought into a country – and that these vary from one country to another. If you go abroad on holiday, you will (or should!) know that there are goods you are prohibited from bringing back to Britain (such as drugs, firearms and offensive weapons) and goods that are restricted in quantity, such as tobacco, alcohol, perfume and gifts/souvenirs. You will also be aware that the import of such items is closely monitored by customs officials. Prohibited goods are clearly not allowed. Goods outside the customs allowance, or imported for resale, require the payment of customs duty before they can be legally brought into the country.

If your boss wishes to take a commercial item abroad, therefore, it is important to check the import regulations that apply in the country being visited. If he or she intends to bring goods back into the UK, regulations also apply. Most import controls within European Union member countries were abolished when the Single European Market was established on 1 January 1992, but this does not mean that all goods, even within the EU, are acceptable. Some goods will still be restricted and will require a licence.

The ATA Carnet system

To facilitate the movement of commercial goods and samples around the world, most countries have procedures allowing for their temporary import – otherwise the situation would be chaotic every time a band played abroad (and needed to import its instruments), when a painting was displayed in a foreign gallery or trade goods were shown in an exhibition abroad! Such importations are generally allowed for up to twelve months and are covered by the ATA Carnet system. (Carnet is a French word, so don't pronounce the 't' – say 'carnay'.) This system was agreed by international convention to reduce the obstacles faced by businesses through the different customs regulations applied in different countries. Today approximately fifty countries in Europe, North America, Asia and Africa are members of the Convention. The initials 'ATA' have been derived from the French/English words 'Admission Temporaire/Temporary Admission'.

Under the ATA Carnet system the exporter obtains one document (called a carnet) which covers all the merchandise taken abroad during the next year – after which time the carnet must be renewed. The goods covered by the carnet do not have to be declared to customs at the time of departure, and are allowed entry into a country without attracting any VAT or customs duty. The type of goods covered can be both personal and professional items, including commercial samples and professional equipment as well as ordinary goods such as computers, cameras, video equipment and cars. The main types of goods *not* covered by the scheme are consumable goods (such as food and agricultural products) and disposable items.

In the UK, ATA Carnets are obtained from the London Chamber of Commerce and Industry, 69 Cannon Street, London EC4N 5AB. A general list of items to be covered must be prepared in advance and an application form for the appropriate type of goods completed. A security deposit is required (usually 40 per cent of the value of the merchandise) in case there are any customs claims if the carnet is used improperly (eg to cover goods not listed). A processing fee is also charged for issuing the carnet. Normally, applications should be made at least seven days before, but it is possible to pay a higher charge to obtain one quickly in an emergency.

Other rules and regulations

Goods being exported for sale cannot be covered by the carnet system and, in this case, it is important to check the import regulations that apply for each particular country. A brief explanation is given in many reference books – such as the *Royal Mail International Business Travel Guide* – and further details can be obtained from the Department of Trade and Industry or from the embassy or consulate of the country concerned. For goods being brought into this country, you can obtain help and advice from HM Customs and Excise offices, although most organisations regularly importing goods will use the services of a specialist import/export house or employ someone who is expert in this area.

Check it yourself

1   Figure 6.4 shows the member countries of the ATA Carnet system.

Countries accepting ATA Carnets

Algeria	Hong Kong	New Zealand
Australia	Hungary	Norway
Austria	Iceland	Poland
Belgium/Luxembourg	India	Portugal
Bulgaria	Ireland	Romania
Canada	Israel	Senegal
Cyprus	Italy	Singapore
Czech Republic	Ivory Coast	South Africa
Denmark	Japan	Spain
Finland	Korea	Sweden
France	Malaysia	Switzerland
Germany	Malta	Turkey
Gibraltar	Mauritius	United Kingdom
Greece	Netherlands	

Figure 6.4   Member countries of the ATA Carnet system

a   Identify those that are currently members of the European Union and those that are not.

b   Can you name four countries not on the list?

c   As a group, how well can you describe the geographical location of each country on the list *and* the other countries you have named? In each case where you are not sure, check your assumptions by referring to a good atlas!

2 Richard Evans has decided to take some commercial samples with him when he visits Australia. Below is a brief description of the main import regulations for this country. Summarise the relevant information he would need in this situation from the details in Figure 6.5 and the information you have just read about ATA Carnets, in the form of a brief memo to him. Keep a copy of the memo safely – you will need to include it in the travel file you start for Richard Evans in the next chapter.

Australia – import regulations

There are limits on the quantities (ie quotas) of four types of goods which can be imported into Australia – textiles, clothing and footwear; motor vehicles; goods produced by certain countries which belong to the South Pacific Forum; and goods from developing countries. Only the first two categories apply to goods exported from the UK. The textile restrictions, which are being gradually relaxed, were introduced as part of the Australian government's policy to protect its native producers, and they cover many items of clothing, footwear and woven fabrics. Quotas on motor vehicles apply only to cars less than five years old.

There are no requirements for exporters to complete special documentation, as Australian customs officials will accept normal invoices, bills of lading or a receipt. Samples and professional equipment may be imported on a temporary basis under the ATA Carnet scheme.

Figure 6.5 Main import regulations applying in Australia

● Other considerations

Business executives who travel regularly on a worldwide basis often revisit the same countries over and over again. They therefore become familiar with the local culture and environment, which may be considerably different from that in Britain. For instance, in some countries nodding the head means 'no' whereas shaking the head means 'yes'; you would be snubbing your host if you wouldn't accept coffee, sweets or even a cigarette when they are offered; and a visitor may insult people deeply by offering a tip or even be jailed for photographing public buildings! Some phrases can easily be misunderstood – even in English-speaking countries – and some words differ. It is well known that Americans call a flat an apartment and a puncture a flat! Hiring a car in America can result in several terms being used which are normally unfamiliar to British people.

Business clothes and business conventions also vary from one place to another and in many countries of the world female executives have to be particularly careful about the clothes they wear. In some areas, of course, it would still not be acceptable for a female to be involved in business negotiations. In many areas, too, the climate is very different from in the UK, which affects the choice of clothes, and there are dry seasons and rainy seasons to consider. A useful hint is to check the humidity as well as the temperature/rainfall averages for a country for a particular time of the year.

When planning a business trip it is also sensible to be aware of forthcoming public holidays in the area, when all business organisations would be closed. It is also often vital to check the current 'safety status' of many countries, particularly those that are known troublespots, such as Columbia and many east African countries, or where there have been recent reports of unrest, terrorist attacks or political strife.

If an executive regularly visits an area and knows it well, then such issues are usually less of a problem. The same applies if you work for an organisation with a network of overseas offices or agents from whom you can obtain relevant information. Otherwise, you will need to research the details yourself – either by using a good reference book, by ringing the embassy or consulate of the country concerned in London, or by accessing an appropriate Internet site.

Check it yourself

1 Use an appropriate reference book, eg *Royal Mail International Business Travel Guide,* and find out

   a the business and social customs
   b the climate
   c the public holidays

   for the five countries listed below:

     Japan, Iceland, Indonesia, Saudi Arabia, Uganda.

2 Access the web site http://city.net/countries and find out the same information for three countries of your own choosing.

3 Access the web site at the Foreign Office on http://www.fco.gov.uk/ to check their 'Do's and don'ts' checklist for another three countries of your own choosing. Alternatively, check BBC Ceefax from page 564 onwards or ring the Foreign Office on 0171–238 4503 for information on a particular country. At the same time, find out the names of three countries to which travel is not recommended at the present time.

4 Use any form of research for one country (to be chosen by yourself or your tutor) and find out as much as you can which would be helpful to your boss, assuming he or she has never been to the country before. Try to select a country with a very different culture from Britain's. Prepare the information in a form of a short fact sheet with appropriate headings.

Review quiz

1 Identify FOUR factors that would influence the method of travel you chose for an executive.

2 List TWO advantages and TWO disadvantages of travelling by train (Eurostar) to Europe rather than by air.

3 State FOUR services a travel agent would provide.

4 Identify FOUR reference sources you would use when planning a business trip within the UK.

5 Describe briefly the type of information available on the Internet which assists travel planning.

6 What is a visa? Explain how you would obtain one for an executive.

7 Identify FIVE risks associated with travelling abroad for which you would arrange insurance cover.

8 Identify SIX items that should be included in a first aid pack for foreign travel.

9 What is an E111? Describe how you would obtain one for your boss.

10 What is a Visa card? Why is one useful for business travellers abroad?

11 Briefly explain why you would need to take the exchange rate into account when ordering foreign currency.

12 Briefly explain the procedure to be followed if your boss wished to take commercial samples abroad on a regular basis.

The previous chapter should have given you an indication of the range of issues you need to consider when planning travel. However, before any reservations can be made, it is important to understand some of the terms used in relation to the various types of travel and accommodation options and to gain a greater appreciation of how some of these systems operate. This enables you to think through the implications of the arrangements you are making – and any alternatives you may be offered. Unfortunately for the unwary, there are several traps involved in making travel arrangements. No executive would be pleased to find that no car was available on arrival because the wrong day had been given to the car hire company (very easy to do, if you misread an international timetable!), that no-one knew which terminal he was in or that his connecting flight from Heathrow departs from Gatwick airport! Neither do you want to show your ignorance to your travel agent by trying to make illegal bookings (such as connecting flights without taking account of the minimum connection times).

This chapter therefore looks at all the different methods of travel in more detail and gives you all the information you need to avoid making any errors that would be the talk of the organisation for months! In addition, you will gain useful practice in finding information on travel yourself and making out clear information sheets. These will be related to the forthcoming trips:

a to Dublin by Joanne Bretherton
b to Australia by Richard Evans.

You could make a useful beginning now by starting two travel files, one for each trip, and clipping to the front of each the relevant checklists from Chapter 6 (pages 209–210).

● Travelling by road

Road transport for business people normally means

* using their own car or a company car

* hiring a car

* booking a taxi or a chauffeur-driven car.

Private or company car

For short trips within the UK, many executives prefer to take their own car as this gives them total flexibility in terms of departure and arrival times and stop-off points on the journey. In most cases, business organisations join (or check that anyone driving their vehicles is a member of) a motoring organisation, such as the RAC, AA or Green Flag, which not only provide a full breakdown and 'get-you-home' service but will also give information on driving abroad and route planning – both in the UK and in Europe.

Often an executive will use his or her car to drive to an airport and will park in one of the special secure parking areas. Spaces in these can be booked in advance. However, you must check whether any company car has to be returned for general use during a long trip, in which case your boss would need to be met at the airport on return.

In some organisations, particularly where executives travel to Europe with goods or need to move around freely, there may be a preference for travelling by car ferry and taking their own cars with them. Another alternative is Motorail, where both the car and the driver travel the main part of the journey by rail through Europe. In this case it is important to check that the car is insured for any damage incurred during the rail journey.

In all cases where someone intends to drive abroad, it is important to be aware of the regulations that apply, particularly in relation to using a British car abroad. Whilst the specific requirements vary from one country to another, in general most countries require that certain accessories are carried on or in the vehicle, ie

- an approved GB plate to be attached to the rear of the vehicle
- headlamps that point towards the nearside to avoid dazzling oncoming traffic – temporary converters are available that can be attached for a short trip, to save having to readjust the headlamps
- a spare set of headlamp bulbs
- a warning triangle – which must be displayed if the car breaks down
- a first aid kit
- a fire extinguisher.

The AA also recommends that the driver takes a spare clutch/accelerator cable as these are different for right-hand drive cars and obtaining a spare on the Continent can be difficult.

The documents that should be carried by the driver include:

- the driver's licence (in Spain an International Driving Permit is required)
- vehicle registration documents
- a copy of the insurance documents plus, preferably, a Green Card (sometimes called the international motor insurance card), which is recognised by the police and other officials abroad as denoting insurance cover

- a European accident statement (again obtainable from car insurers), which enables drivers to exchange facts after an accident without admitting liability

- a Bail Bond for travellers to Spain. This is required because the Spanish police can detain the driver after an accident unless it can be proved that any claim for damages will be met. Bail Bonds are available free of charge from most insurance companies. In the case of an accident the bond must be handed to the police.

Hiring a car

If the traveller does not own a car or is travelling to a country by rail or air, but wishes to travel around freely without the restrictions of taxis and public transport, then it is usual to hire a car. This is a particularly useful alternative abroad, especially if a left-hand drive car is appropriate. Note, however, that many car hire companies only accept a driver who is over the age of 21 (23 in some cases), has been driving on a full licence for at least a

Driving you to distraction!

Most people are aware that Britain is unusual in driving on the left-hand side of the road, and they expect to drive on the right in most other countries. However, they may be less prepared for other changes to their driving habits, such as reading signposts and speed limits in kilometres, giving way to cars coming from the right, being charged a fee to drive on a toll road, and on-the-spot speeding fines. In the US drivers can turn right on a red light. In Australia, motorway drivers have to become used to being overtaken on both sides!

It is easy for the uninformed to break the law. In Gibraltar, for instance, it is illegal to use full headlights at any time – even in the pitch dark. In Sweden, Norway, Denmark and the Czech Republic, dipped headlights must be used even during the day. In the Ukraine and Romania you can be arrested for driving a dirty car!

To help drivers abroad, information on basic driving regulations is given in many reference books (see page 217) or can be obtained from the tourist office, embassy or consulate for a particular country. Motoring organisations will also give advice – AA members can obtain information on motoring abroad by ringing 0990 500600, and can join the AA Five Star Europe scheme and receive a special information pack. Reputable car hire companies should issue a booklet on driving regulations applying in the relevant countries – which the driver should read carefully.

year (longer for some models of car) and has a clean driving licence – which must be produced, together with proof of identity, when the car is collected.

It is normally better to reserve the car before the trip, and make all the arrangements in the UK, particularly as many car hire companies operate on an international basis (such as Hertz and Avis). In other cases your travel agent can contact a broker who will negotiate the hire with a local company. Generally you have the choice of having the car delivered to and collected from the hotel or the airport. You will have to specify clearly the collection and delivery points – not all car hire companies allow for different ones.

It is important to make sure that you deal with a reputable company. In Britain check that the hire company is a member of the British Vehicle Renting and Leasing Association (BVRLA), whose members have to operate to a specific code of conduct. In addition, state that you require a relatively new vehicle with a low mileage. Check the preferred model with the hirer – and ask for details if you are offered an unfamiliar model (the names and types are often different abroad). The last thing you want is to hire the American equivalent of a Mini Metro for your MD who required a prestigious car to impress clients in California!

You will find that the standard hire charge usually includes unlimited mileage and basic insurance cover for passenger liability and third party risks. You will also be offered the opportunity to pay a premium for collision damage waiver (CDW). This covers the hire car in the case of an accident (although there may be an excess to pay, eg the first £100 of any repair costs). In the UK, CDW is usually included in the price, but it is worth checking. In Europe and elsewhere it is usually bought as an extra. Finally, your executive may be covered for personal accident insurance on his or her own policy if it also covers hiring a car. This is essential as it covers the driver in the case of injury, and it can be purchased from the car hire company.

Finally, business travellers driving in the US need to make sure that they are fully covered for any liability in the case of an accident. Many claims in the US are for huge amounts of money and normal insurance cover would not extend to this amount. Extra liability insurance can be arranged with some companies before travelling to the US, and in other cases it can be taken out with the US company when the car is collected.

Taxis and chauffeur-driven cars

The major differences between an ordinary taxi and a chauffeur-driven car are the type of vehicle and the level of service provided. A brief look through your local Yellow Pages should give you all the information you need to discern the difference! Some organisations have their own car pool to be used for taking people to the airport or train station, or as a 'meet and greet' service for executives and visitors. Otherwise, you need to find a local organisation that can provide a good, reliable service and knows the ropes about business travel. This includes:

- *never* being late for a pick-up at the airport or train station

- having clean, well-serviced vehicles with space for luggage

- employing smart drivers, preferably in a suit or uniform

- knowing that they should check with the airport or station that there are no delays before setting off to collect a client

- arriving in the right place and holding up a clear printed sign, preferably displaying the company name and logo and the person's name for ease of recognition. A small point to note is that, when important visitors arrive, it does not do anything for the company's image if their first sight is of a hastily written name, scribbled on a piece of old card!

Of course, it goes without saying that you will have given the driver all the information he or she needs to collect or meet your executive without difficulty. For the outward journey, the details required are the collection address, the destination and the time of collection. For inward journeys by air, more details are required, including name of airport, terminal number, airline, flight number, place of departure and estimated time of arrival – often termed ETA. Most arrivals halls have designated meeting points. For train arrivals you should state the name of the station, the starting point of the train (which may be different from where your executive boarded the train), the ETA and a location point, if possible. It is also sensible to give the person arriving the name and telephone number of the firm hired to meet them. If there are any misunderstandings or problems, it is then a simple matter to ask the information desk to page the driver – or even telephone the firm direct. This is particularly useful if the ETA is late at night or during the early hours of the morning.

Planning a route

The final aspect of car travel with which you are likely to be involved is route planning. Having the ability to work out the best route from A to B – via C and D if necessary – is useful for numerous reasons, not least in your personal life! In business, your boss may have to take a journey in an unfamiliar area of the country. In this situation good, clear directions are invaluable to a driver – especially when coping with unknown roads, heavy traffic and bad weather simultaneously. Knowing the route your boss is travelling means you can calculate the distance and also estimate the departure and arrival times. You should, of course, be capable of giving clear directions to any visitors driving to your place of work – and know the main roads nearby, the road numbers, nearest motorways and useful landmarks. Calculating distance is either a matter of referring to a mileage chart, or finding the places on a map (usually denoted by a red pointer) and working out the total.

Map reading is not difficult, particularly if you have a good road map. This must be up to date so that new ring roads and motorways are shown. For a

Metfax, Metweb or Metcall – the choice is yours

Checking the weather, not only in Britain but worldwide, is now a simple matter of picking up the phone, using the fax machine or switching on your computer! The Met Office has now introduced a new service, in operation 24 hours a day, 365 days a year, giving details of weather conditions and weather maps all over the world. You can also find out about traffic information at the same time.

MetCall commercial service information is available on 0374 505 177, with world forecasts available on 0336 411 211. Anyone with a fax machine can dial 0336 400 41 plus the area number on their fax machine for a regional five-day forecast. Other Metfax services include a national forecast and a regional forecast updated every three hours. On the Net, you can reach them on http://www.met-office.gov.uk.

city, a street guide is more useful, particularly one that clearly identifies one-way streets and parking areas. If you are a driver yourself you will appreciate that clear directions should include estimated distances, that routes should be focused on motorways and main (A) roads, and that junction numbers should be included when the driver must join or leave a motorway. You will also realise why it is better to give directions as a list of spaced points and not as continuous text – particularly if the driver is trying to glance at the page while stopped briefly at traffic lights!

Always allow extra time for travelling by car to allow for traffic hold-ups and other minor delays. It is better for the driver to have time to stop for a cup of coffee on a journey to an important customer, rather than be panicking behind the wheel with several miles still ahead and the appointment time already past. Finally, be prepared to allow for weather conditions and to check these on bad days. Both weather and traffic bulletins are regularly given on Ceefax and Oracle as well as on radio. Major road works are listed in many daily papers, and the Met Office has introduced a new service for giving weather reports (see above).

 Check it yourself

1 As a group, find out the specific driving regulations that apply to one particular country or one American state. If any member of the group (or the tutor) knows someone who is a member of the AA,

you can call 0900 500600 for information. Alternatively, ask a friendly local travel agent for information – preferably one that frequently arranges car hire abroad for organisations. A final option is to use a reference book or the Internet – although here you are likely to find that the guidance is very general, apart from certain areas in the United States which are well documented on the Net.

2 Write out a list of clear directions for someone visiting your college from a location about 50 miles away. Try to include the use of the nearest motorway network, if possible – together with junction numbers. Check the style and content of your directions with your tutor.

3 Using an up-to-date road map, prepare directions for your boss, who is driving from your company offices in Leeds first to visit a client in York and then to Hull before travelling to Lincoln where he will stay the night. For each leg of the journey, either find out or calculate the mileage. If your boss travels at an average of 40 mph, how long will each journey take? Check your answers with your tutor.

4 In the checklist you prepared for Joanne Bretherton's trip to Ireland on page 210, you should have noted that she required information on the route from Dublin to Galway and details of the mileage. Find out this information and make a note of the time to be allowed for the journey, assuming Joanne drives at an average speed of about 45 mph. Make clear notes giving this information and put them into the relevant travel file.

5 On his travel request form (Figure 6.2), Richard Evans asked you to find out about driving in Australia. One of your colleagues has passed you a short article on this subject which she read in a magazine (Figure 7.1). Use this information to produce a brief factsheet containing *relevant* details for Richard. Submit this to your tutor for his or her approval and then keep it safe in the appropriate travel file.

• Rail travel

Within the UK

Rail travel is a popular choice for business travellers in the UK. Not only are most stations sited in city centres but it is possible to relax on the journey, read a paper and eat a meal, or do paperwork whilst travelling – all of which are impossible for the car driver.

Driving in Australia

Driving in Oz is easier for the British than the Americans – mainly because Australians drive on the left-hand side of the road. There is no need for that major irritation, therefore, of having to think about which side of the road you should be on for the first week or so, and constantly climbing in the wrong door of the vehicle whenever you forget! As in Britain, seat belts must be worn by drivers and passengers at all times.

The roads are mostly modern and in good repair but Australia hasn't the cross-country motorway network established in Britain (or the freeway network used in the States). Instead, mainly because of the distances involved between cities and the fact that Aussies usually fly between major cities, most roads are two-lane, and involve the 'stop and go' traffic normally encountered on this type of route.

The maximum speed limit in cities and towns is 35 mph – 60 km/h on the signposts, as Australia uses the metric system. On country roads and highways the speed limit is between 100 km/h and 110 km/h (62–68 mph) unless the signs indicate otherwise. Fines are severe and the traffic police are not inclined to look the other way, nor to accept lame tourist explanations as an excuse for speeding. Both radar and speed cameras are used and radar detectors are strictly forbidden.

The other area where the law is severe is drink driving, with alcohol limits much lower than in Britain. RBT is the code in Australia for Random Breath Testing, undertaken at road blocks where drivers are stopped and asked to breathe into an alcohol measuring device. Anyone caught driving whilst over the 0.05 limit receives a punitive fine and licence suspension for the first offence.

In some cases the regulations are different depending upon the state in which you are driving. In Melbourne, for instance, traffic often overtakes on both sides of the road and you use the left lane to make a right turn! Most car hire firms will quickly bring you up to speed on the regulations that apply in their particular area. Remembering them all, however, can be a different matter!

Wherever you drive, always carry your licence with you, in addition to your passport. An International Drivers Permit on its own is not enough. You need a valid overseas drivers licence for the class of vehicle you are using in Oz.

Finally, remember that petrol is sold by the litre, both leaded and unleaded, but it is quite expensive at about A$0.70 a litre. It is even more expensive in rural areas, where fuel may be completely unavailable after nightfall. Most petrol stations accept international credit cards.

Figure 7.1 A magazine article on Australian motoring

As you may remember from the last chapter, since the railways were privatised, 25 train operating companies now run trains in different areas of the country. Some concentrate on InterCity routes, which are the most commonly used by business travellers. Other routes are run by regional railways.

The cost of rail travel was briefly mentioned in Chapter 1, as were the various types of tickets available. The first point to establish is whether you should be reserving First Class accommodation or Standard Class for your boss. In many cases, additional services and facilities are available to First Class passengers, such as free car parking, London underground tickets, refreshment vouchers and the ability to buy meal vouchers in advance. You need to find out the times of different trains on the routes he or she wants to use and the name of the operating company. You should note that you can book a return journey with one company, even if the route involves changing trains and using the services of another.

There are various ways in which you can obtain the information you need – either by contacting the National Rail Enquiry Line on 0345 48 49 50, ringing the operating company direct, using the Internet (see page 217) or visiting your local station. The other alternative, if your boss frequently travels by train, is to keep a copy of the GB Passenger Railway Timetable in your desk drawer, or a booklet for the regular services you use. However, you must be able to read a timetable properly to give accurate information (this means checking all the footnotes *carefully!*) and should be able to check each of the following points.

- The correct departure and arrival times.

- The length of time the journey will take.

- Whether it is direct and, if not, the number of 'legs' on the journey – try to keep these to a minimum and remember that you must allow a connection time which varies from one station to another. Additional time must, of course, be allowed if the connecting train leaves from a different station – in London a minimum of at least one hour is required.

- The type of catering facilities on the train (eg restaurant car, buffet counter or at-seat trolley). If you are booking Standard Class, check if the restaurant is reserved for First Class passengers only.

- The availability of seats and whether reservations are compulsory or recommended.

- The availability of both First Class and Standard Class seating.

- The type of train (eg Pullman trains are usually more comfortable and have a greater range of facilities).

You are *always* wise to make a seat reservation for your boss, even on trains not listed as being particularly busy. Knowing there is a seat waiting, and which carriage it is in, is far better than hunting for an empty seat on a full train with a briefcase in one hand and an overnight bag in the other!

If you make a reservation more than seven days in advance, not only may you be able to save money for your boss, but the operating company will also post the tickets to you. If the reservation is made less than seven days in advance you will be given a booking reference number which must be quoted at the station when the tickets are collected prior to departure. You should note that if you are booking over the phone, you must pay by credit card and the name on the credit card must match that of the traveller. In addition, your boss will have to sign for the tickets and may be asked to produce the same credit card to prove identity. A sensible alternative for many organisations is to open an account with an operating company and take advantage of the businesses services it offers. These include being billed for bookings on a monthly basis, travel planning advice and assistance, car rental at the point of destination and reservation of hotel accommodation both in the UK and in Europe. In addition, most train operating companies link with Eurostar, so that if you work outside London you can make arrangements with your local operator for your boss to travel from the nearest InterCity station to London and then by Eurostar to Paris or Brussels (see below).

Finally, if you live in a city where there are several stations, do make sure that your boss knows which one he or she is using! The same applies, obviously, if you are making arrangements for collection on arrival.

European rail travel

Rail travel to Europe was revolutionised in the 1990s, when it became possible for business travellers to make rapid journeys across the Channel. In 1994, when the first Eurostar services began from London to Paris and Brussels via the Channel Tunnel, this became an obvious option for travellers wishing to journey rapidly to Europe. There are now connections from many parts of England to many parts of the Continent, although a dedicated high-speed link has yet to be built.

Currently, Eurostar trains depart from London Waterloo to Paris sixteen times a day, and to Brussels ten times a day, with increasing numbers calling at Ashford, Kent. Some stop at Calais and Lille en route and passengers arriving in Paris or Brussels can link with European trains to other parts of France and Belgium as well as to destinations in Germany and Holland.

The main classes of accommodation on Eurostar are Premium First, Normal First, Standard Plus and Standard. Cheaper fares are available for Leisure and Excursion passengers and to those who book a promotional return.

Eurostar (UK) Ltd

The range of additional services for Premium First passengers is considerable and includes a free taxi to any central Paris destination (or central London destination) on arrival. Dedicated check-in areas and a fast-lane reduce check-in time to ten minutes, but those who arrive earlier can use the Clubhouse lounges at Waterloo or Ashford or the Salon Eurostar at Paris Gare du Nord or at Brussels Midi. In addition, on board the Premium First passenger is served a three-course meal and complimentary drinks and, should there be any need to change the method of travel, can exchange tickets for a British Midland Diamond EuroClass air ticket from London or Paris.

In common with many airlines and hotels (see pages 260 and 270), Eurostar operates a Frequent Traveller programme. Business people who travel regularly can earn points; the more points they earn, the greater the number of facilities they receive, moving from Blue status through Silver to Gold. Again in common with many organisations, Eurostar operates a 'partner programme' whereby making reservations with its partner hotels and car rental company will also earn points.

Finally, if you are booking Eurostar from a regional base, do note that special connecting fares are offered. Do not, therefore, simply add together the Eurostar fare and the normal train fare to London without checking with your local operator first!

International rail services

In many places in Europe, taking the train between cities in different countries is easier (and sometimes faster) than catching a plane – between Frankfurt and Basle, the German ICE train completes the trip in three hours, which is ten minutes faster than the plane, and the cost is a mere £71 as opposed to £178 for the airfare. To travel from Geneva to Milan costs £204 (one way) by air yet only £69 in a Pendolino tilting train (and only takes 25 minutes longer) and between Paris and Brussels the savings are even greater – executives prepared to spend one extra hour travelling on the French TGV train will pay £38, compared with £167 for an air ticket. However, obtaining information on some of these services in Britain can be extremely difficult, as many travel agents are not well informed on international rail schedules and services.

Another bonus of rail travel is that several places and routes are accessible by train which cannot be reached easily by plane. The problem is that executives and PAs often think 'plane' but not 'train'. You may therefore spend hours puzzling how to get your boss easily from Paris to Lausanne or from Frankfurt to Berne, without considering the rail options. However, with new high-speed services (see below) this attitude may change in the future.

Anyone who regularly needs to access international rail information should obtain a copy of the Thomas Cook European Timetable, which is published monthly. Alternatively, useful telephone contacts are Rail Europe on 0171 491 0356 and European Rail on 0171 387 0444. To travel further afield, you or your travel agent will need to find out information directly from the

'I know where I'm going . . .'

In the future, it is likely that even more travellers will opt to travel around Europe by train, rather than fly. This is particularly true as high-speed line and tilting trains (which can travel at speeds up to 140 mph) become available on more and more routes. In Europe, a new stretch of high-speed line in Belgium is about to reduce the Eurostar London–Brussels trip by 30 minutes, and German Rail plans to extend its ICE trains from Munich to Vienna and Milan. New stretches of high-speed line are also being constructed between Frankfurt, Cologne, Amsterdam and Brussels, which will drastically reduce journey times.

In Britain, the major development is the high-speed track between London and Folkestone, originally scheduled for 2003, which will reduce Eurostar timings to two hours for Brussels and two hours twenty minutes for Paris. In addition, new international stations are planned at Ebbsfleet, St Pancras and Stratford. The Eurostar service is also being extended to the regions, initially to Manchester and Birmingham and later to Scotland's east coast. Some TOCs such as Virgin are already announcing plans to introduce tilting trains starting in 2001, which will drastically cut some InterCity travel times.

country concerned – contacting the tourist office is a sensible starting point. However, you should bear in mind that rail travel is a practical option in Europe because of the speeds at which trains travel, the distances involved and because European air fares are generally very high. The situation can be very different elsewhere in the world!

Check it yourself

Joanne Bretherton's associate, Paul Livesey, lives in Liverpool. He has two trips to make by train in the next two weeks. Use the timetable and symbols guide shown in Figure 7.2 to identify and suggest appropriate trains for him according to his preferences (see below).

Scotland → North West England, West Midlands → London

Mondays to Fridays

Station		VT	VT	NW	VT	NW	VT	VT	VT	VT	VT	CT	NW	VT	VT	VT	NW
Notes				A								C		D			
Edinburgh	d	09 10														08 50	
Haymarket	d															08 55	
Glasgow Central	d			09 10			09 38										10 10	
Motherwell	d			09 27			09 53										10 24	
Carstairs	d																	
Lockerbie	d	10 08															
Carlisle	a	10 35		10 42			11 00										11 32	
Carlisle	d	10 35		10 42			11 00										11 35	
Penrith	d	10 51					11 15										11 52	
Windermere	d						11 11											12 05
Oxenholme Lake District	d				11 17		11 41									12 18	12 24
Barrow-in-Furness	d					11 11											
Lancaster	d	11 32		11 59	11 45		11 56					12 04				12 35	12 45
Preston	a	11 52		11 59	12 08		12 19					12 27				12 58	13 08
Blackpool North	a	12 28	12 32				12 58							13 13			12 26
Blackpool North	d	11 08				11 26	11/47									12 08	12 26
Preston	d	11 53			12 09	12 20								12 27		12 59	13 09.
Wigan North Western	d	12 06			12 25	12 34								12 47		13 13	13 25
Liverpool Lime Street	a					13 19								13 24			14 19
Warrington Bank Quay	d	12 18				12 44										13 25	
Bolton	a				12 43	12g59								13g25			13 43
Manchester Piccadilly	a				13 03	13g23								13g49			14 03
Manchester Airport	a				13 20	13g41											14 20.
Manchester Piccadilly	d	*11 40*			12 17		12 30			12b33						*12 40*	13 10
Stockport	d				12 26		12 38			12b42							13 17
Wilmslow	d	*12 09*								12b50						*13 09*	
Liverpool Lime Street	d									12 45			12 49				
Runcorn	d									13 02			13 06				
Hartford	d												13 17				
Crewe	a	12 41								13 25			13 31			*13 49*	
Holyhead	d				10 48												
Bangor (Gwynedd)	d				11 16												
Chester	d				12 26											*13 17*	
Crewe	d	12 42			12 52					13 25			13 33			*13 52*	
Macclesfield	d				12 40					12 52							13 32
Stoke-on-Trent	d				13 01					13 12			13 16				13 53
Stafford	d	13 03			13 16		13 22			13 45				13 54			14 16
Lichfield Trent Valley	d																
Tamworth Low Level	d																
Nuneaton	d									14 12							
Shrewsbury	d											13 00			*13 25*		
Wolverhampton	d	13 29			13 36		13 42					14 14		14 19	14 28	14 35	
Sandwell & Dudley	d													14 29			
Birmingham New Street	a	13 49			14 09		14 00					14 29		14 42	14 49	14 51	
Birmingham New Street	d	14 06												14 45		14 59	
Birmingham International	d	14 16			14a45							14 25		14 55		15a09	
Coventry	d	14a27			14a57						15a08	14 37		15 07		15a27	
Rugby	d									14 28						16a11	
Northampton	a									14 58							
Milton Keynes Central	a						14 19	14 25	14 40	15 23				15 40			
Watford Junction	a								15 04			15a31					
London Euston	a						15 00	15 05	15 25	15 30		15 55					

A Bicycles cannot be conveyed on this service
C From Morecambe (Table 98)
D The Cornish Scot
b Change at Crewe
c Change at Dundee
e Via Glasgow Queen Street and Glasgow Central. Passengers make their own way from one station to the other
f Until 16 January and from 16 February
g Change at Preston

Code   Train company name
CT   Central Trains
NW   North Western Trains
VT   Virgin Trains
Italic timings indicate connecting trains

References and Symbols used in this Timetable

Date and Time Symbols

a	Arrival time.
d	Departure time.
p	Previous night.
s	Stops to set down only.
u	Stops to pick up only.
x	Stops on request. Customers wishing to alight must inform the on-train staff, prior to departure from the previous station, and those wishing to join must give a clear hand signal to the driver.

M	Monday.
T	Tuesday.
W	Wednesday.
Th	Thursday.
F	Friday.
S	Saturday.
Su	Sunday.
•	Adding 'O' to the abbreviation for the day or days (eg **WO**) means the train runs **only** on the day or days preceding the 'O'.
•	Adding 'X' to the abbreviation for the day or days (eg **FX**) means the train runs on all the days in this section of the timetable **except** the day or days preceding the 'X'.

Wavy line between train times indicates that this train does **not** run during the full period of the timetable on which the train is shown.

BHX	Does not run on Bank Holiday Mondays **13 April and 4 May.**
GHX	Does not run on Glasgow Holiday Mondays **29 September, 13 April and 4 May.**
→	Train continued in a later column.
←	Train continued from an earlier column.

Station Symbols

⊖	Stations having interchange with London Underground services.
10	Figure in box indicates the minimum Interchange Time in minutes to allow between trains at this station: example shows 10 minutes—see also **Connections** page.
⛴	Shipping service.
✈	Airport Link – station for interchange. See also Airport Links pages.
⛴	Hovercraft, Catamaran or Hydrofoil.

Accommodation

All services shown in this timetable convey Standard accommodation only unless otherwise shown.

Train Numbers

On certain tables, mainly in South East England, route codes are shown as part of the column heading information. These codes correspond with numbers that will be displayed on trains which are equipped to display such information.

Train Symbols

On Board Services.

IC	Train with: • First Class and Standard accommodation. • Light refreshments and hot and cold drinks (available for whole or part of the journey). • Reserved Seats available.
ICS	Shuttle train with: • First Class and Standard accommodation. • Reserved Seats available. • Frequent and regular service. • Enhanced welcome and access at London Terminal Stations. • At-seat service of food and hot and cold drinks in First Class and Standard accommodation.
P	First Class Pullman service (available to First Class ticket holders).
✕	Restaurant service (available to First Class ticket holders).
×	Restaurant service (available to First Class ticket holders, also Standard if accommodation is available).
S	Silver Standard.
A	Alphaline service with: • Reserved Seats available. • At-seat catering service of cold snacks, sandwiches and hot and cold drinks for whole or part of journey. • British Telecom card phone. • Air-conditioning. For cycle carriage details see separate publicity.
TE	Turbo Express train with: • First Class and Standard accommodation. • A service of cold snacks, sandwiches and hot and cold drinks available for whole or part of journey. • Air-conditioning.
∅	A Buffet counter service of hot food, sandwiches, hot and cold drinks available for whole or part of the journey. Many of these trains offer a Menu service with tables near the buffet made available for customers enjoying hot meals.
⎁	A service of snacks, sandwiches, hot and cold drinks available for whole or part of the journey.
⏄	At-seat Trolley service of cold snacks, sandwiches and hot and cold drinks available for whole or part of the journey.
R	Seat reservations recommended. See also **Reservations** page 6.
R	Seat reservations compulsory. See also **Reservations** page 6.
◇	Seat reservations available. See also **Reservations** page 6.
▼	Cycles only carried with advance reservation. See separate publicity for full details.
1	Also conveys First Class accommodation.
⛐	Bus service. (Heavy luggage, prams, bicycles, etc. may not be conveyed.)

Figure 7.2 Railtrack timetable and symbols guide. Reproduced by permission of Railtrack

Prepare your information in the form of two separate memos to him, each containing your recommendations.

1 Next Wednesday, Paul has to attend meetings in Manchester and Birmingham. He will be travelling to Manchester in the Marketing Director's car and then going on to Birmingham New Street by train. He is hoping to leave Manchester at lunchtime and wants to arrive in Birmingham before 2.30 pm as he is meeting the Birmingham representative at that time, who will be accompanying him on the visit and bringing him back to Liverpool on Thursday. Paul has asked you to find a suitable train from Manchester to Birmingham and to check if this has 'at seat' or 'buffet' catering facilities.

2   Paul is attending a meeting in Edinburgh with Joanne the following Monday. They will be travelling to Scotland in Joanne's car on Sunday evening. Joanne will remain in Scotland to see some other clients on Tuesday. Paul has asked you to recommend the best train he can catch back to Liverpool on Tuesday morning – and to let him know if he will have to change trains at all en route.

Check your train information with the key on page 300 and the content and layout of your memos with your tutor.

3   As you will have seen, working through a rail timetable is not easy (which is probably why most people prefer to ring the National Rail Enquiries line instead!). However, you can hardly claim to be an efficient travel arranger and shy away from timetables. For further practice, study the symbols guide carefully and then, as a group, work through alternative journeys that would be possible from the timetables shown in Figure 7.2.

Test yourself

As a group, why not consider the possibility of travelling to Europe on Eurostar yourselves? Before you dismiss the idea out of hand, cost it out carefully. If you take advantage of the cheaper fares and book at an excursion or leisure rate, you may find it is much cheaper than you thought. If you don't like the idea of visiting Paris or Brussels, then don't forget that Eurostar also runs to Disneyland Paris (although the entrance fee is not included in the price so would have to be costed separately).

To obtain the information, contact Eurostar on 0345 30 30 30. If you live outside London, you also need to ask for information on connecting fares and any discounts available for group travel. Ask for timetables and booking information and work out when you could arrange for the trip to take place. Alternatively, you can visit a local travel agent who handles Eurostar bookings, call your local station or access the Eurostar web site on http://www.eurostar.com. However, for up-to-the-minute accurate information on your own particular needs, you are recommended to ring Eurostar direct.

Keep your costings safely. Later in this chapter you can compare this option with travelling by air to the same places, and then add on the price of hotel accommodation for two or three nights.

There is no need to be restricted to the suggestions given above. If you are feeling more adventurous you can work out how much it would cost to continue on to Antwerp or Amsterdam. If you are feeling less adventurous, then – as a group – decide where you would like to go for a day trip or a short break in the UK, find out the Apex fare and the times of trains on which you could travel (either by obtaining a timetable from your local station, ringing the National Rail Enquiry Line, ringing the operating company or surfing the Net).

Finally, put all your information and ideas (individually) in a memo to your tutor. Make sure you clearly list times and prices. Then arrange a group meeting to discuss the options further. Note that if your group is also studying Conference and Meetings Organisation, you could usefully send out a notice and agenda and take minutes of the meeting.

● Air travel

The majority of business trips overseas are still made by air because of the speed and convenience of this type of travel – particularly over long distances. Even within Britain, many internal flights are used daily, particularly on the Shuttle service that departs every hour between London Heathrow and Belfast, Edinburgh, Glasgow and Manchester. Ticketing and check-in are fast and easy, and can be done electronically. Even check-in can be done by means of a self-service machine rather than queuing at a flight desk.

Internal flights within the UK are known as domestic flights. Because they do not travel out of Britain there are no customs areas to clear and anyone travelling with only hand baggage can leave the airport within minutes of arrival.

Airlines and airports are well aware of the problems of travellers arriving from city centre locations, and express rail links are currently available from Gatwick and Manchester airports. In 1998 the Heathrow express link becomes operational – aimed primarily at business travellers.

Both European and international flights are frequently used by business travellers – so much so that on all flights there is Business Class seating (often given other names, such as Club Class), business lounges for departure and arrival, and frequent flyer programmes for anyone who uses an airline (or its partner hotels and car hire companies) regularly. In some cases airlines have joined together so that points awarded on all the airlines in a group count towards the same scheme.

To make an airline booking you first need to be able to identify appropriate flights that fit in with your executive's appointments. You can, of course, ask your travel agent to do this for you, but many PAs prefer to look through the alternatives themselves. This is because a variety of options can often be chosen, which will depend upon the boss's preferences – and they feel they can offer a more personal service to their boss than the travel agent is likely to do. The options available normally include:

- place of departure (eg Gatwick, Heathrow or London City Airport)

- time of departure/arrival (preferences may depend upon whether your boss is a night owl or a morning lark)

- the airline – most executives have personal preferences in this area, with certain airlines they strongly like and others they strongly dislike!

- routing – particularly if the flight will not be direct; in this case executives often have a preference about whether they travel via say London, Amsterdam or Zurich – depending upon which airport they find the most efficient and easiest to use and, sometimes, the range and price of the duty free goods!

- alternative flights, if the first choice is fully booked – in this case you will be offered the opportunity to 'wait list' your first choice, in case any cancellations occur

- whether or not specific seat reservations can be made – and, if so, where the traveller prefers to be seated, particularly on a long journey.

Jet lag and international time zones

Before you select a flight, an important factor to consider is jet lag – an unpleasant experience caused by travelling across different time zones. This is always worse if the journey is from west to east and is a long one. As an example, an executive leaving San Francisco at 6 pm to fly to London faces a ten-hour journey. However, when it is 6 pm in San Francisco it is already 2 am the following day in London. By the time the executive arrives at Heathrow, his or her body clock is saying 4 am, whereas in London it is now 12 noon. This means such travellers feel at low ebb, whilst everyone around them is busily working. If you have booked an appointment for 2 pm, you can hardly expect energy and productivity – particularly as it is often very difficult for people to sleep on the journey. It is therefore much better to leave the rest of the day clear (which also means fewer problems if the flight is delayed) and schedule the first appointment – at the very earliest – for the next morning. You should note, however, that travel from east to west over shorter distances often gives you some time to play with! A journey to New York takes eight hours and the eastern seaboard of the US is five hours behind the UK. Therefore, if your executive left on a 9 am flight, the arrival time would be 5 pm UK time but 12 noon in New York. An appointment could then be made for 2 pm, given that the executive's body clock would be registering 7 pm.

Jet lag can be kept to a minimum if the traveller:

- avoids alcohol and caffeine during the flight (especially in quantity!)
- is physically fit and takes plenty of exercise
- wears comfortable clothing and footwear in-flight and drinks about 8 oz of water each hour
- sets his or her watch for the time at destination as soon as possible to get in the right frame of mind
- tries to avoid overnight flights
- has comfortable seating or is able to get a good night's sleep. This is much more likely if travel is First Class or Executive Class. BA, for instance, provide separate cabins for First Class passengers with seating that converts into a bed – rather than just reclines. In addition, a window seat means fewer disturbances from fellow passengers.

The ultimate cure for jet lag?

Many travel organisations have realised that there is money to be made from curing – or alleviating – jet lag for business executives. An American organisation, Jet Ready Travel Services, offers a computer software program that provides a customised set of recommendations based on a proposed flight schedule entered into the computer, together with personal details of the traveller. Virgin Atlantic offer Upper Class passengers the opportunity to have an aromatherapy massage from a therapist either in the Virgin Clubhouse at Heathrow or during the flight – and many hotels offer similar treatments, special diets, health spa treatments and even, in one case, the free use of a flotation tank for residents suffering from jet lag. For those with greater concern for comfort than cost, some specialist hotels, such as the Rembrandt in London and the Tudor in New York, offer circadian suites – at the price of about £400 a night! These are specially designed rooms that enable the traveller to simulate his or her own time zone throughout the stay, by the use of special blackout curtains, full spectrum artificial lighting (to simulate daylight) and round-the-clock room service. More prosaic travellers are likely to buy an over-the-counter sleep aid to help them to sleep, or to wait until they next visit the US where melatonin can be purchased from health food shops. This helps to control the body clock and, although concerns about its long term use have prevented it from being put on sale in Britain, for short-term use it is recommended and endorsed by many business executives.

The best way to check time zones is by looking in your Phone Book. Against all international codes is shown the time difference. However, you have to allow for other factors, such as adjusting clocks for daylight saving time – some countries such as Britain, change their clocks twice a year to make the maximum use of daylight. In Australia, each state may do this on different dates! Your best way of checking, if you know the length of a flight, is to look at the timetable – the arrival time is always given as local time. This is why your boss's ticket from San Francisco to London will show about 18 hours' time difference between departure and arrival.

One final, but important point. Time differences also mean that you and your boss should note beforehand the sensible times for making contact – otherwise you are in serious danger of ringing at 3 am with some routine information! This aspect is covered in more detail in the final chapter.

Reading an airline timetable

There are several ways in which you can find out information about flights – as you saw in Chapter 1. You can ring your travel agent or contact an airline directly over the Internet to access current timetables. However, most PAs prefer to look in a standard (paper) reference guide. The *ABC World Airways Guide* is the most comprehensive, as this gives flights for all airlines worldwide. However, if your boss is a member of a frequent flyer programme, or regularly uses one or two particular airlines, you can obtain a small booklet containing all their latest timetables. Do bear in mind, however, that this will limit your options to the flight schedules offered by those airlines.

Before you start, you are strongly recommended to learn some of the terms used in 'airline speak' (see page 259) and to read the sub-sections and footnote keys carefully. Otherwise you can easily misread the information.

Making the booking

Once you have made your choice, it is sensible to talk this through with your travel agent, which also protects you in case you have made a mistake! The agent will then make the booking, confirm it to you and send you the ticket just before the departure date. Do keep this safely. It is also important to check it carefully *immediately* you receive it (mistakes are not unknown) and to make sure that there is a flight coupon for every sector of the journey and that the airport/flight numbers are correct. Check that the ticket is marked 'OK/NK' or 'KK' in the status boxes against each flight. Check the baggage allowance for each passenger – if the traveller's luggage is over the prescribed weight, an excess baggage fee may be charged.

Finally, check that the name on the ticket is correct in every detail (it must match the passport). You should be aware that flight tickets are *not* transferable. If, therefore, Richard Evans was taken ill at the last minute, his place could not be taken by someone else unless the ticket was cancelled and another one issued in the substitute's name.

Courting the PAs – the British Midland way

Airlines don't try just to appeal to executives – they also try to encourage PAs to use them. If you organise business travel for your boss, you are eligible to join British Midland's High Flyers Club, designed to keep PAs and secretaries up to date with business travel news. A quarterly magazine contains articles, features on different destinations and other news from British Midland. In addition, if your boss is a Diamond Club gold or silver card member, you are automatically eligible for 'gold' High Flyer membership and earn rewards yourself for your bookings.

For details contact the High Flyers Club on 01332 854454. Further details of the Club and other services offered by British Midland can be found on their web site on http://iflybritishmidland.com.

Check it yourself

1   Figure 7.3 shows all the airline terms you are likely to need to know. Read the description against each carefully, and check with your tutor if there is anything you do not understand.

2   Figure 7.4 is an extract from British Airways Worldwide Timetables, which explains the information given on their timetables. Read this carefully and work through it with your tutor to check you understand how to interpret the information given.

3   You should have already started a travel file for Richard Evans, following the instructions on page 238. Refresh your memory about his requirements from pages 208–210, 235 and 244–5. Your next task for Richard is to identify some suitable flights for him and his party. Use the timetables given in Figure 7.5 to do this. Make sure you make a clear note of the *date* of arrival in both cases.

Notes to help:

a   The return flight will be Melbourne to London and then London to Glasgow and you will have to look up both legs (as opposed to the outward timetable, which includes both flights). Make sure that the return connecting flight in London leaves from Heathrow and not Gatwick!

b The minimum connection time between Terminal 4 at LHR and Terminal 1 (domestic flights) is 75 minutes.

Check your answers with the key on page 301. Then write out your notes neatly and put them into your travel file for Richard Evans.

4 Richard Evans has informed you that he would prefer seats on the earliest flight outwards and the one with the minimum stops on the return. Mark these options clearly on your information sheet. You also need to reserve his hire car, which he wants to collect at the airport, both in Sydney and in Melbourne. Richard does not know much about Australian cars but would prefer one similar to a Ford Sierra. He will pay by credit card. You wish to make both the flight and hire car reservations through your travel agent, Instant Travel Solutions, and you also want them to arrange for Australian visas for all members of the party. As their telephone has been engaged for the last half hour and you have several other jobs to do, you decide to fax your contact there, Mark Griffiths.

Prepare the fax required and check your finished work with your tutor. Put a copy of the fax into your travel file.

5 Mark rings you back promptly to confirm the flights and hire car have been booked. He also needs the passport of each person travelling in order to obtain the visas.

You now wish to book a taxi to collect Richard Evans and his colleagues from home to travel to Glasgow airport. Richard has informed you that the journey will take about one hour – but you also need to allow for the minimum check-in time required (see Figure 7.6) and any traffic delays that might occur. A taxi must also be booked for the return journey and the company will need the flight number and estimated time of arrival (ETA).

a Prepare notes on the details you would need to give to the taxi firm when you make your booking. Check your timings with the key on page 301.

b Your taxi company is J D Executive Drive, 43 Maxwell Road, Glasgow, G2 4MP, tel 248–4949. You have rung the manager to book both taxis and he has asked you to confirm this in writing. Write the letter required and check it with your tutor. Put a copy of the letter into the travel file and make a note of the telephone number – as you will need this later when you compile the itinerary.

Air travel reference guide

Airline prefix
The code letters shown before a flight which denote the airline – eg BA = British Airways, EI = Aer Lingus, QF = Qantas.

Airport
Cities often have several (eg Heathrow, Gatwick, Stansted, London City airport). Always check connecting flights use the same airport.

Airport code
The air travel identifier which consists of a three letter code, eg LHR – London Heathrow, LCY – London City airport. Be careful of duplicate names, eg Birmingham, UK (BHX) and Birmingham, Alabama, US (BHM).

Business Class
The class of travel most frequently used by business travellers – cheaper than First and better than Economy. Sometimes called Club Class.

Carrier
Another name for airline.

Check-in time
The time at which the traveller must register at the airline desk before the flight, which varies between flights, class of travel and airports. Usually kept to a minimum for business travellers where possible. For connecting flights, no second check-in is usually required at the intermediate airport.

Code sharing
A system to watch for on flight timetables where one airline uses another airline for certain parts of the route, eg British Airways may use Qantas flights for some routes, but still prefix the flight with the BA code.

Concorde
The British Airways flagship which flies London–New York in 3 hours 40 minutes (against the usual 8 hours). All First Class seating/service, fast-track check-in and many other services.

Domestic flight
A flight that does not cross international borders.

Electronic ticketing
A new method of ticketing, known as E-ticket, where no paper ticket is required.

Estimated time of arrival (ETA)	Flight arrival times are often described as ETA because many factors – including weather – can make a difference to the exact time of arrival. You should therefore always check the latest ETA before leaving to collect someone from an airport.
Frequent flier programme (FFP)	A 'club' for frequent travellers, eg Executive Club (British Airways), Diamond Club (British Midland), Freeway (Virgin), Raffles Class (Singapore Airlines), Le Club (Air France). Benefits include valet car parking, priority booking and check-ins, business lounges, discounts and mileage awards including free flights. Miles or points can be collected on airline bookings and bookings with their hotel and car hire 'partners'.
Long haul	A long distance intercontinental flight. There are usually stop-overs for refuelling.
Minimum connection time	The minimum time permitted between connecting flights – which depends upon the arrival/departure airport and terminal. See the *ABC World Airways Guide* for details.
Open-dated return	A pre-paid return ticket with no specified return date.
Open jaw	On an open jaw journey, a passenger flies to one destination and returns from another, travelling between the two by air, train or car (eg outward London–New York, return Washington DC–London). This may be available only if the outward and return flights are with the same airline.
Red eye	The term used for the overnight flight from New York to London, because the time change means passengers lose a night's sleep.
Round the world (RTW) ticket	This is often cheaper for travel to Japan, Australia or other parts of the Pacific – the traveller continues the journey in the same direction, rather than returning by the same route.

Short haul	The opposite of long haul, eg European flights.
Shuttle	The walk-on, hourly domestic UK air service between major airports.
Terminal	The airport building from which a flight departs or at which it arrives. Identified by a number (Terminal 1, 2, 3, etc). This is vital information for all travellers and anyone meeting a person from a flight.
Time zones	The hourly segments into which the world is divided. West of Britain is earlier than GMT, east is later. The date line runs through the Pacific so that travellers crossing it westwards find it is a day later and those crossing it eastwards find it is a day earlier. The easiest way to remember this, if you saw Michael Palin's Pacific Rim adventure on television, is to remember that when he travelled from Alaska to Siberia (only a short way, east to west) he travelled over the date line and 'jumped onwards' a day.
TOD	Ticket-on-departure system for business travellers.
Wait list	The reserve list for a scheduled flight that is currently full – cancellations may be received.

Figure 7.3 A glossary of air travel terms

HOW TO USE THIS TIMETABLE

---

[1] **From BELFAST (City)** [12]

Depart Belfast City Airport (minimum check-in time 30 mins: JY 60 mins)
Reservations tel 0345 222111

[2] ▶ **NEW YORK (John F. Kennedy)**   *HC IC MC RD RZ TJ TX AV*   [11]

| 123456- | 0700 | 1240a | BA7800♦ | ATP | 1 | MAN | 0800 | 1000 | BA1503 | 767 |
| --------7 | 0700 | 1335a | JY961 ○ | 146 | 1 | LGW | 0830 | 1040 | BA2173 | 767 |

[3]   [4]   [5]   [6]   [7]   [8]   [9]   [10]

[1] Departure city.

[2] Arrival city.

[3] Period of operation if other than the timetable validity dates.

[4] Days of operation.   1 Monday   2 Tuesday   3 Wednesday   4 Thursday
                         5 Friday   6 Saturday   7 Sunday

[5] Flight information.   Departure/Arrival times with Terminal indicator (if applicable) and Flight Number.
                          Terminal indicator: Ⓝ Ⓢ Gatwick terminals:
                                                           ①②③④ Heathrow terminals.
                          ♦ Operated by one of British Airways alliance partners.
                          ○ Smoking service.

[6] Aircraft type.

[7] Number of stops en-route.

[8] Transfer connection airport.

[9] Transfer connection flight information. Departure/Arrival times and flight number.

[10] Aircraft type.

[11] Ground partners: *BC* *BCP Parking and Travel services*   *TX* Travelex Foreign Currency.
     - Hotels   *CO* Concorde Hotels
                        HC Hilton Corporation
                        HL Hilton International (including Hilton National)
                        HY Hyatt Hotels
                        IC   Inter-Continental Hotels and Restaurants
                        LW The Savoy Group of Hotels and Restaurants
                        MA Maritim
                        MC Marriott Hotels Resorts and Suites
                        RD Radisson Edwardian Hotels, London and Radisson Hotels Worldwide
                        RZ   Ritz-Carlton Hotel Company
                        TJ   Taj Group of Hotels
     - Car Rental   *AL* Alamo   *HZ* Hertz
                        AV Avis   *SI*   Sixt

All British Airways passengers can benefit from the exceptional value car rental offered in the Hertz Worldwide
Drive partnership programme. Executive Club members who rent on the Executive Club Worldwide Drive
programme are offered a discount of up to 60% off standard tariffs plus an upgraded car (when available) and
Executive Club Miles (Air Miles for UK members). All other car partners offer members the ability to earn
mileage only.

Partner hotels offer benefits including a preferred Executive Club rate, late check out, room upgrades (when
available) double occupancy for single room rate and Executive Club Miles (Air Miles for UK members) at
properties worldwide.

For further details and to make a booking please call British Airways, the hotel/car partner or your travel agent.
Executive Club members quote a membership number when booking and produce the card at check-in.

British Airways other ground partners include Hewlett Packard, AT&T, Vodafone and Visitel:

Hewlett Packard are setting up a new business centre in the Executive Club/Club Europe Lounge at Heathrow
Terminal 1 and regularly offer Executive Club members opportunities to collect miles on purchase of Hewlett
Packard products.

The BA Travelphone is a mobile phone offered to Executive Club members through our partner, Vodafone.
Executive Club members can earn miles on purchase, spend and receive regular bonus miles.

The AT&T global cashless calling service allows Executive Club members to stay in touch while away from
home. There is no need for a separate card, your Executive Club number is your calling card number. Miles are
earned on spend.

With Visitel Executive Club members earn miles on phone hire.

Lounge access available for Silver and Gold Executive Club members.

Access at Lagos, Mumbai and Sofia is restricted to Gold members.

Please note that the example schedule shown is for demonstration purposes only.
Additional notes are provided at the foot of flight pages.

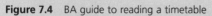

Figure 7.4   BA guide to reading a timetable

From	To	Days 1234567	Depart	Arrive	Flight number	Aircraft	Stops	Transfer Information Airport	Arrive	Depart	Flight number	Aircraft

FROM GLASGOW

▶ SYDNEY

HL HY IC MC RZ   TX   AV HZ

		Days	Depart	Arrive	Flight number	Aircraft	Stops	Airport	Arrive	Depart	Flight number	Aircraft
		67	0815	2045†	BA1475	757§	2	LHR	0940	1215	QF2	744
		12345	0915	2045†	BA1477	737§	2	LHR	1035	1215	QF2	744
		1234567	1815	0610‡	BA1495	757§	2	LHR	1930	2130	BA009	744

FROM SYDNEY

▶ MELBOURNE

HY TX   AV HZ

		Days	Depart	Arrive	Flight number	Aircraft	Stops
		1234567	0725	0855	BA009	744	0

FROM MELBOURNE

▶ LONDON

HC HL IC LW MC MO RD TJ   TX   AL AV HZ BC

		Days	Depart	Arrive	Flight number	Aircraft	Stops
		234567	1430	0540④†	BA010	744	2
		1	1430	0555④†	BA010	744	2
		1234567	1705	0530④†	BA7309◆	744	1

FROM LONDON

▶ GLASGOW

HL MC   TX   AL AV BC

		Days	Depart	Arrive	Flight number	Aircraft	Stops
		12345	0700Ⓝ	0820	BA2956	737	0
		12345	0715①	0830	BA1472	737§	0
		123456	0815①	0930	BA1474	757	0
		12345	0915①	1030	BA1476	737	0
		1234567	0930Ⓝ	1050	BA2958	737	0
		1234567	1015①	1130	BA1478	757	0
		1234567	1215①	1330	BA1482	757§	0
		1234567	1400Ⓝ	1520	BA2962	737	0
		1234567	1415①	1530	BA1484	737	0
		12345 7	1515①	1630	BA1486	737§	0
		1234567	1615①	1730	BA1488	757§	0
		12345 7	1645Ⓝ	1805	BA2964	737	0
		12345 7	1715①	1830	BA1492	737§	0
		1234567	1815①	1930	BA1494	757§	0
		1234567	1900Ⓝ	2020	BA2968	737	0
		12345 7	1915①	2030	BA1496	767	0
		1234567	2015①	2130	BA1498	757§	0

Heathrow Airport
① Depart/Arr Terminal 1
② Depart/Arr Terminal 2
③ Depart/Arr Terminal 3
④ Depart/Arr Terminal 4

Gatwick Airport
Ⓝ Depart/Arr North Terminal
Ⓢ Depart/Arr South Terminal

1 Monday 2 Tuesday 3 Wednesday 4 Thursday 5 Friday 6 Saturday 7 Sunday
◆ Operated by one of British Airways partner carriers.

† Next day
‡ Two days later
§ Aircraft may vary

Figure 7.5 BA timetables

Guide to minimum business travel check-in times at major UK airports

Notes

Precise check-in times depend upon the airline and the destination, and should always be checked individually with the travel agent or airline. Generally you should note that there are shorter check-in times for Executive Club members of all airlines travelling on business than for holiday travellers, particularly if there is only hand-baggage (see over).

For domestic flights, the time shown below is the minimum time for arrival for a BA Shuttle flight before the flight is due to depart.

The times given for all domestic flights assume hand baggage only. Longer time is needed if luggage also has to be checked in.

Assume a minimum of 30 minutes (maximum 120 minutes for Israel) for travellers taking a domestic flight to London with an onward connection from Gatwick or Heathrow with the same airline.

Airport	Domestic	International short-haul	International long-haul
Belfast	15 mins	30 mins	
Birmingham	15 mins	30 mins	
Edinburgh	10 mins	30 mins	
Glasgow	10 mins	30 mins	
Leeds Bradford	15 mins		
Liverpool	15–30 mins		
London City	10 mins	10–30 mins	
London Gatwick	15–20 mins	30–60 mins	60–90 mins
London Heathrow	20–30 mins	45–60 mins	90–120 mins
Manchester	10 mins	30–60 mins	90–120 mins

Figure 7.6 Minimum check-in times

Test yourself

On page 252 it was suggested that you find out details of travelling by Eurostar, as a group, to Paris or Brussels. An alternative method of travelling would, of course, be by air – although you may consider that the Economy fare on a scheduled service is a little beyond your means.

If that is the case, investigate the possibility of travelling on one of the 'no-frills' air services given on page 201. Although Paris and Brussels trips may not be on offer, other alternatives may be Amsterdam (from £78 return) or Geneva (from £118 return) – both from Luton. Ring EasyJet on 01582 700 058 or BA's offshoot company, Go, at Stansted to find out about their current offers. Alternatively, contact Ryanair for details of their no-frills flights to Ireland (to Cork, Knock or Kerry), which are even cheaper. Don't forget that you can also find out about domestic flights to destinations such as Inverness, Aberdeen or Edinburgh.

Compare your findings with the information you obtained on pages 252–253 and see which type of trip and which method of travel is favoured by the majority of your group.

● Sea travel

The only time business travellers are likely to use this form of transport is when they are travelling to Ireland or the Continent and wish to take a vehicle with them. Needless to say, in the case of journeys to the north of France, the Channel Tunnel's Le Shuttle service has often proved more attractive than making a sea crossing. In addition, there are sometimes advantages for executives located on the east coast if they use a ferry service to visit northern Europe.

Alternatives – depending upon the route involved – include car ferry (usually termed 'ro-ro' ferries for 'roll-on, roll-off'), hovercraft and Seacat. Jetfoil, another option, is passenger only. If your ideas of ferries are several years out of date, then you should familiarise yourself with the range of facilities and services (and the looks!) of many of the modern fast ferries – such as those operated by Stena Line to France, Ireland, Holland and Scandinavia. You might get quite a surprise!

To make a reservation you must know the make, length and registration number of the vehicle and whether your executive requires sleeping accommodation. This is optional on some routes and essential on others – in which case you may be given a choice of standard or de luxe cabin. Only the latter is likely to include private facilities.

On some routes passengers can pay a small surcharge to use a private lounge and have access to a fax and photocopier en route. On other services a special executive club operates for regular business travellers.

All passengers must check in at the ferryport before sailing – usually about an hour before departure, but times vary and must be checked. For last-minute bookings you can arrange for the tickets to be collected from the ferryport on departure.

Top of the league – or bottom?

The 1997 Observer Travel Awards gave top marks to North Sea Ferries for the fourth year in succession for their sailings from Hull. Brittany Ferries were second with their sailings to France and Spain from Portsmouth and Plymouth, followed by Le Shuttle – which gained more marks than all the Dover ferry companies.

Scandinavian Seaways were awarded fourth position, with their sailings from Harwich and Newcastle to Denmark, Germany and Sweden, with Hoverspeed – who run crossings on Seacats and hovercraft to Ireland and France – in fifth place.

P&O European ferries were awarded sixth place for the second year in succession with their links from the UK to France, Spain and Ireland. P&O and Stena, awarded eighth place, are due to merge into a new line, called P&O Stena Line, which will probably be operational from mid-1999. You should also note that another P&O company, P&O Scottish Ferries, offers sailings from the UK to the Scottish Islands, Norway and Iceland.

One above Stena was B&I Irish Ferries, and one below was Sea France – a new service offering sailings across the Channel. Finally, in last place was Sally – with their Ramsgate to Dunkirk fast service.

✓ Check it yourself

You have already started a travel file for Joanne Bretherton in relation to her forthcoming trip to Ireland. Refresh your memory about her requirements by looking back at your checklist. You have now contacted a ferry company and been provided with the information shown in Figure 7.7. Remember that Joanne's trip will be made in late March. She has now informed you that she wishes to make both journeys in a morning – but not too early! Refer to Figure 7.7 to prepare a short memo giving Joanne details of a suitable ferry and the cost for herself and her car. Check the information you have obtained with the key on page 301, and the content and layout of your memo with your tutor. Put a copy of the memo into your travel file for Joanne.

HOLYHEAD–DUN LAOGHAIRE

	1 Oct–15 Dec 5 Mar–6 June	16–24 Dec	27 Dec– 4 Mar	7 June– 30 Sept
Mon-Fri	0600 0930 1430 1830	0600 0930 1430 1830 2130	0630 0930 1400 1730	0600 0930 1130 1430 1830 2030
Fri/Sat	as above plus 2130	as above	as above plus 2030	as above plus 2230
Sun	1000 1500	1000 1500 1800	1000 1500	0930 1400 1830 2030

DUN LAOGHAIRE–HOLYHEAD

	1 Oct–15 Dec 5 Mar–6 June	16–24 Dec	27 Dec– 4 Mar	7 June– 30 Sept
Mon-Thurs	0645 1015 1515 1915	0645 1015 1515 1915 2215	1015 1445 1815	0645 1015 1215 1515 1915 2115
Fri/Sat	as above plus 2215	as above	as above plus 2115	as above plus 2315
Sun	1045 1545	1045 1545 1845	1045 1545	1015 1515 1915 2115

Check-in time: with car 30 mins, foot passengers 15 mins
(Note: Dun Laoghaire is approximately 45 minutes' driving time from the centre of Dublin – and Laoghaire is pronounced 'Leary')

Sailing time: approximately 105 minutes

ALL-IN SINGLE FARES (£)

Band A applies before 0900, after 1800
Band B applies 0900–1200
Band C applies 1200–1800

	1 Oct–15 Dec 5 Mar–6 June	16–24 Dec	27 Dec– 4 Mar	7 June– 30 Sept
Car (max 6.5m long) driver and up to 4 passengers	Band A £112 Band B £120 Band C £130	Band A and B – £190 Band C – £210	Band A – £105 Band B – £115 Band C – £125	Band A – £140 – Band B – £180 Band C – £205
Car (6.5m–10m long), driver and up to 4 passengers	As above × 1.2	As above × 1.5	As above × 1.2	As above × 1.4
Caravan or trailer	£60	£150	£60	£150
Motorcycles and bicycles	free	free	free	free
Foot passengers – Child under 5 yrs Child 5–16 yrs Adult Senior Citizen Student	free 12 25 20 20	free 18 32 28 28	free 12 25 20 20	free 16 35 30 28

Notes: Cars over 10 m long, price on application.

EXECUTIVE LOUNGE

Free coffee/tea, biscuits, newspaper, magazines

Photocopy and fax facilities

At-seat service

All-in price – £10 each way

Figure 7.7 Ferry travel to Ireland

Test yourself

As a group, obtain literature or information from *at least* six of the ferry companies listed on page 266 – either through your travel agent, by contacting the company directly or accessing their web site. The travel world web site mentioned on page 218 gives useful links to most companies (http://travel.world.co.uk/index.htm).

Calculate the cost of sailing to Europe or Ireland as a group, rather than travelling by rail or air. Bear in mind that as a foot passenger the cost will be much less than if you were taking a car. However, don't forget that, unless you live near a ferryport, you will also have to include the cost of travelling there.

Now design a chart, as a group, showing four alternative destinations, with the current prices of each possible method of travel. Decide which TWO destinations are the favourite and keep your work safely – in the next section you can find out how to cost and book accommodation.

● Arranging accommodation

The choice of accommodation for a business trip is critical. A poor hotel with restricted check-in times and limited facilities in a noisy or remote location can put additional pressure on a business executive who is expected to be at his or her best for meeting – and often entertaining – clients throughout the trip. For this reason, most organisations use the well-known hotel groups, which are familiar with the needs and expectations of business customers, such as Ramada, Holiday Inn, Hilton, Inter-Continental, Marriott, Forte and Sheraton. However, this type of chain is usually expensive and may not be appropriate in all circumstances – particularly for a short UK trip made by a middle manager or junior executive.

For that reason, when considering accommodation you need to revert back to your Kipling list. It is sensible to consider the items in the following order:

- **what** organisational and budgetary regulations apply to hotel bookings and reservations?

- **who** will be travelling – and what are their needs and preferences?

- **why** is the trip being made?

- **when** is the accommodation required (dates and times)?

- **where** can you find information on suitable hotels?

- **how** will payment be made?

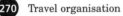

What organisational regulations apply?

These may include constraints on:

- the distance travelled before overnight stays are permitted

- the amount of money that can be spent per night on accommodation – which may vary depending upon the location, the reason for the trip and the status of the executive

- the classification of hotel that can be used under different circumstances.

In some organisations you may find that you are confined to one or two particular hotel groups to maximise corporate loyalty points – either because certain hotels are linked to airline loyalty schemes, or because your organisation is a member of an honoured guest scheme offered by a hotel group. In this case, make sure you know the membership number as you will need to quote this whenever you make a booking. Alternatively, you may be instructed to use the services of a particular hotel booking agency. In other cases you may have free choice within a particular budget range. Note that hotels may quote you their standard rate (called the rack rate). A travel agent or booking agency is often able to obtain a discount on this rate because they make reservations regularly.

Who will be travelling?

This factor, together with the reason for the trip, is likely to influence your choice of accommodation considerably. Obviously there is a substantial difference between making a one-night reservation for a technician visiting a company 50 miles away, and booking accommodation for a major sales trip to South East Asia by your MD and Sales Director!

It is useful to note the following facts about reserving hotel accommodation for business travellers.

- Unless there is an emergency, it is not normal for business executives to share a room.

- Executives are likely to prefer king-sized rooms, large twin rooms or even suites. Be careful that you do not inadvertently reserve a small single room for an important executive, particularly in the UK. As a point of note, in hotel parlance, a 'double' room has a double bed, whereas a 'twin' room has twin beds. A large twin usually comprises two large double (or even king-sized) beds.

- Always book a room that has private facilities unless (because of the location) this is impossible.

- You should specify whether your boss wants a smoking or no-smoking room, particularly if you are making a booking with a major hotel group.

In such groups, room categories are often given codes, eg NSK = non-smoking king-sized room.

- Most large hotel groups give a 'room only' rate, which does not include breakfast. This is always the case in the States, whereas in Britain you may still be quoted for room and breakfast (or bed and breakfast). Make sure you check whether any meals are included in the rate.

- Some hotels have room service, others have tea and coffee making facilities in the room; some offer both. Find out your boss's preferences in this direction. The MD may like being waited on with 24-hour room service, while your own boss may prefer in-room facilities (which usually work out cheaper).

You may be fortunate enough to work for well-travelled executives who know exactly where they prefer to stay in virtually all the major cities in the world! In this case, provided that you accede to their requests, you cannot go far wrong. The situation is likely to be more complicated, however, if the trip is to an unknown destination, your boss will be entertaining important clients upon his or her arrival and/or has very discerning tastes and preferences about personal and business requirements. Your task is even more complicated if the location is somewhere off the beaten track, such as Ulan Bator or Sumatra!

A useful first step is to prepare a brief checklist for yourself of 'must have' facilities for your executives. These are likely to include all the standard facilities you would associate with a top hotel plus, in many cases, specific business facilities – such as rapid check-in and check-out (to save queuing), a large working area and desk within the room including power outlets, and printer/fax/copier facilities. Many large business hotels now have dual-line speaker telephones installed in the rooms with an integral modem, so that business executives can access and send e-mails by laptop from the privacy of their own rooms. In some cases, such facilities may be considered more important than extras such as a health and fitness centre – although this also may be considered a very welcome bonus on a particularly long or stressful trip!

Why is the trip being made?
The reason for the trip and the type of work being undertaken often has a direct influence on the type of facilities required. In some circumstances, for instance, your boss may wish to use a meeting room during the visit (often termed a 'syndicate' room) and may need specialist presentation equipment to be available (see Section 1, pages 93–95). In this case you would have to request such facilities when you make the initial booking.

If important customers are being entertained at the hotel, you may wish to make the reservation with one that has two or three prestigious restaurants – and to check that the hotel has a good reputation in the local business community.

The business itinerary and the means of transport will also affect the choice of location for the hotel. City-centre hotels are invaluable if there are many central meetings to attend or if the reason for the trip is to visit an exhibition or other event held in the vicinity. City-centre hotels are also normally more appropriate for those arriving by public transport, as parking can be difficult. If your boss is using his or her car and travelling from one place to another (particularly in the UK), hotels on main roads or near motorway links – but outside town or city centres – are often easier to find and much quieter places in which to stay! Finally, if your boss is travelling by air, do remember that all major airports worldwide have a large number of executive style hotels in the vicinity.

Airport facilities par excellence!

Hilton Hotels have introduced Business Guest rooms at their London Heathrow hotel – sited on their new 'business floor'. All are equipped with their own workstation and have adjustable lighting, a PC line, stationery kit, personalised fax that operates in four languages, and an automated messaging service together with secretarial support. Each room is also equipped with a special, ergonomically designed '8-hour' chair, designed to reduce fatigue drastically. Guests have free use of a PC and printer and also receive ten free acetates and up to 50 free photocopies. An express check-out service speeds travellers on their way if they become absorbed for too long!

In the United States, Hilton, American Express and IBM are currently testing new smart cards to speed up check-in at eight Hilton hotels across the US. The IBM chip is programmed to contain information on the executive and his or her individual customer profile (and preferences for different facilities), and the card can be used to obtain information on room types and rates, to make or amend reservations and to check and print the final bill. If the trial is successful it is likely to be introduced throughout the Hilton group over the next few years.

When is the accommodation needed?

In the international hotel trade, rooms are normally booked from 12 noon one day until 12 noon the next. If your boss is arriving in the early morning, it is normal for baggage to be left in the porter's lodge after checking in until the room is ready for occupancy. You may be able to reserve a courtesy room if your boss will want to freshen up before a first appointment and before the room is available. If the arrival will be late (normally after 6 pm) it is important that this is clearly specified, as otherwise the hotel may re-let the room.

On the day of departure, the room must normally be vacated by noon, but some British hotels have different rules (eg 10 am!), so it is worth checking this when you make the booking. If your boss will not be leaving until late in the day, you should check if a courtesy room could be made available (or if the check-out time could be extended). This is particularly useful if your boss will be attending meetings in the same hotel all day, as he or she then has a private 'base', rather than just the use of the public rooms.

Where can you find information?

Once you have the basic facts about a trip your next task is to find information on suitable hotels. Your source of information will depend mainly upon whether you are looking for a suitable hotel in the UK or abroad.

Within the UK, you can access *Yellow Pages* for the area, ring the local Tourist Office or use a tried and trusted reference book, such as *Hotels and Restaurants in Great Britain, The Good Hotel Guide* or the *AA Handbook*. If

you want a hotel in a particular chain, ring the London hotel in the same group to find out about those in other areas of the UK or worldwide. In most cases there are also London-based reservations offices to handle bookings worldwide. An invaluable book giving details of hotels in a variety of towns and cities is the *ABC Worldwide Hotel Guide*, and *Michelin Guides* are indispensable for information on hotels in the Europe.

Your travel agent will be able to give you information on hotels worldwide, as will any of the international hotel reservation agencies that specialise in corporate reservations. You can also find out information yourself from the Internet. Virtually all the major hotel chains have web sites, and in many cases you can make the booking on-line. If your executives regularly favour particular hotel chains, it is sensible to contact them for a booklet listing all their hotels worldwide and to ask to be included on their mailing list – so that you will also receive details of any special offers or discounts. If your boss is a member of any honoured guest or favoured guest programmes, then you will automatically receive regular information from the relevant hotel group.

Note that many airlines also offer a hotel booking service, and for international trips it is sensible to check with your travel agent if a room can be reserved at the same time as you make the flight booking. Often the price is considerably lower than if you made the reservation separately, which is an added bonus!

How will payment be made?

There are three ways in which payment can be made.

- Through the hotel reservations agency or through your travel agent.

- By asking the hotel to invoice you for the amount.

- By credit card.

The last option is the one most commonly used. The executive will settle the bill when checking out, on either a personal or corporate credit card. In the case of the former, the money will be reclaimed by completing an expense claim.

Usually, hotels are not willing to send an invoice unless your organisation has an account with them. This will only be the case if you use the hotel or hotel chain regularly, or if your boss or your organisation is registered as a member of a loyalty scheme. If so you need to quote the membership number when you make the booking.

If you make the reservation through a reservations agency or travel agent, the overall bill for accommodation may be invoiced to your organisation but your executive would still be expected to pay for extras (such as room service, telephone calls and newspapers) on departure.

If you make the booking directly with the hotel, do make sure that you specify how they should expect to receive payment. The last thing you want is for an important client travelling with your boss to be faced with an unexpected bill prior to departure!

Making the reservation

Unless your travel agent is making the booking for you, it is usual to telephone the booking agency or the hotel to make the reservation and then to write or fax confirmation of the booking. In most cases it is *not* usual for the hotel to write back to you to confirm the arrangements, unless you specifically request this. For that reason, you should make certain that your boss takes a copy of the fax or letter in his or her travel file (see Chapter 8), in case there are any disputes. If the trip is to a particularly distant part of the world where hotels may be more casual about reservations, then you may also want to provide a list of a few alternative hotels in the area or, at the very least, the address and telephone number of the local tourist office or British consulate!

Today's date

Reservations
The Grand Hotel
Riverside Walk
HIGHTOWN
HG1 5ML

Dear Sirs

I refer to our telephone conversation of today and confirm my reservation of a non-smoking room with facilities for Mr Simon Figari for the nights of Wednesday and Thursday, 14 and 15 June 199-. Please note that Mr Figari will not be arriving at the hotel until at least 2000 hours on Wednesday, 14 June.

I confirm that your room rate of £120 per night includes breakfast. Please note that Mr Figari will settle the account by credit card at the end of his stay.

Yours faithfully

(Your name)
(Your designation)

Figure 7.8 Example of confirmatory letter to a hotel

To make a basic booking is a three-stage process.

1 Write down your requirements clearly. Ensure you include:

- the names and initials of all executives
- the date and times of arrival and departure
- specific room requirements
- any additional requirements and queries
- information as to how payment will be made.

2 Telephone the hotel and ask for 'Reservations'. In many large hotels this is a separate office and is not undertaken by the switchboard operator. Make your requests clearly and don't become rushed or confused – remember that you are the customer. If you are ringing an international hotel abroad, it is very likely that the reservations staff will be multilingual. Your first question, therefore, should be to talk to someone who speaks English! When you have worked through your list, tell them you will write or fax to confirm the reservation.

3 Prepare a letter or fax (on company headed paper) giving all the key information discussed over the telephone. In many cases it is normal to write a letter of confirmation for a UK booking (unless it is made at the last minute) but to fax confirmation to a hotel abroad. Usually the document is brief and simply details the main requirements that have been agreed – as shown in the example confirmation letter in Figure 7.8.

Bear in mind that although it is now possible to book hotel rooms over the Internet by quoting a credit card number, many people are still wary of giving such details because of the lack of security on the Internet at this time. In many cases, hotels will allow you to reserve accommodation over the Net without quoting a credit card number and will then write to you or telephone you to confirm the booking.

Check it yourself

1 As a group, hold a brainstorming session to decide the facilities you consider most business executives would wish to find in a hotel. Compare your list with the suggested key on page 302.

2 One of the executives in your organisation, June Franks, is visiting Bristol next week and has asked you to book accommodation on her behalf. She will be driving to Bristol and arriving on Tuesday evening at about 8 pm and leaving on Thursday morning. She

wants a room with private facilities and breakfast on Tuesday and Wednesday. She will settle the bill by credit card but wants you to find out the rate and to check if this includes breakfast.

a Use an appropriate reference book or access the Internet to find an appropriate four-star hotel. Useful starting points include the electronic yellow pages on http://www.eyp.co.uk and http://www.britain.co.uk.

b From the instructions above, make out preparatory notes which you could use as an aide memoire when you make the telephone reservation. Then role play the situation, with a colleague or your tutor playing the part of the hotel receptionist.

c Prepare a short letter confirming the arrangements, and invent any details you need to make this realistic. Check the contents with your tutor.

3 Joanne Bretherton (refer to your travel file) needs a hotel for three nights in Dublin and one night in Galway. Use an appropriate reference book or access a search engine on the Internet to obtain information on suitable hotels. Produce this neatly, preferably in typed format, giving details of at least two hotels in each location, together with information on facilities and room rates. Put a copy into your travel file.

4 Richard Evans has asked you to fax your Australian agent, Harry Canter in Melbourne, to ask him to book appropriate hotels in both Sydney and Melbourne and to confirm the details directly to you once the bookings have been made. Prepare a fax detailing his requirements and put a copy in the appropriate travel file.

Check all your work with your tutor.

Test yourself

If you have been working on the idea of going away as a group yourselves, then you now need to find some suitable accommodation at the destination of your choice – and to establish the price. By now, following the exercise on page 269, you should have selected two alternative destinations. A wealth of information about tourist accommodation is available on the Internet and you can find out details by entering 'hotel – [place'] into most search engines. Alternatively, you can visit your local travel agent, look in an appropriate reference book or ring the tourist office of the place in which you are interested.

As a group, obtain information on about six hotels in your price range, in each destination. Present your findings and put the selection to the vote. Don't forget that in this situation you may wish to check if you can obtain any discounts for a group booking.

Finally, if you have still not decided where you would like to go – or why – then you could visit as a group one of the travel exhibitions that are held around the country (see below), even if only on a day trip!

Travel fairs – is there one near you?

Each year a number of travel fairs are held in major exhibition halls around the country for those involved in organising business travel. In 1998, for instance, there was Business Travel 98 at the Business Design Centre, London on 10–12 February, and the British Travel Trade Fair at the NEC, Birmingham on 25 and 26 March. Each November, the World Travel Market fair usually takes place at Earls Court in London.

Although you may think all these exhibitions are mainly for the travel trade and professional travel organisers (which they are), each one normally has lots of information you can obtain to help you make more sense of business travel. In addition, there are often useful seminars you can attend. For instance, at Business Travel 98 you could attend Reed Travel's session on 'The beginner's guide to planning and arranging travel', or even find out more about electronic travel information or how to save money when booking hotel rooms. Even if you have missed the 1998 fairs, it's not too late. Most of these fairs and exhibitions are held annually – either surf the Net for details or ring Reed Travel Exhibitions on 0181 910–7691 for information.

Review quiz

1 Identify THREE reference sources you could use for selecting a hotel in the UK.

2 State FOUR items which should be carried by a UK car driver who is driving his or her own car abroad.

3 Name SIX facilities that would be required by a business person staying in a hotel.

4 Briefly explain how and why you would take account of time zones when planning your executive's appointments on a trip abroad.

5 Identify FOUR ferry routes between the UK and Europe.

6 Describe the main facilities you would ensure are available on an InterCity train journey before making a reservation for your boss.

7 A hotel in Paris quotes you the room rates in French francs. How would the final cost of accommodation to your organisation be affected by the exchange rate in force at the time of the visit?

8 State THREE advantages and THREE disadvantages of travelling by air.

9 A junior member of staff has received the following message from your travel agent whilst you were at lunch. 'We have had to **wait-list** your request for a **Business Class** seat on the 1000 flight to Paris next Monday and have meanwhile booked a seat on the flight departing at 1100 hours from **LHR**. Both flights connect with the local **shuttle** service from East Midlands airport. We have arranged for an **open-dated return** as requested.'

Your junior is perplexed by the terms in bold. Explain briefly what each one means.

10 A new executive has heard that he has to make a trip to Canada and take some small samples of finished goods to show potential customers. He is worried that he might be stopped by customs officers unless he has a special import licence. What would you advise him and why?

Putting it all together – and maintaining communications

If you are inexperienced at making travel arrangements, you may consider that once you have planned the trip and made the reservations your work is over. Unfortunately this is far from the truth. In reality you still have other important tasks to undertake if you are taking your role as a PA seriously.

Let us start by reviewing what you have done so far. Ideally you have:

- obtained detailed information on the requirements for the trip

- made out a checklist of jobs you have to do

- obtained information on travel, accommodation and other aspects of the trip from various sources

- found out comparative costs, where appropriate

- agreed the final choice of travel, and timings, with your boss

- made and confirmed all bookings and reservations.

All of these aspects have been covered in the previous two chapters.

At this stage you need to:

a prepare all the paperwork that will be needed by your boss on the trip

b make arrangements for staying in contact while he or she is away.

● Preparing and assembling the documentation

Most of the relevant documentation for the trip should already be in your travel file. If you refer to your travel files for Joanne Bretherton and Richard Evans you will find:

- checklists relating to the jobs you have to do

- information on travel options and preferences

- information on accommodation options and/or faxed requests for the same

- other relevant information and confirmatory documents you have been asked to obtain or send.

In reality, by now you would also be receiving tickets from your travel agent and, in the case of Richard Evans, faxes from the Australian agent confirming the hotel booking and a voucher from the travel agent relating to the hire cars.

The eventual number of documents within a travel file can vary considerably. A two-day visit to Milan to see one customer may only entail the collation of four or five documents. A file containing all the documents and information for a month long tour of South America and Australasia involving several meetings, dinners and conferences is likely to be a very different matter!

Basically, however, all the documents your boss will need can be grouped into seven different categories:

1   The **itinerary** – which you have yet to prepare – summarises all the travel and accommodation arrangements for the trip, from leaving home to returning home. Many executives prefer a comprehensive version to include all the visits arranged, stating where they will take place, when and with whom – giving a contact name and number – and including any social functions they must attend. It is often useful to clip or staple this longer version to the front of the travel file and to provide a shorter version of essential travel details that can be carried in a pocket.

2   **Travel** documents include airline, rail or ferry tickets and car hire documents (together with any notes on driving regulations you have prepared).

3   **Accommodation** documents include copy letters and faxes confirming reservations, or hotel documents or vouchers issued by a travel agent.

4   A copy of the **insurance** policy covering the trip should be included.

5   Additional **notes** on other contacts, eg the full names, addresses, telephone and fax numbers of organisations being visited, are useful if these are not included in the main programme itinerary. Other customers in the area, local representatives or agents and other useful numbers should be added in case of any emergencies.

6   A separate category comprises all documents relating to forthcoming business **meetings and visits** (eg presentation documents, slides and/or OHTs, copies of letters or faxes confirming meetings, copies of relevant contracts, etc). These should be numbered separately for each meeting and a cross-reference entered in the main programme itinerary (see below).

7   **Miscellaneous** documents include invitations to events, information sheets you have prepared on places to be visited, social customs or public holiday information, organisational advertising materials and booklets, and a supply of business cards for your executive.

In a *separate* folder or wallet you should provide any currency or travellers' cheques that have been requested.

✔ Check it yourself

Most PAs have a checklist of items their executive needs to take on standard business trips. You may obtain some comfort from the fact that this does not normally need to include personal items, clothing or toiletries! After some time, both you and your boss will know this list by heart, but at the beginning – and any time when a trip is being undertaken in a hurry – it is useful to use it as an aide memoire to avoid the most obvious items (such as passport or driving licence!) being left behind inadvertently.

As a group, brainstorm the items you think you would be required, using the letters A–Z as your guide. Then check your list against the key on page 302.

Compiling the itinerary

The importance of the accuracy of this document cannot be overstated! A wrong date, time or flight number can easily cause chaos. It is therefore important not only that you prepare it very carefully indeed, but that you check it line by line with someone else's help before you give it to your boss – who may also wish to check it for peace of mind!

It helps enormously if you are working from a finalised information sheet that clearly identifies each and every one of the arrangements you have made, such as those you have been preparing so far. Additional information you will have to make sure you have obtained includes the following.

- The point of departure and return – and whether this is home or office. In many cases, you can use your common sense. On other occasions it is wise to check. If an executive is travelling early in the morning, is going a long distance or will be away for some time, it is usual for home to be the point of departure. If, however, the trip starts late in the day and is only for a short distance or short time, most executives will go to the office first and travel from there. The same applies in reverse on their return – early morning arrivals from a short distance mean the executive will often travel straight from the point of arrival to the office and work all day. This would not be the case if your boss was just returning from a three-week trip to the Pacific, and was both tired and jet lagged!

- The travel arrangements you have made to and from the different airports or train stations, assuming the executive is not taking his or her own car. You must remember that to be absolutely correct, an itinerary should not have any 'gaps' for travel. Therefore you need to check:

  - how your boss will be travelling to the airport, ferryport or train station
  - whether anyone will be meeting him or her on arrival

- the time that your executive will need to leave the hotel on the day of departure to get to the airport in time. You can usually find out this information from your travel agent or from any local representative who knows the area, or even from the hotel itself. Most hotels can easily arrange a taxi for the final journey on the day of departure, if required.

Do note that if a taxi firm has been hired to take your boss anywhere it is wise to include the telephone number in the itinerary so that they can be contacted immediately if there are any problems. This might save you from having to solve a serious transport problem at midnight on a Friday!

- All information on any appointments or social arrangements. Always include the name of the person, the address and telephone number (in case it is needed in an emergency) together with details of the files containing any relevant papers (see below).

- In many cases, PAs also include a reference to the currency and travellers' cheques that are being taken.

Let us assume that your boss, Tara O'Connor, is travelling from your Birmingham office to Brussels next week – the third week in January – to visit a client. She is leaving on Monday evening on the 1655 British Airways flight BA 1748, which arrives at 1905. She will return on Wednesday morning, departing Brussels at 0945 and arriving at Birmingham at 0955, on flight number BA 1745.

You have made a reservation at the Hotel Le Meridien, Carrefour de l'Europe 3, 1000 Brussels – tel: 02/548–42–11, fax: 02/548–30–30 – which is about an hour's journey from Brussels airport. Tara has two appointments during her visit. At 9 am on Tuesday she is meeting Amelie Boudoux at the Belgian Foreign Trade Board, World Trade Centre – Tower 1, Boulevard Emile Jacqumain 162/36, B1000 Brussels. At 2 pm on Tuesday afternoon she has a meeting with Emile Huret of the Clothing Industries Federation at Rue Montoyer 24, B1000 Brussels. She is also meeting another contact for dinner in the evening – Ingrid Theys from the Belgian Chamber of Commerce. A table has been booked in the hotel restaurant for 7.30 pm, though they have arranged to meet in the foyer at 7 pm.

Tara is travelling from the office to the airport by taxi and that this will take 45 minutes. She also needs at least 30 minutes for checking in (see Figure 7.6 on page 264) so, to be on the safe side if traffic is busy, it would be sensible to arrange for a taxi to collect her from the office 90 minutes before departure time. She will arrange her own taxis in Belgium. For the trip you have obtained £50 in Belgian francs and £200 of sterling travellers' cheques.

With all this information it is possible to make out her itinerary for the trip. This is shown in Figure 8.1 on page 284. Before you look at this, however, you may wish to consider how *you* would draft it out from the information given above.

Visit to Brussels – 23–25 January 199–

Monday 23 January

1425 Taxi from office to Birmingham airport (J D Supercars – tel 0121–387–9901)

1525 (latest) Check in at airport

1655 Depart flight BA1748

1905 Arrive Brussels (take airport taxi to hotel)
Accommodation reserved at Hotel Le Meridien, Carrefour de l'Europe 3,
1000 Brussels – tel: 02/548–42–11
(Confirmatory fax attached)

Tuesday 24 January

0900 Meeting with Amelie Boudoux at Belgian Foreign Trade Board, World Trade Centre
– Tower 1, Boulevard Emile Jacqumain 162/36, B1000 Brussels – tel 02/516–28–39

For relevant papers see folder 1

1400 Meeting with Emile Huret of Clothing Industries Federation, Rue Montoyer 24,
B1000 Brussels – tel 02/439–16–20

For relevant papers see folder 2

1900 Dinner with Ingrid Theys, Belgian Chamber of Commerce – tel 02/613–20–39. Meet
in the foyer at Le Meridien.

1930 Table reservation in hotel restaurant at Le Meridien.

Wednesday 25 January

0815 Depart hotel for airport

0915 (latest) Check in at airport

0945 Depart flight BA1745

0955 Arrive Birmingham airport. Taxi booked with J D Supercars for transport to office
(tel 0121–387–9901)

Currency

£50 Belgian francs

£200 Sterling travellers' cheques

Figure 8.1 Itinerary for Tara O'Connor

Check it yourself

1 Work through the itinerary from the information given above. Note
in particular the layout and the fact that the 24-hour clock is used
throughout. Assume you are Tara. Have you all the details you
need, in the order in which you are likely to need them? If the
answer is 'yes', then the itinerary is set out as it should be.

2 From the times given it appears to take over two hours to get to Brussels and only ten minutes to return. By now you should realise why! If not, check with your tutor!

3 Tara has asked you to summarise her travel and hotel details *only* on a card she can carry in her pocket. Identify the information she will require and draft this out neatly on A4 card or paper.

4 Figure 8.2 shows a finalised information sheet for Tara's visit to London and Oxford the following week. From the information

---

Visit to London and Oxford – 1–4 February

Travel

Birmingham New Street to London Euston - InterCity - 1 Feb

Options - 0745 and every half hour onwards throughout the morning.
Travelling time 1 hour 40 mins ✓ *0815 train - seat reserved*

London Paddington to Oxford - 3 Feb

Options (direct trains - no changes) - dep 1418 arr 1515, *dep 1448 arr 1546,* ✓ *seat reserved*
dep 1520 arr 1621, dep 1548 arr 1649, dep 1618 arr 1720

Oxford to Birmingham New Street - Feb

Options - dep 1418 arr 1540, dep *1516 arr 1639,* dep 1616 arr 1740 ✓ *seat reserved*

Accommodation

Single room with facilities reserved at

London Marriott, Grosvenor Square tel 0171-493-1232

The Randolph, Beaumont Street, Oxford tel 01865 247481

Confirmed by fax.

Other arrangements/appointments

1 Feb - 2 pm - Meeting with Denise Fuller, Abercrombe International, Armada Crescent, WC3. Tel 0181-409-2208.

2 Feb - all day - visit to IT 2000 Exhibition at Earl's Court

3 Feb - 9.30 am - Meeting with Stanil Pachevsky, DJV Solutions, 18 Corby Place, W1. Tel 0181-208-1749.

3 Feb - 7.30 pm - Dinner with Charles Davidson from Linton Software, Abingdon Road, Oxford. Tel 01865 319278. NB CD will collect TO'C at hotel at 7 pm.

4 Feb - 10.00 am - Attend presentation at Linton Software, followed by lunch.

Figure 8.2 Finalised information sheet

given, make out an itinerary for the trip, assuming she will take her own car to Birmingham station from her home, allowing 50 minutes to drive there, and leave it in the long-stay car park.

5 Joanne Bretherton has sent you the memo shown in Figure 8.3 confirming her hotel requirements and giving details of her

---

MEMO

TO   You

FROM   Joanne Bretherton

DATE   23 February 199–

Forthcoming visit to Ireland

Thank you for the information you recently gave me on hotels in Dublin and Galway. However, following a discussion with our contacts over in Ireland, I have decided that I would prefer to stay at The Drury Court while I am in Dublin and the Great Southern Hotel in Galway. For your information, the address of the Drury Court is 28–30 Lower Stephens Street, Dublin 2, tel 01–475–1988. The Great Southern's number is 91–564041. While you were at College yesterday I asked Pauline to make the reservations and I think she has put the confirmatory faxes on your desk.

I will be visiting Patrick O'Nealy at Ryans Electronics, Shelby Road, Dublin on the first afternoon. I've arranged to be there at 2 pm and will be there for the rest of the day. The phone number is 01–428–3922. I'll also be meeting him the following morning at 9 am and will be there until just after lunch, when I then want to call in on Gabrielle Lagan at Multimedia Inc on O'Connell Street, at about 3 pm – tel 01–373–2009. Pauline booked a table in the hotel restaurant on Tuesday night at 7.30 for Gabrielle and myself. I will also be meeting up with Gabrielle on the Thursday and will be working with her at Multimedia – probably from about 1 pm onwards.

In Galway, as I think you know, I'm seeing Peter Griffiths from Virtual Solutions of Boston as he's in Ireland at the same time, and this will save a trip to the States! Pauline has booked a seminar room at the Great Southern for the afternoon – I'm leaving it to Peter to make arrangements for dinner! I've arranged to meet him in the foyer at 2 pm.

Can you sort all this out for me please, and draft out an itinerary I can look at to check there are no obvious clashes or problems. I think I had better allow two hours for driving to Holyhead, by the way. Incidentally, you may find it useful to note that if you need to ring me, the code for Ireland is 00–353.

Figure 8.3 A memo giving Joanne's requirements

appointments in Dublin and Galway. Using this document and the information you have already obtained on ferries and road distances in Ireland (saved in your travel file), draft out an itinerary for her approval.

Check all your work with your tutor and compare your finished itineraries with the suggested keys on page 304.

Contact lists and contact information

There is a limit to the amount of information that can usefully be contained in an itinerary. However, many executives welcome the addition of other useful information – particularly that which would be useful in an emergency. Therefore most PAs prepare a list that includes other relevant details. Many of these names, addresses and numbers will be standard items you can keep on disk, simply adding and deleting individual items to customise your list for a particular trip. Typical contents include the following.

- The name, address and telephone number of any company branch offices in the country or vicinity and the home address and telephone number of the office manager or person in charge. The same would apply if the organisation has appointed a particular agent or representative who lives in the area.

- The name, address and telephone number of other customers and clients in the area who may be visited if there is enough time to spare – or if any other appointments are cancelled at the last minute. In some cases, it is useful if a brief synopsis is attached (or recent copies of file correspondence) about the latest business transactions with each company.

- The name, address and telephone number of a reputable local car hire company (often useful even if a car has not been reserved in advance).

- The local address and telephone number of your travel agent (if worldwide) and the airline (in case return flight arrangements have to be changed during the trip).

- The UK code from the country being visited. Note that this will vary depending upon whether your boss is using a chargecard or not. Details can be found in the BT booklet *Step by step guide to calling the UK.*

- The name, address and telephone number of

  – the local bank where any missing travellers' cheques should be reported

- the British embassy or consulate
- the nearest Thomas Cook office where a MoneyGram can be received
- any Government offices or local Chamber of Commerce or other organisations that could provide useful advice and information.

• The telephone number of

- insurers' 24-hour help line (or other number to which any claims must be reported immediately)
- card protection agency (in case any credit cards are stolen).

• A note of the company telephone and fax number and the direct dial extension number for yourself and any key executives with whom your boss may wish to make contact. You may also be expected to provide the home phone numbers of these executives – as well as your own – in case there is an emergency out of office hours!

Business meetings and business documents

The number of associated documents to be taken on the trip will depend very much upon the reason for the visit. If several customers will be visited to discuss a potential sale or other issues, relevant documents relating to each particular customer will be taken. Do not, however, be tempted to hand over a set of office files to your boss, as these will probably be required during his or her absence! Rather, briefly review the documents in the file with your boss, note anything that would be useful, and take a photocopy. Then fasten the photocopies in a file folder, in date order with the most recent document on the top. If several folders are being assembled, mark each one clearly with the name of the customer.

The same approach can be used for other types of documents, such as presentation materials, speeches or contracts. However, do be careful before you hole-punch any documents that this is permissible – it would not be suitable, for instance, for overhead transparencies or sales brochures, which should be put into separate envelope wallets or small boxes.

● Keeping in contact

Many PAs actually take their notebook to bed with them during the time their boss is away on an important, long-distance business trip! This is particularly the case if the trip involves visiting parts of the world such as Japan and New Zealand where time differences make it difficult to establish contact during normal working hours. Thankfully the advent of mobile phones, e-mails and computer networks has meant that the need for very late night or early morning calls has virtually gone – unless a real crisis occurs.

Many new PAs have the mistaken idea that life will be a doddle once the boss actually leaves on a trip. Others may take the optimistic view that at least there will be time to catch up on routine jobs, such as filing. In reality, this can be the *busiest* time for the PA – who now becomes the key contact and link person between her organisation and her executive. If several executives are away simultaneously she may find herself very stretched indeed responding to all the requests and queries she receives – and keeping her travelling executives up to date on events occurring at home. The only way to cope effectively is to plan how and when contact will be made, and to discuss what issues are likely to become critical, before the trip takes place.

Before the trip

Once the itinerary is finalised it is sensible for the executive and PA to go through this together to check that it includes all essential items and notes. The next part of the discussion should be concerned with work-in-progress and items that will need to be handled in the office during the executive's absence. You can prepare for this session by putting all current papers in a file and working through them with your boss, making clear notes as to the action you have to take in each case. In some instances, your boss may wish you to take some action and then, depending upon the response you receive, check with him or her as to what to do next. In other cases, of course, new problems and situations may arise once he or she has left.

You should next decide the best method of contact and the best times for contact. You should make a brief note on the itinerary when the first few calls will be made – because there will be nothing more annoying than for your boss to phone you from the other side of the world only to find you are at lunch or away from your desk and cannot be located by the switchboard! Equally it can be very frustrating for you, if a serious and urgent problem arises, if you have no way of tracking down your boss for days. Setting agreed times for incoming calls, particularly from a very long distance, saves both time and money. However, do be aware that in some countries telecommunications are less advanced and connections may be difficult to make, or there may be delays. In this case, an alternative method of communication (eg fax or e-mail) may have to be considered. Fortunately the development of international, modern telecommunication systems is rapidly increasing the alternatives in this respect (see below). It is important that you agree between you which main method of communication you will use for routine matters, and you also both know an emergency number that can be called if a crisis occurs. Decide also whether you will send a routine or even daily 'news e-mail' containing current items of note, to reduce the amount of time spent on the telephone. Finally, check what action you should take if any mail is received that is marked Personal during the trip – particularly if this is also marked Urgent!

Keeping in touch – in the millennium and beyond

There was a time when business executives on the move were out of touch with anyone until they had arrived at their destination. Today, most people are familiar with pay-phones on trains and aeroplanes for making outgoing calls. Alternatively, many executives carry their own mobile phones which they can use on train journeys, although these are not permitted on flights.

However, a range of new options exists for the business traveller who wants to stay in constant contact with his or her base while away from home.

- GSM digital mobile phones can be hired from some travel operators. These phones can be used in most countries in Europe and many countries worldwide. British Airways, for instance, operates its Visitel mobile phone hire service, where the hirer is notified of the mobile phone number two or three days before departure and this number never changes regardless of the countries being visited. A voice mail/messaging service operates when the phone is switched off and these stay in memory for up to 72 hours for retrieval. The disadvantage is that there is usually a charge for receiving as well as making each call on a mobile phone.

- Most executives carry a BT Chargecard or other equivalent card (such as the Thomas Cook Worldwide telephone card) which can be used for calling from phones all over the world. This saves the need for local currency and also keeps costs down – as hotel telephone charges are often very high indeed.

- BT operates an international 'follow me' telephone service called BT Onenumber International, where there are no charges for receiving the call. Calls received on the user's personal 07071 number can be diverted to most fixed and mobile phones in Europe, the United States and Canada – in other countries the mobile number must be used.

- Satellite telephones are expensive but will work anywhere in the world. Portable versions are now available which weigh as little as 2.3 kg and can be carried as hand-luggage.

- Laptops mean that executives can dial into their organisation's computer network to send and collect e-mail messages. Alternatively, anyone with an Internet subscription/electronic mail box can use the Internet for the same purpose.

When the boss is away

The golden rules for good communications whilst your boss is away are as follows.

- Prepare for each daily contact in advance, to maximise the usefulness of the time you are on the telephone. Do this by

  - opening all the mail and sorting this and any messages into three groups

    a urgent items needing your boss's comments/attention/approval
    b non-urgent items your boss should know about
    c all items you can deal with yourself

  - sorting every document, in every group, into priority order
  - if there is any long or complex matter to be discussed, sending this either by fax or e-mail to your boss in advance so that he or she will have had time to read and consider it.

- Before the telephone rings, make sure you have all your files, folders and documents in front of you and your notebook ready. Start by working through the contents of your group **a** items. If there is time, you can continue to group **b**. This will very much depend upon your boss's schedule and the number of items arising out of the trip that he or she wants to discuss, and the jobs that need to be done as a result.

- Before you ring off, agree the next point and time of contact. Remember, times may have to be changed to allow for time differences if your boss is travelling around.

After contact time you will often have several jobs to do, clearing all the documents from group **a** and possibly **b** as well, moving forward items from group **b** that weren't discussed but which are becoming progressively more urgent, and undertaking any tasks your boss has asked you to do.

It is also considerate to remember your boss's family – particularly if he or she is in a part of the world where communications may be difficult. Checking if he or she has been in touch recently, passing on any messages and even posting pre-written birthday cards are all jobs which are often part of the PA's role!

On your boss's return

Don't forget that jet lag affects many people upon their return – particularly if they have travelled a long distance. For that reason, many executives do not necessarily return to work the day after they arrive in the country. The first day in the office will be a 'catching up' day, when your boss will need peace and quiet for all the items that need attention. You can help if you keep appointments to a minimum and have prepared a summary of everything you have dealt with in his or her absence, plus a list of urgent matters that need attention. Make sure all relevant papers are in priority order attached to the list and have your own routine jobs up to date so that you can concentrate on assisting your boss and expediting any urgent tasks.

Final feedback

One useful tip is to schedule a five- or ten-minute meeting with your boss to review the organisation of the trip, the arrangements made and the things that went smoothly – and those that didn't. Make notes which will help you to modify or improve your arrangements next time. These may relate to organisational details or simply to your boss's preferences – which usually become more and more marked with each subsequent trip!

Finally, you may also be responsible for returning any unused travellers' cheques or currency to your Finance section and for checking that your boss has completed the relevant expense claim by its due date. In some cases, you may even be handed a mountain of receipts and asked to draft the claim for approval. At this point, do remember that a PA is employed for both efficiency and discretion. If you find that your boss ran up a substantial bill in the hotel minibar or spent a fair amount entertaining clients in a local nightclub, this should not be your main item of gossip for the next six weeks. If anyone is likely to query it, let it be the company accountant and not you!

Test yourself

Instead of a review quiz, this chapter concludes with two assignments for you to carry out – one in small groups and the other on your own.

1 Throughout the travel section of this book, reference has been made to the role of embassies and consulates (specifically from page 215 onwards). Their function has been mentioned in relation to visas, import and export regulations, health advice, and business protocol – to name but a few. In addition, on page 220 (j), it was suggested that you use the Internet to find out more about them.

Your task now is to divide into small groups (about four is ideal) and prepare a fact sheet containing the following information:

a the difference between an embassy and a consulate

b the information that can be obtained from foreign embassies and consulates in the UK which would be helpful for a business trip

c the assistance that can be given to travellers by British embassies and consulates abroad.

How you approach this task is up to you. Some useful starting points may be for one person to backtrack through this book to list points of note, for another to visit and interview a travel agent who can give useful information, for a third to visit the college (or local) library to check reference books, and for a fourth to contact an embassy or consulate for information.

Type up your fact sheet and compare it with those compiled by other groups. (Note that it is suggested that groups liaise about which embassy or consulate they are contacting – rather than have each group contact the same one!)

2 The second assignment is linked to the work you have already undertaken for Richard Evans' visit to Australia. Start by familiarising yourself with the documents in your travel file and refresh your memory by looking back at his requirements, which were specified in Figure 6.2 on page 208, and the checklist, which was shown in Figure 6.3 on pages 209–210.

You should also have in your file:

- information on ATA Carnets and Australian import regulations you researched on page 235

- information on Australian driving regulations, which you summarised at page 244

- the flight details you researched on page 257

- a copy of the fax sent to the travel agent arranging the car hire and flights

- information on the taxis you have booked and the copy letter to the taxi company

- a copy of the fax you sent to the Australian agent requesting hotel accommodation.

You have now received the following documents:

- a fax from Harry Canter in reply to yours, shown in Figure 8.4

- a memo from Richard Evans, shown in Figure 8.5

- a memo from John Laraby, one of Richard's colleagues, shown in Figure 8.6

Use these to undertake the following tasks:

a Write a memo to the Finance department requesting the foreign currency required. The current exchange rate is £1 = A$2.5. Note that you must specify the amount of currency you require in Australian dollars and *not* in sterling.

b Prepare a fax to the Blue River Hotel, Hobart, Tasmania, confirming the accommodation booked by Harry Canter (see his memo in Figure 8.4).

c List TEN useful items you think Richard Evans and his team should take with them.

d Write out a checklist for yourself listing all the different documents relating to the trip which Richard Evans will need to take.

e Make out a comprehensive itinerary for the visit, including all appointments, as requested by Richard Evans.

f Prepare an information sheet, containing the items specified by Richard Evans in his memo.

g Write a short memo to Richard Evans, suggesting some suitable contact times during the first week he is away, in response to his request.

Check all your answers with your tutor. Note that a suggested comprehensive itinerary is shown in the key on page 305 but this is not definitive – slight variations from this may be acceptable provided that all the important information is included in the correct order.

TO　　You

FROM　Harry Canter, Australian agent

DATE　10 February 199–

Richard's visit to Australia

Thanks for your fax. I've reserved and confirmed accommodation as requested at the following hotels:

Sydney – Park Regis Hotel, 27 Park Street, Sydney NSW2000,
Fax 61–2–6383–4010, tel 6383–4040 (26–28 Feb)

Melbourne – Sheraton Vista Hotel, 131 Spring Street, Melbourne Vic 3005,
Fax 61–3–2873–3048, tel 2870–3020 (1, 2, 3, 5 and 6 March)

Please advise Richard that I will meet them at the Park Regis for breakfast at 0800 on the 27th. We are meeting Brian Colraine of Pacific Fabrics, Riverside Drive at 1030 (tel 4098–3951) and then going on to see George Combes of Westway Interiors, Jolumunga Way (tel 3003–5768) at 2.30 pm – he's also invited us to a barbie at his house in the evening! Richard already has the details for the 27th.

In Melbourne, we'll be at Jonaster Brothers, Coolridge Park, from 10 am on Friday with Sid Hawkes and will meet him again at 9.30 the following day. Tel: 61–3–2928–3030. On Monday we're going on to Hobart to see Peter Meades at Tasmanian Carpets at Goolonga Lake (tel 0380–2828) – I've made all the arrangements. We're travelling outwards on flight QF 405 from Melbourne at 0820 (arriving 0930) and returning on the 1640 flight QF 460 on Tuesday, arriving Melbourne at 1750. I've reserved four rooms at the Blue River Hotel, tel 61–02–0398–0129, fax 61–02–0318–8447 for the night of the 4th. We meet Peter at 10.30 on the first morning and 9.30 on the second. Back in Melbourne on the 6th we have a final call to Jan Rylance at Rivershade Design on Park Street at 10 am (tel: 04977–9891), which leaves the last afternoon free for sorting out any problems.

If you've any queries please ring or fax me. Don't forget that to contact us, you'll have to insert 00 before the county/city code. Incidentally, check-in times for Australian domestic flights is half an hour – 90 minutes for outward international flights. I'll make sure we leave the hotels at the right times!

Finally, could you do me a favour? The Blue River fax was out of order when I tried to confirm the booking and I'll be away for the next few days. Could you fax them to confirm the booking and the payment method please (corporate plastic, as ever!)

Regards

Harry

Figure 8.4　Fax message

MEMO

TO   You

FROM   Richard Evans

DATE   15 February 199–

Forthcoming trip to Australia

I think most of the details are in place for this visit, but there are one or two aspects we need to finalise.

1   Please note the visit arranged for the 28th to see Marilyn Potter of Ethnic Designs, Spencer Street – tel Sydney 7301–3797. We'll be there all day from 10 am onwards.

2   We have finally decided on the currency we'll need. I think you had better obtain £800 for us in Australian currency and £1000 in sterling travellers' cheques. Please request this from Finance immediately.

3   I know I have already asked you to look up driving regulations for me. However, as Jack McCormack might be staying out there now, after we have left, we could do with some additional information. I've asked John Laraby to send you a copy of an information sheet he has on the area – can you please sort through this and extract relevant information on

    a)   useful contact addresses we might need
    b)   public holidays that could affect Jack if he stays until June
    c)   any health requirements we should know about
    d)   the banking hours
    e)   business customs and practices over there
    f)   some indication of the time difference – so I don't ring home (or you!) at an unsociable hour!

    If you could prepare this as a concise information list under suitable headings it would be very useful indeed. Don't forget I also need the information on driving and import regulations that I asked for earlier – it might be useful if you included this in the same document.

4   I think it would be useful if you could draft out the itinerary, including all appointments. We'll need to go through this carefully to ensure there are no problems.

5   Finally, could you suggest some appropriate contact times for the first week I'm away, particularly given the time difference. I'll need to stay in touch with you regularly, as apart from work emanating from the trip itself, I'll need updating on what's happening here.

Thanks
RE

Figure 8.5 A memo from Richard Evans

MEMO

TO   You

FROM   John Laraby

DATE   Today

Australia information

Attached is the information I promised Richard I would send you. I compiled most of it for my visit there last year when I also visited Perth – so you may have to customise it a little for Richard's trip. Hope it is helpful!

JL

AUSTRALIA – FACT SHEET

Passport and visa requirements
All British citizens require passport, visa and return tickets. Thomas Cook has a new procedure for obtaining Australian visas electronically in a matter of days (or hours). British Visitor Passports are not valid.

Currency
Australian dollars and cents. Coins are 10, 20 and 50 cents, also for A$1 and A$2. Notes are for 5, 10, 20, 50 and 100 dollars. Check the exchange rate regularly – it can be very volatile.

Health
No vaccines required for UK travellers, but high factor sunscreen recommended during (Australian) summer months, and wraparound eye protection. Tap water safe, sanitation excellent.

Voltages
Electrical voltage is 240 volts, 50 cycles AC. Adaptors should include a three-pronged plug. Hotels have razor adaptors.

Business hours
Shops open every day – often on Sunday. Usual working hours 9–5.30 pm, 4 pm on Saturday. Late night shopping in most cities. Post offices open Monday–Friday 9 am–5 pm – also Post Office Shops which open during main shopping hours and Saturdays until noon. Banks are open Monday–Thursday from 9–4 pm and on Friday until 5 pm. Some banks now opening 9–5 and also on Saturdays until 4 pm.

Public holidays

New Year's Day – 1 Jan, Australia Day – 27 Jan, Good Friday and Easter Monday (as UK), Anzac Day – 25 April, Queen's Birthday Holiday – 9 June, Labour Day – 6 Oct, Christmas Day and Boxing Day (as UK).

Tipping

Not expected except in larger hotels and restaurants. Taxi fares: usual to tip about 10% or round up to next whole dollar. Restaurants about 5% – 15%, depending upon service and size of bill, hotel porters about one or two dollars per bag.

Business customs and practices

Business hours for visiting normally between 9 am and 4 pm, much business done over lunch (1 pm–2.30 pm – late by British standards). Alcohol often consumed on these occasions. Australians very hospitable and mix social and business activities. Business dress quite traditional – for women, fashionable and feminine usually has more appeal than 'power' dressing.

Weather

Warm summers and mild winters (colder in Melbourne than Sydney). Rainfall heaviest between March and July – particularly in Perth. Seasons reversed – also winds! South wind = cold! Average temperatures in March in southern states is between 65 and 70 degrees Fahrenheit, in June 55–60 degrees (Tasmania is colder, being further south).

Emergency number

000 = police, fire and ambulance. 0103 = directory enquiries. Time = 0055 12 582, temperature = 0055 33 124. International access code for England is 0011 44. Most public telephones now cardphones. Note that code for Australia from England is 00 61 followed by 9 for Perth, 3 for Melbourne, 2 for Sydney and 02 for Hobart.

Time zone

Australia's west coast (Perth) is 8 hours ahead of GMT and the east coast is 10 hours ahead of GMT. Therefore 9 am in Sydney = 11 pm in London. Daylight Saving Time is observed between late October and early March, which means there may be an additional hour's difference.

Contacts and useful addresses

In the UK:

High Commission of the
Commonwealth of Australia
Australia House
The Strand
LONDON WC2B 4LA
Tel: 0171 379 4334,
fax: 0171 240 5333

Australian British Chamber of
Commerce
Suite 10–16
Morley House
314–322 Regent Street
LONDON W1R 5AE
Tel: 0171 636 4525,
fax: 0171 636 4511

In Australia:

British High Commission
Commonwealth Avenue
Yarralumla
CANBERRA
ACT 2600

Tel: 270–6666, fax: 273–3196

British Consulate-General
17th Floor
90 Collins Street
MELBOURNE
Victoria 3000

Tel/fax: 9650 2990

Australian Tourist Commission
Level 4
80 William Street
Woolloomooloo
SYDNEY 2011
NSW

Tel: 360–1111, fax: 331–3385

Australian–British Chamber of
Commerce
Suite 302a
CML Building
Level 3
14 Martin Place
SYDNEY
NSW 20000

Tel: 221–0355, fax: 221–0116

British Consulate-General
Level 26
Allendale Square
77 St George's Terrace,
PERTH
Western Australia 6000

Tel: 221–4422, fax: 221–2344

British Consulate-General
Level 16
The Gateway
1 Macquarie Place,
Sydney Cover
SYDNEY 2000
NSW

Tel: 247–7521, fax: 233–1826

Chamber of Commerce and
Industry of Western Australia
190 Hay Street
EAST PERTH
Western Australia 6004

Tel: 365–7555, fax: 365–7550

Figure 8.6 Memo and report from John Laraby

A final note!

If you have now organised and arranged a trip for yourselves – even if only for a day – do take the opportunity to prepare a real itinerary and to obtain some useful information on your destination before you depart.

Finally, after the trip, hold a review session – not just to consider which aspects you enjoyed (and didn't), but also to review the travel plans you made and to see if you could learn from experience if you repeated the exercise.

Section 2 – Keys

● Key to Check it Yourself on page 210

Checklist for Joanne Bretherton – proposed visit to Ireland
(Correct current dates should be entered here)

Travel
Ferry – Holyhead to Dublin return – outward Monday (date), return Friday (date)
Car plus driver
Check ferry times and make booking

Accommodation
1 × single room (en-suite)
Dublin – 3 nights – Monday, Tuesday and Thursday (include dates)
Galway – 1 night – Wednesday (give date)
Obtain information on suitable hotels and make reservations

Currency
£200 in Irish punts

Other
Check mileage and route from Dublin to Galway.

● Key to Check it Yourself on pages 250–252

Train information for Paul Livesey

1 Trip from Manchester to Birmingham

   Depart Manchester Piccadilly   Arrive Birmingham New Street
   1217   1400
   (Note: the following train at 1310 would not arrive until 1451 – too late
   for Paul Livesey's appointment)

2 Trip from Edinburgh to Liverpool

   Depart Edinburgh 0910, arrive Lime Street 1319 – change at Wigan
   North Western (arrive 1206, depart 1225).

   (Note: the earlier 0850 train takes longer as it goes via Glasgow)

● Key to Check it Yourself on pages 257–258

Question 3

Glasgow–Sydney – departure date Monday, 25 February

Dep GLA 0915	Arr LHR 1035	Flight BA 1477
Dep LHR 1215	Arr SYD 2045 (following day)	Flight QF 2

or

Dep GLA 1815	Arr LHR 1930	Flight BA 1495
Dep LHR 2130	Arr SYD 0610 (2 days later)	Flight BA 009

Sydney–Melbourne – transfer date Friday 1 March

Dep SYD 0725	Arr MEL 0855	Flight BA 009

Melbourne–Glasgow – return date Thursday 7 March

Dep MEL 1430	Arr LHR 0540 (following day)	Flight BA 010
Dep LHR 0715	Arr GLA 0830	Flight BA 1472

or

Dep MEL 1705	Arr LHR 0530 (following day)	Flight BA 7309
Dep LHR 0715	Arr GLA 0830	Flight BA 1472

(Note: latter option has fewer stops)

Question 5

Check in at Glasgow airport must be *at least* by 0845 for the early flight. However, at this time of day when traffic is busy you would be sensible to book a taxi for about 0715 and to allow about an hour and a quarter for the journey and 45 minutes at the airport.

On the return, the taxi will be meeting flight BA 1472 arriving from London Heathrow at 0830 hours. The key point is to get the date correct, as Richard will be arriving on 8 March, because of the time difference.

● Key to Check it Yourself on page 266

Possible ferry times for Joanne Bretherton's trip to Ireland and return:

Holyhead to Dublin – check-in 0900, depart 0930, arrive 1115

Dublin to Holyhead – check-in 0945, depart 1015, arrive 1200

Cost: £240 return plus additional £20 for use of executive lounge.

• Key to Check it Yourself on page 276

Hotel facilities

- high standard of decor and furnishing

- en-suite rooms – choice of smoking or non-smoking, suites or rooms

- 24-hour room service and porterage

- laundry services

- within the room – shower, hairdryer, trouser-press, colour TV with cable channels, radio and international direct-dial telephone, air conditioning/variable central heating, tea/coffee making facilities

- work space/desk in room plus phone and fax/modem link

- close to major road routes, railway stations/underground and relatively convenient for the airport, if possible

- at least one public restaurant of a high standard

- multilingual reception staff

- pre-bookable car parking (essential if he or she is arriving by car)

- complimentary newspapers

- health and fitness centre

- secretarial support

- high-speed check-in/out

- concierge services for car hire, theatre tickets, etc

- hotel shops selling key items, such as toiletries

• Suggested Key to Check it Yourself on page 282

A–Z checklist

A ATA Carnet
Audio tapes

B Baggage labels (spare)
Batteries (spare – for razor, dictating machine, etc)
Briefcase

C Calculator
Car keys
Car (or car hire) documentation

Credit/charge cards
Confirmation documents (hotels, appointments, etc)
Customer contact lists, details, contracts, correspondence, etc

D Diary

E Emergency contact numbers
Eurocheque book and card
Eye mask (for long haul travel)

F Floppy disks
Foreign currency
Flight bag

G Guide books

H House keys

I Insurance documents
International driving licence
Itinerary

L Laptop with integral modem

M Maps
Medical packs
Mobile phone

N Notebook

P Passport
Phone cards
Phrase book
Presentation aids

S Sales documentation
Sales literature
Samples
Screwdriver
Spectacles (and spares!)
Sterling
Suitcase
Sunglasses

T Tickets
Travellers' cheques (and separate list of numbers)

V Vaccination certificates
Visas
Visiting cards

• Keys to Check it Yourself on pages 284–287

Question 4 – suggested itinerary for Tara O'Connor

Visit to London, 1–4 February

Monday 1 February

0725   Depart for Birmingham Station

0815   Depart on London train – seat reserved

0955   Arrive London Euston – taxi to hotel
Room reserved at London Marriott, Grosvenor Square,
tel 0171–493–1232
If room is not available, baggage can be left with the porter and a
courtesy room can be used.

1400   Meeting with Denise Fuller, Abercrombe International, Armada
Crescent, WC3 – tel 0181–409–2208

Tuesday 2 February

Visit to IT 2000 Exhibition, Earl's Court

Entrance ticket attached.

Wednesday 3 February

0930   Meeting with Stanil Pachevsky, DJV Solutions, 18 Corby Place, W1 –
tel 0181–208–1749

1400   Depart for Paddington station

1448   Depart on Oxford train – seat reserved

1546   Arrive Oxford – taxi to hotel
Reservation at The Randolph, Beaumont Street, tel 01865–247481

1900   Collected at hotel by Charles Davidson, Linton Software for dinner at
1930 hours

Thursday 4 February

1000   Presentation at Linton Software, Abingdon Road, Oxford – tel
01865–319278

1430   Leave for Oxford station

1516   Depart on Birmingham train – seat reserved

1639   Arrive Birmingham New Street

Question 5 – suggested itinerary for Joanne Bretherton

Visit to Ireland, 26–30 March

Monday 26 March

0700   Depart for Holyhead

0900   Check-in at ferryport

0930   Depart for Dublin

1115   Arrive Dun Laoghaire ferryport

1200   Arrive Dublin
Room reserved at The Drury Court Hotel, 28–30 Lower Stephens
Street, Dublin 2, tel (00–353) 01–475–1988

1400   Meeting with Patrick O'Nealy, Ryans Electronics, Shelby Road, Dublin, tel (00–353) 01–428–3922

Tuesday 27 March
0900   Continuation of meeting with Patrick O'Nealy, Ryans Electronics, Shelby Road, Dublin, tel (00–353) 01–428–3922
1500   Meeting with Gabrielle Lagan, Multimedia Inc, O'Connell Street, Dublin, tel (00–353) 01–373–2009
1930   Table reservation at The Drury Court for dinner with Gabrielle Lagan

Wednesday 28 March
0900   Check out of Drury Court – drive to Galway on N6 (130 miles)
1200   Arrive Galway
       Room reserved at Great Southern Hotel, tel 91–564041
1400   Meet Peter Griffiths from Virtual Solutions, Boston in foyer of hotel, then seminar room

Thursday 29 March
0900   Check out of Great Southern Hotel – drive to Dublin on N6
1200   Arrive Dublin
       Re-register at The Drury Court Hotel, Lower Stephens Street
1300   Continuation meeting with Gabrielle Lagan, Multimedia Inc, O'Connell Street, tel 01–373–2009

Friday 30 March
0845   Check out of The Drury Court, drive to ferryport at Dun Laoghaire
0945   Check-in at ferryport
1015   Depart on ferry
1200   Arrive Holyhead

● Keys to Test Yourself on pages 293–294

Suggested itinerary for Richard Evans and colleagues

Visit to Australia, 25 February–8 March

Monday 25 February

0715   Taxi from home to Glasgow airport (booked with J D Executive Drive, tel 248–4949)
0845   (latest) Check-in at Glasgow
0915   Depart flight BA 1477
1035   Arrive Terminal 1, London Heathrow. Transfer to Terminal 4
1215   Depart flight QF 2

Tuesday 26 February
2045   Arrive Sydney airport
       Hire car reserved with Avis Rent-a-car for collection at airport
       Accommodation reserved at Park Regis Hotel, 27 Park Street, Sydney, tel 61–2–6383–4040.

Wednesday 27 February

0800   Breakfast at hotel with Harry Canter

1030   Meeting with Brian Colraine, Pacific Fabrics, Riverside Drive,
tel 4098–3951

1430   Meeting with George Combes, Westway Interiors, Jolumunga Way,
tel 3003–5768
Evening barbecue at George Combes' house

Thursday 28 February

1000   Meeting with Marilyn Potter, Ethnic Designs, Spencer Street,
Sydney, tel 7301–3797

Friday 1 March

0655   Check-in Sydney airport

0725   Depart flight BA 009

0855   Arrive Melbourne

1000   Meeting with Sid Hawkes, Jonaster Brothers, Coolridge Park, tel
61–3–2928–3030
Hire car reserved with Avis Rent-a-car for collection at airport
Accommodation reserved at Sheraton Visa Hotel, 131 Spring Street,
Melbourne, tel 2870–3020

Saturday 2 March

0930   Continuation of meeting with Sid Hawkes, Jonaster Brothers

Monday 4 March

0750   Check-in Melbourne airport

0820   Depart flight QF405

0930   Arrive Hobart, Tasmania

1030   Meeting with Peter Meades, Tasmanian Carpets, Goolonga Lake,
tel 0380–2828
Accommodation reserved at Blue River Hotel, tel 61–02–0398–0129

Tuesday 5 March

0930   Continuation of meeting with Peter Meades

1610   Check-in Hobart airport

1640   Depart flight QF 460

1750   Arrive Melbourne
Accommodation reserved at Sheraton Visa Hotel, 131 Spring Street,
Melbourne, tel 61–3–2870–3020

Wednesday 6 March

1000   Meeting with Jan Rylance, Rivershade Design, Park Street,
tel 04977–9891

Thursday 7 March

1535   Check in Melbourne airport

1705   Depart flight BA 7309

Friday 8 March

0530	Arrive London Heathrow, Terminal 4. Transfer to Terminal 1
0715	Depart flight BA 1472
0830	Arrive Glasgow airport
	To be met by J D Executive Drive, tel 248–4949

Index